NEW TOOLS FOR ECONOMIC DEVELOPMENT

NEW TOOLS FOR ECONOMIC DEVELOPMENT: THE ENTERPRISE ZONE, DEVELOPMENT BANK, AND RFC

edited by
George Sternlieb
David Listokin

CENTER FOR URBAN POLICY RESEARCH

RUTGERS UNIVERSITY • P.O. Box 489
PISCATAWAY • NEW JERSEY • 08854

Published in the United States of America by the
Center for Urban Policy Research
Building 4051--Kilmer Campus
New Brunswick, New Jersey 08903

Grateful acknowledgment is made to the following for permission to reprint their articles:

Sir Geoffrey Howe for his speech entitled *A Zone of Enterprise to Make All Systems "Go,"* presented to the Bow Group, June 26, 1981.

Stuart M. Butler for *Enterprise Zones in the Inner City*, Heritage Foundation, Washington, D.C., 1980.

George Richard Meadows and John Mitrisin for *A National Development Bank: Survey and Discussion of the Literature on Capital Shortages and Employment Changes in Distressed Areas*, Economics Division, Congressional Research Service, Library of Congress, April 1979. Reprinted in Fund for Public Policy Research, Studies in Taxation, Public Finance and Related Subjects - A Compendium, Vol. 3, Washington, D.C., 1979.

James M. Bickley for *An Evaluation of the Reconstruction Finance Corporation with Implications for Current Capital Needs of the Steel Industry*, Economics Division, Congressional Research Service, Library of Congress, Feb. 26, 1980. Reprinted in Fund for Public Policy Research, Studies in Taxation, Public Finance and Related Subjects - A Compendium, Vol. 4, Washington, D.C., 1980.

The papers by George Sternlieb, Robert W. Burchell and David Listokin were funded by the U.S. Department of Housing and Urban Development.
The statements and conclusions contained therein are those of the authors and do not necessarily reflect the views of the U.S. Government in general nor the U.S. Department of Housing and Urban Development. Neither the Federal Government nor the Department of Housing and Urban Development makes any warranty, expressed or implied, or assumes responsibility for the accuracy or completeness of the information therein.

Library of Congress Cataloging in Publication Data

Sternlieb, George.
New tools for economic development.

Bibliography: p.
Includes index.
1. Economic assistance, Domestic—United States—Addresses, essays, lectures. 2. Urban renewal—United States—Addresses, essays, lectures. 3. National Development Bank (United States)—Addresses, essays, lectures. 4. Reconstruction Finance Corporation—Addresses, essays, lectures. I. Listokin, David.
II. Title.
HC110.P63S72 338.973 81-10087

ISBN 0-88285-074-1 (pbk.) AACR2

Cover Design by Francis G. Mullen

Contents

INTRODUCTION

George Sternlieb
David Listokin

CITIES IN THE POST-INDUSTRIAL ERA

A tide of decentralization—in jobs, housing, entertainment, and, indeed, all the money-begetting activities of Americans—has been running against the cities for many years. Through the expansionist decades since World War II, federal programs have abetted the growth of suburbia and, more recently, of exurbia. The factors need no retelling here: mortgage policy, tax policy, highway policy—all have favored the new over the old. In contrast to this rich fare, the country's malnourished older central cities have been fed a subsistence diet of federal aid: kept going "just in case"; kept breathing—though raggedly—on grounds that the penalty of not having them, if priorities should alter, would be vast.

Now things are changing. There is a growing uneasiness about the nation's capacity to sustain, let alone extend, post-World War II development patterns. Energy problems will not go away. The cities' density, cited so often as a crippling disability, is once again acquiring allure. As real incomes in the United States diminish, particularly in housing and transportation buying power, the central city may begin to look like a good speculation. Reuse and recycling are in; sprawl and the profligate use of resources are losing their appeal.

A new perspective on the cities' labor pool is also beginning to emerge. De facto policy certainly encouraged a migration of redundant labor from the nation's newly mechanized, superefficient agricultural sector to its cities. The United States now has the smallest proportion of its people involved in agriculture of any major food-producing nation. By way of comparison, the Soviet Union has ten times the proportion of its population living on the land.

This country-to-city migration of job seekers is far from an exclusively modern American phenomenon. What is novel is its breathtaking pace since the forties—and the simultaneous outflow of the middle class. What is also new is that the economy of the central city, out of tune with the post-industrial era, has not been able to offer jobs to this latest wave of incoming unskilled workers, as it always had in the past. The upshot is that most major cities have a welfare population ranging from 15 to 25 percent of their total population.

Absorption of these in-migrants into the working force has been further inhibited by an enormous growth in the number of U.S. workers. The bulge is a function in part of the post-war baby boom, but much more strikingly, of the surge of women into the labor force. From 1947 to 1977, for example, the number of employed husbands in husband-wife families increased by 23 percent, while the number of employed wives increased by 208 percent. To state the contrast another way, nearly twice as many women as men were added to the job market.

By now, the impact of these social forces has almost peaked, and a different demographic curve is shaping up. The same phenomenon that has emptied the elementary and junior high schools of the country and has made teaching credentials a passport to the ranks of the unemployed will soon make the nation labor-short. The rates at which people join the labor force are scheduled to decline quite abruptly in the early 1980s. As a result, the young people of the central city who now top the lists of the jobless, may in a few years find themselves looked on more as a national resource and less as an economic liability. (This scenario makes a large assumption: that they will be competitive with their equivalents in other countries that are becoming focal points for worldwide manufacture.)

Out of a convergence of new social and economic forces, a new pattern of American economic growth may be emerging. Now we import labor-intensive products, while a surplus or marginal labor force in central cities is minimally cared for. We may be moving toward a time when the central city will be a significant economic entity and its unemployed, hitherto disregarded, will have work to do.

Is this a realistic picture of the future? Can the central city be once again a vigorous part of the economy, or, at a minimum, be stabilized? The answers to these questions are far from definitive. Tough, practical issues of the post-industrial economy must be addressed.

Up to about 1970 the decline of the central city was a uniquely American phenomenon, viewed by European observers particularly, as an exotic happening confined to the United States—home of a wide set of aberrations.

Since 1970, however, there is increasing evidence that this is a phenomenon of post-industrial urban economies. France, Italy, and Germany, as well as Japan show the beginnings of parallels with the American experience. The shift of manufacturing out of the central city is far from unique to the United States. Restoration efforts, therefore, must probably face a much more potent underlying economic dynamic rather than a simple idiosyncrasy of American land-use and investment patterns.

The nature of the new businesses in the central city—increasingly, service and office activities—continues to accentuate the mismatch between the cities' jobless and the new work opportunities. Studies by the Center for Urban Policy Research have shown, for example, that about 70 percent of persons employed in manufacturing within the city of Philadelphia also lived in the city, but only 30 percent of new office employees were city residents. So, it is not possible to conclude that more jobs in the city will necessarily mean lowered unemployment among its residents.

As we move further and further into the post-industrial state, one issue bulks ever larger: For whom is the city to be revitalized? Should it be a refuge for the falloff from the old industrial mass employment? Or should the goal be to optimize the new, exciting "city within a city," that is attracting the young and well-educated to live in the city were they work—at jobs in the banks, insurance companies, consulting facilities, and production service employments that are growing within the core? The de facto new towns-within-towns—Soho in New York, Capitol Hill in Washington, Society Hill in Philadelphia, and the many equivalents elsewhere—epitomize the second alternative. This dichotomy constitutes one of the major problems in government/private efforts at economic revitalization within the central city. The issues of relocation, for example, are evident as the childless, young, high-incomed look for one-of-a-kind housing accommodations—sometimes at the cost of low-income individuals, many of whom indeed are welfare recipients.

Racial issues further complicate this dilemma. Whereas the new middle class is by no means all white, the bulk of the poor in central cities belong to racial and ethnic minorities. An economic revitalization of the central city that disturbs their living accommodations yet does not yield them jobs is bound to lead to racial as well as class friction. Indeed, in cities where the new middle-class neighborhoods are developing, the conflict is already evident.

PUBLIC POLICY AND THE CITIES

Analysis of the problems of central cities has gone through many permutations, each of them generating equivalent remedies. Initially, the decline of the cities was seen as a transient problem caused by faulty or archaic land use, by the intrusion of slums into viable economic areas, as well as by the difficulties of assembling suitable large tracts of land for new job-begetting purposes. These interpretations underly the 1950s era of physical improvement typified by urban-renewal clearance and highway development.

The turbulence of the 1960s refocused the issues to those of structural unemployment: the mismatch between the education and training of central-city residents and the kinds of jobs that are emerging in a post-industrial society. Much of the Model Cities program and the great wave of training initiatives that ensued were the result.

Only within the last half dozen years has the very unavailability of jobs—the decline of employment opportunities and of entrepreneurial activity in the central city—become the focus of concern. This concern spurred the formulation of a veritable alphabet soup of programs to spur urban economic development.

The Community Development Block Grant (CDBG) program consolidated scores of categorical housing and community development subsidies. Although it did not focus on economic revitalization, it could be used for a multitude of reinvestment activities, including planning and technical assistance and the acquisition of real property for economic development purposes.

The Urban Development Action Grant (UDAG) was a child of CDBG with an emphasis on economic redevelopment. It was applied in financially and socially "distressed" communities and attempted to leverage private commitments of capital and state and local assistance. UDAG funds could be used for a wide variety of purposes, including the acquisition and development of land or public-works facilities and the provision of direct financial assistance to firms or nonprofit entities.

The Economic Development Administration (EDA) offered an array of measures to encourage reinvestment, including: loans and grants designed to improve or expand public facilities; loans and guarantees that could be used to finance economic development in designated areas; technical assistance for economic development; and special grants to impacted areas (for example, those affected by the closing of a major steel mill or a coal mine) or to communities experiencing "long-term economic deterioration."

The limited results of these and other programs from the Farmers Home Administration (FmHA) and Small Business Administration (SBA) highlighted the difficulty of spurring urban economic development in the face of changing regional, national, and even international demographic and economic forces. The scale of the problem is epitomized in manufacturing and can be seen as the end result of three trends: the movement of jobs from central city to suburbia (and now to exurbia); the shift of jobs regionally, often at the cost of the areas in which old, large cities dominate—the Northeast and older North Central sections of the country; and the changing nature of employment opportunities in the United States as a whole.

Behind a facade of hotel and high-rise office development in older central cities, there has been a devastating shrinkage in the job base. With it has come a decline both in population and in the buying power of that population, as wealthier residents have left and the less fortunate have remained. From 1976 through 1978, a net total of nearly three million individuals migrated from central cities. In the same period, because of selected migration, the income of central-city residents went down approximately $9 billion a year, with concomitant shrinkage in retailing, service, and small-scale, for-local-consumption manufacturing.

In a United States suddenly grown fearful of its competitive status in the world economy, there is an unfortunate tendency to think that support for one sector—the nation's distressed cities—can be won only at the cost of another. Missing is the perception that if new growth is generated there, the country as a whole will benefit. This attitude has inhibited the execution of a variety of programs earmarked specifically for the poor and those urban regions where the poor increasingly predominate. The report of the White House Task Force on Balanced National Growth in the spring of 1978 and the responses made to it reflected some of this conflict.

Despite the stress, there is the beginning of a major consensus. The first item in this new ordering is an agreement that what is required in order to revitalize ailing urban economies is a broad based constructive partnership between government at all levels and private industry. It is becoming clear that the former cannot "go it alone"; that within a competitive economy, there must be a reshaping of the environment and the incentives given the private sector, if appropriate job-generating activities are to be secured. Government aid and direct employment opportunities certainly are necessary, but unless they are complemented by an increase in the private sector they are doomed to fall of their own weight. The second element that is gradually emerging is the understanding that this issue is not one of merely parochial interest—of a few geographic loci or of a particular segment of the population—but rather one of national urgency; that, on both fiscal and moral grounds, the costs of welfare and non-self-support of individuals is nationally debilitating.

Flowing from this conceptual grasp is the sense that reform of older programs and/or the development of new is far from a monopoly of either the right or the left, nebulous as those directions may be within the political spectrum of the United States. There is rather a long-term, complex, and often confused process of attempting to understand the nature of the problem environment, with the latter frequently in flux, and bringing to bear on the issues, as they come into focus, a variety of tools, until an appropriate fit can be obtained.

NEW TOOLS FOR ECONOMIC DEVELOPMENT

This volume brings together some of the principal approaches that are currently under review or have been advocated in the last several years to spur urban economic development. Three strategies are considered. One is the *Enterprise Zone*—entrepreneurial islands within urban areas spurred by preferential tax and regulatory treatment. A second is a *National Development Bank* designed to secure financing to capital-short distressed areas. The third—the *Reconstruction Finance Corporation (RFC)*—has as its goal the provision of financial aid and other support to aging, basic industries.

These strategies represent different forms of public intervention with one common denominator—not to provide a public dole but to stimulate private initiative and investment. It is vitally important to avoid parochialism in viewing the approaches that are presented. They all have as their ultimate goal stimulating the seemingly moribund, if not declining, economies of our impacted areas. In the heat of advocacy, there is a strong temptation to attempt to enhance the virtues of one's own brainchild by denegrating the alternatives; by suggesting that one's own sponsored bill is the Magic Bullet. Although one can hope that such magic may sometime evolve, at least as of this writing there is clear need for a package of mechanisms.

ENTERPRISE ZONE

Perhaps the most striking current effort is the series of proposals that have been grouped under the rubric of the Enterprise Zone. Conceptually, it can be viewed as a fiscal extension of urban renewal. The latter's emphasis was essentially a physical one, the grouping of land parcels, and, if necessary, demolition and write-down of values to make buildable sites available, with the implicit belief that there were developers who would flock into these ready locations. The Enterprise Zone groups a variety of benefits that are to be made available to impacted areas. The latter are to be defined under federal guidelines by local municipalities. If the cost of doing business is too high in central cities some options are to reduce the costs through preferential tax treatment, to minimize government regulations, or to slice labor costs by cutting social security payment requirements.

The original suggestions along these lines emerged from the desperate straits of the British industrial establishment. They have been voiced most coherently by the Honorable Sir Geoffrey Howe, former opposition spokesman on treasury and economic affairs. In his essay *Liberating Free Enterprise: A New Experiment*, Sir Geoffrey decries the overregulation and high taxation of British businesses and advocates the establishment of Enterprise Zones in impacted cities. The Zones would be freed from public regulations such as rent control and land use restrictions; only basic public health and safety standards would be imposed. In addition, the Zones would be granted preferential tax treatment for many years. These conditions would create a unique business environment attractive to private entrepreneuers. Public authorities owning land within the Zones would, in fact, be required to dispose of their holdings to private parties within a specified period of time. Sir Geoffrey's proposal is far more sweeping than the political realities of the United States would permit—or for that matter than have been implemented in Britain. They are included here as a "pure" form of the Enterprise Zone concept.

The evolution of the Enterprise Zone and the translation of the concept into legislation and programs is discussed by Stuart M. Butler in *Enterprise Zones: Pioneering in the Inner City.* Butler traces the origins of the Zone strategy to the "Freeport" plan—a 1977 proposal by Peter Hall of Reading University advocating the creation of islands of "shameless" free enterprise in depressed, depopulated areas. The "Freeport" plan was the conceptual basis for Sir Geoffrey Howe's Enterprise Zone proposed in 1978. Sir Geoffrey's recommendations were considered and then adopted with certain modifications by Britain's Conservative Government in 1979-1980. At the same time, the Enterprise Zone was introduced into the United States as a concept for action by the Heritage Foundation. Shortly afterwards it entered the legislative agenda, most prominently in bills proposed by U.S. Congressmen, Jack Kemp and Robert Garcia.

The Kemp-Garcia *Urban Jobs and Enterprise Zone Act* is currently under perusal in the United States Congress. It has received the endorsement of both sides of the aisle and, whether as an entity or as a series of concepts and actions to be implemented separately, it clearly will be a very potent input into the debate on breeding new economic vitality into depressed areas. How would the proposal, if implemented, realistically work? What will be realized and at what cost? These questions are addressed by George Sternlieb in *Kemp-Garcia Act: An Initial Evaluation.* This paper summarizes the incentives provided by this legislation, compares these attractions to existing economic development bonuses and provides some simple dollars-and-cents elaboration and projection of the potency of the Kemp-Garcia mechanisms. Sternlieb concludes that Kemp-Garcia offers perhaps the most substantial incentives ever given to companies in impacted areas. The major bonus is provided by the Kemp-Garcia provisions involving depreciation and income tax policy as opposed to social security reductions and property tax exemptions.

Projecting the basic arithmetic of a program is a dangerous activity. The counterintuitive nature of reality provides all too many instances of fallacious costing and evaluation of benefits. This is especially true in new programs and clearly an even greater threat in those that are still at the conjectural stage. Within those limitations we would suggest that the elements of the Kemp-Garcia plan although promising, require much more in the way of pencil pushing and cost/benefit analysis. A first effort in this regard is the focus of the paper that is presented here.

NATIONAL DEVELOPMENT BANK AND RFC

The Enterprise Zone strategy, whether in the guise of Kemp-Garcia or other proposals, can provide strong incentives for locating firms in declining areas. It does so by providing a buffering of the stream of income that will be secured by the successful operation of a new enterprise within a designated zone. In this fashion, it is a complement rather than a competitor of programs that focus on the front-end requirements, such as making capital and/or loans available with which to set up the enterprise.

The provision of capital to economically impacted areas is the subject of the paper by George Richard Meadows and John Mitrisin—*A National Development Bank: Survey and Discussion of the Literature on Capital Shortages and Employment Changes in Distressed Areas.* The National Development Bank (NDB) was an important financing vehicle in the original urban recommendations of the Carter Administration in 1978. While it was defeated at that time, it is a concept that is deserving of more vigorous debate than it has been afforded. Meadows and Mitrisin provide an opportune examination of the NDB. They discuss the forces contributing to a capital shortfall in distressed areas, outline the operational administration of the NDB, identify its unique contribution in the face of "competitive" programs, and examine alternative NDB strategic financing approaches and the payoff matrix of these alternatives.

Enterprise Zones and the NDB provide important props for economic development but fall short for declining industries that do not meet banking criteria and for which the tax virtues and depreciation allowances of the Enterprise Zone may be only of marginal utility. Older, impacted urban areas particularly suffer from dependence on industries or particular players within industries that are in decline. The generic problem is part of the broader issue of redirecting the economy of the United States; the particular case of central cities requires even more care.

These problems have been a decade in the making and so ingrained that some observers recommend reviving the strong economic rescue vehicles devised in the Depression when the nation's basic industries similarly faced problems of disfunction under new economic realties. This strategy is considered by James M. Bickley in *An Evaluation of the Reconstruction Finance Corporation with Implications for Current Capital Needs of the Steel Industry*. Bickley discusses why the RFC was formed in 1932, traces its early activities as an important financial prop to lenders (financial institutions and agricultural credit intermediaries) and basic economic sectors, examines the RFC's expanded scope during the 1940s and considers why it was disbanded in 1953. This discussion serves as background for considering the timeliness of reviving the RFC or some variant in the 1980s to support aging industries in decline. The steel industry is used as an illustrative example.

THE FISCAL DIMENSION

One of the major goals of the different economic development tools is to stabilize and revive the fiscal health of impacted communities. The topic is considered in *Fiscal Impact of Economic Development* by Robert W. Burchell and David Listokin. Incorporated within this paper is a brief review of the principal HUD (UDAG), EDA, and FmHA efforts at revitalization as of 1980. Prototypical projects aided by these agencies are then selected and a comparison is made of the public benefits versus public costs in each case. Burchell and Listokin conclude that the economic development projects had a significantly positive impact on the local fisc of the host communities—the local revenues generated by the projects exceeded local service costs by a wide margin. There was also a positive multiplier effect of the federal dollar of investment to the net revenue gained by the host community.

As we painfully attempt to stabilize the financial condition of our municipalities and weigh alternative uses of scarce stimulative dollars, it is essential that very rigorous evaluation be undertaken of the payoffs—not the least of them the rebuilding of the independence of the municipal storehouse. Tools for this purpose are presented in the fiscal analysis paper.

Whether all of the vehicles presented are either necessary or desirable—or equally significant, affordable—are issues on which people of goodwill and talent may well differ. The importance of the ultimate target of all of them—thorough rejuvenation of impacted areas and providing real futures for their people—at the very least deserves a full consideration of the state of the art. It is our hope that the materials assembled here will provide a beginning.

New Tools for Economic Development

LIBERATING FREE ENTERPRISE: A NEW EXPERIMENT

Sir Geoffrey Howe

THE DECLINING ECONOMY

For some years now, Great Britain's economy has been sliding into decline. Our living standards have been falling relative to the rest of the world. Seediness is the order of the day. While whole communities have been virtually blitzed by "planning" and stagnation, whole industries (in which Britain should still have a stake) have fallen off the edge of our economic table. And the businesses and industries of the future have not sprung up in their place.

Look out of the window on a train journey to any corner of Britain, and you can literally see the dangerous extent to which we have been living off the industrial and social capital that was accumulated by earlier generations—and failing to amass our own. Resources have been diverted to maintain consumer living standards today. But no seedcorn has been saved for tomorrow.

This is the key to understanding the developing sickness of our society. The consequent lack of economic success is breeding social tensions and threatening to destroy the framework of civilized existence.

THE POLITICAL CHOICE

In the face of these problems, two distinct philosophies are on offer. On the one hand, there is the Socialist alternative. On this view, prosperity can be achieved only by State direction of our resources, with the trade unions in partnership with a less than entrepreneurial political elite; the capital that is necessary will have to be accumulated through the tax system.

It is in this strictly economic sense that we are entitled to argue that the route maps provided by Messrs. Anthony Benn and Aneurin Bevan for Transport House will lead Britain to an East European destination. It is not a police state that they have on the drawing board—but an increasingly sullen and seedy economy, with authoritarianism as an inevitable consequence.

On the other hand, there is the libertarian approach—which is, or should be, common not only to Conservatives but to many Liberals and some Social Democrats as well. This does not imply any flat rejection of a role for public authority. There are many things that can be undertaken only by Government. But for the mainspring of the economy, we look to private initiative, widely dispersed and properly rewarded. In many areas, we believe, the burgeoning of State activity now positively frustrates many healthy private initiatives. Over-regulation is a major part of Britain's present disease.

The Conservative case is founded not simply on prejudice but on the proof of experience, in our own past and in the rest of the world even today.

The countries which are currently raising their living standards faster than any other, even in a hostile world economy, are those whose economic policies are still nearest to our ideal. We find surprising—but convincing—examples in Taiwan, South Korea, Hong Kong and Singapore. And from the more successful developed economies—Germany, Japan, and the United States, for example—the lesson is the same. We should take heed of the extent to which observers of even those economies are growing anxious at their development of some of the early symptoms of the British desease. The United States Secretary to the Treasury, Mr. Michael Blumenthal, observed the other day:

> Investment is lagging for the simple reason that it has become less profitable . . . . For too many businesses, particularly small and new ones, the gap between a productive idea and a foreseeable profit has widened into a forest of red tape.

Even here in Britain, the positive side of our message still manages to get through from time to time. In South Wales about 10,000 men are employed to make 2.5 million tonnes of steel a year at British Steel's Llanwern. Only a mile or two away, at the privately owned mini-mill of Alpha Steel, built and brought into production in under three years at a cost of less than £100 million, fewer than a thousand men will soon be producing 1 million tonnes a year. The comparison is revealing.

SELF-DEFEATING STATE INTERVENTION

Of course, the State can point to some apparent successes. Britain's post-war new towns have promoted the growth of prosperous communities. But it is anything but clear that their capital cost has even been properly counted. Operating on near green-field sites, armed with substantial State money and cut-price compulsory purchase powers, it would not have been easy for any management to fail.

But in other more complex areas, the more the State has become involved, the less obvious its success in hitting even those targets for which the original intervention was designed.

For a quarter of a century, the centre of my hometown in South Wales saw its commercial life ebbing away while "plan" succeeded "plan." The citizens of Redhill have just celebrated the twentieth anniversary of their first town centre development plan—with scarcely a brick to show for it so far.

Even the prosperity of county communities is now being stifled by structure plans which set out ruthlessly to limit future commercial activity to businesses that are already based within the county. Is it not perverse to be tearing down tariff barriers within Europe at the same time as we are erecting ring fences to prevent the movement of enterprises within our own country?

APPETITE WITHOUT RESOURCES

But it is in the big cities that the appetite of the State has almost out-run its capacity. In Liverpool in December 1976, 1100 acres of inner-city land (15 percent of the total) lay vacant; but only 150 of these were included in any firm programme for development. A third of all this vacant land was allocated to highways, none of which were unlikely to be implemented; half of this land had been vacant for 5 years. The same story can be told of many other of our major cities.

Large parts of the London borough of Lambeth, in which I live, continue to crumble in the name of "housing action areas" and the like. At the very gateway of Lambeth on the southern end of Vauxhall Bridge stands a huge site, that has been vacant for years. When Peter Shore recently asked Councils to provide a list of derelict land, this was duly reported to him by the Stockwell and Vauxhall neighbourhood Council. It is owned by the Department of the Environment!

The Broad Sanctuary site in Parliament Square has been empty for nearly thirty years. I daresay Vauxhall will have to wait longer than that.

The public purse has been quite unable to provide the funds, or the enterprise, to match the planners' aspirations. No wonder one Lambeth squatter, on whom I called not long ago, displays in his window the mildly worded poster: "More and more people are coming to believe that the Lambeth Council Planning Department are wreckers." It is easy to sympathize with the painted slogan on one Camberwell hoarding: "Corrugated iron is the character armour of the Council."

BUREAUCRATIC NIGHTMARE

This is the background against which successive governments have introduced bill after bill and shuffled much the same amount of money from one new fashionably named urban programme to another. But all attempts at reform seem only to multiply the bureaucracy. The Department of the Environment's 1976 Report on Birmingham's Inner Area is at its most characteristic with its proposal "to give initial momentum to industrial investment" by the establishment of a "multi-authority inter-departmental steering committee under the chairmanship of the Department of Industry, the county or the district as appropriate."

Is it any wonder that a *New Statesman* author, writing only two weeks ago about this part of London, observed that "the complex interrelationships between the various local authorities and other agencies involved have created an inertia," which have turned London's docklands into a "bureaucratic nightmare"?

This "progress" seems to have reached its reductio ad absurdum with the recent failure of the Docklands Joint Committee to persuade either of the two very suitable top candidates (there were 260 applicants) to take on the job of Docklands Manager (at £24,000 a year).

As Judy Hillman wrote in the *Guardian* the other day, docklands are "sinking under the weight of the planners' grand design." The local MP, Ian Mikardo, apostle of an entirely planned Socialist society, has rightly defined the effect of planning on his constituency:

> One does nothing until one is absolutely sure that it is right. Since it takes many years to ensure that one is doing the right thing one does not do anything at all for many years.

Tacitus put it more crisply (he was describing the Roman scorched-earth policy in first-century Germany): "Faciunt solitudinem, pacem appellant."

But, of course, London's dockland is only one example. The frustrating domination of more and more of our urban communities, by a combination of widespread public land ownership and public intervention into virtually all private activities, has produced a form of municipal mortmain which will not be shifted without a huge effort of will.

MUNICIPAL MONASTICISM

Henry VIII may or may not have had good reason to dissolve the monasteries. Many medieval communities certainly gained a new lease on life from the dispersal of monastic property to freebooting individuals. And long before the monasteries were dissolved, it had proved necessary to pass

Statutes of Mortmain, specifically to prevent land being held idle in moribund monastic ownership.

Today's prelates, at once the leaders and the prisoners of municipal monasticism, are in town and county halls or the head offices of nationalised industries and public corporations. I do not question their goodwill and sense of commitment to "the public interest." Just as zealously as the monks and abbots strove to do the will of God, today's chief executives and planning officers seek to serve the will of democracy—but alas, with less fruitful results.

In the outcome, tens of thousands of people are unwillingly involved in frustrating each other's efforts, as well as those of their fellow citizens. I sadly echo the comment of one frustrated planner[1] that:

> One is forced to question the current priorities of a system of planning which spends so much time and energy exercising strict controls over the extensions of individual houses and minor changes of use, while allowing whole areas to be demolished and laid to waste for years, even decades, at the heart of the most populous cities in the country.

THE RETURN TO ECONOMIC VITALITY

This dismal story of disappointed expectations surely represents the highwater mark of our general case for the fundamental change of approach. It is essential to restore the competitive diversity of our economy, as quickly as possible. Inventiveness, marketing, and development—all must be properly rewarded. New, small enterprises have a vital role to play. So too do established companies, with the experience which will enable them to respond to rapidly changing world trading conditions. The much-maligned multi-nationals have done, and can still do, more for economic progress than all the meditations of Karl Marx.

This return to economic vitality crucially depends upon the fundamental reform of our tax system. Post-tax differentials in Britain are now even narrower, according to a recent statement by a Treasury Minister, than they are in China or in Poland.

It is often said that prescription of tax reform has already been tried and failed. Sadly, even under the last Conservative Government, that was not really the case.

Between 1970 and 1973, income tax on wages and salaries plus surtax and employees' national insurance contributions declined, as a percentage of all wages and salaries, by only 0.3 percent, from 20 to 19.7 percent. And our top marginal rate of 75 percent remained far above the average which prevailed in other countries.

Tax cuts have a real creative importance. For they can allow the rapid accumulation of post-tax wealth by the comparatively small (and necessarily unidentifiable) band of people who have the capacity to identify and exploit new commercial opportunities (in services as well as in manufacturing industry).

That is why we must restore the legitimacy of becoming rich by taking risks (apart from those which arise from doing the football pools). *That* is the way to promote the creation of real new jobs.

The other almost equally urgent need is to set about the sensible deregulation of our economy. By this I do not mean anything resembling a wholesale abandonment of those laws (for consumer protection or against racial discrimination, for example) which are an acceptable feature of most modern prosperous economies. I refer more specifically to economic interventionism—price and dividend control, for example; and to the consequences of our planning system, which I have already tried to spell out.

That is our general case for transforming the tax system, so as to restore incentives, and for liberalising the entire planning system, for challenging the effectiveness of Industrial Development Certificates (IDCs), Office Development Permits (ODPs), and all the other paraphernalia.

INNER-CITY GHOST TOWNS?

But one must be very doubtful whether these general changes will bring speedy or sufficient relief to the worst-afflicted areas with which we are concerned.

Some might even argue that they are beyond help and would abandon them as inner-city ghost towns—a doleful monument to our collective incompetence. That would be a feckless and inhumane conclusion.

These areas are then the biggest challenge. Can we, if we have the courage and imagination, transform them into our greatest opportunities? Are we perhaps driven to the conclusion that the remedies that need to be applied generally should be even more dramatically applied in the worst afflicted areas?

They still have, after all, some very real advantages. They are often close to other thriving commercial centers, almost as often close to rivers that have been great harbours. Much of the land is already cleared: the dereliction is itself an opportunity. And they still house communities who cherish a sense of civic pride but yearn for jobs, real jobs—who are looking for a window of hope for the future.

Even in today's inhospitable, even hostile, conditions, *some* jobs are still coming into existence, *some* profits are still being made.

Some pioneering efforts (for example, the thirty-strong craftsmen's cooperative called Waterside in Rotherhithe Street; the Action Resource Centre; or the Clerkenwell Workshops) are still trying to blaze a trail, in the teeth of institutional inertia. But it isn't often fun. Nor will it be, if we go on as we are.

"Public enterprise," which has been making more and more of the running for the last thirty years, has certainly not delivered the goods.

Isn't it time to consider the alternative approach? The original prosperity of our cities was founded on the pursuit of profit. Why should we not again seek a solution that is based primarily on the view that those who help to restore prosperity are entitled to expect financial reward—and on a substantial scale?

TOWARDS A RICH SOCIETY

We cannot, I believe, create a rich society unless we are prepared to accept and welcome the fact that some people will, as individuals, become richer. Unless people are able to earn and keep significant reward for the investment and effort that we wish them to put into our urban deserts, they are just not going to be interested. More pleasant, they may well feel, to run an antique shop in Winchester, or a restaurant at Aldborough. Or, if they fail to get planning permission even for that, to settle for an inflation-proofed pension from something like the dis-Location of Offices Bureau.

I repeat: it can hardly be said (even by Mr. Ian Mikardo) that the State-directed alternative has been a wild success.

HONG KONG IN GLASGOW?

Against this background, I was delighted last year to discover that a distinguished Socialist, Professor Peter Hall, was beginning to reach for the same prescription as myself—and I emphasize that I am now offering a purely personal view.

Why not, he argued (and so do I) *consider highly unorthodox methods*? Why not, he suggested to the RTPI (Royal Town Planning Institute) Conference at Chester last year, aim to recreate the Hong Kong of the 1950s inside Inner Liverpool or Inner Glasgow? Small selected areas of inner cities, he argued, should be simply thrown open to all kinds of initiatives, with minimal control—based on the idea of "fairly shameless free enterprise." (Note the Fabian reserve which convinced Professor Hall that freedom could only be "fairly" shameless!)

The germ of this revolutionary idea springs from the experience of other communities where something like a Freeport solution has laid the foundations of economic liberation. Independent countries like Hong Kong and Singapore have been entirely free to make themselves magnets for enterprise, with generally benevolent tax and customs regimes, freedom from exchange control, and an absence of unnecessary regulations and of heavy social or other obligations on commerce and industry. Special tax and other concessions for pioneer businesses have been guaranteed for a substantial period of time.

On a more modest scale, places like West Berlin (for special reasons) and Shannon in the Irish Republic have developed a similar approach. Even within our own [United] Kingdom, the Channel Islands and the Isle of Man offer some instructive lessons.

THREE ALTERNATIVE IDEAS

It is important to distinguish between the three different concepts that are involved in all this:

1. *THE FREEPORT IDEA*

A Freeport is simply a "free trade zone," generally near a sea or air port. Customs and excise duties and tariffs are not payable on goods and raw materials imported into the zone. They may be exported from the zone similarly free of duty, generally after having been reprocessed. Such items as tobacco, food and drink, radio and television, cameras, chemicals, and electrical equipment are the kind of products suitable for such treatment.

Freeport facilities already exist in several continental ports. Shannon is an example of the same kind of thing.

The Greater London Council [is] now considering a proposal to establish a Freeport on 300 acres of London's dockland. The idea certainly deserves consideration. But the Report submitted by the GLC's Controller of Planning and Transportation identifies some limitations:

> The provision of such sites is difficult in London and would almost certainly involve rehabilitating some land. It would also be impossible for the development to service interest on market value of 300 acres from the start.

Now is not *this* a little odd?

There are said to be 5,000 acres of empty land in London's East End, more than half of them in public ownership. If 300 of these acres cannot be assembled fairly quickly, it is a further criticism of the existing state of affairs. And loan charges must surely be being paid, by one form of public authority or another, on far more than 300 of the 5,000 acres now standing idle?

2. *THE "CROWN COLONY" IDEA*

This is Professor Hall's fully fledged proposal for a largely independent community—tariff free—and exempt from most legislation and indeed from the Welfare State as well. In his own words it is an "extremely drastic last-ditch solution" which could be tried "only on a very small scale"—probably in an area that was "largely abandoned and denuded of people." UK passports, he observes, would still be valid in the area!

This proposal—which is *not* the one that I am putting forward—would indeed be "drastic," if only because those who already lived in the area would lose all state benefits along with most of their tax liabilities. If one went as far as this, then (as with the Channel Islands) it would be necessary to ensure that the new "colony" did not become a tax haven for every individual citizen and footloose company office.

As I say, I should not at this stage support an experiment as dramatic as this; but the idea should be kept at the back of one's mind—if only as a yardstick against which to judge more modest proposals.

3. *THE ENTERPRISE ZONE*

This is the approach which I personally believe to be well worth studying. It would be designed to go further and more swiftly than the general policy changes that we have been proposing to liberate enterprise throughout the country.

This suggestion would *not* be based on considerations of regional policy (which is an entirely distinct subject, with its own complexities and counterarguments). Rather the idea would be to set up test market areas or laboratories in which to enable fresh policies to prime the pump of prosperity, and to establish their potential for doing so elsewhere.

Nor are these proposals suggested only for former port or dockland areas; although they would certainly be appropriate in some such areas, and could easily be combined with the simpler Freeport concept.

The idea would be to designate, in four or five places for a start—Clydeside, Merseyside, the West Midlands, and East London, say—substantial areas of land with the intention that most of them could be developed with as much freedom as possible—to make profits and to create jobs. The key elements might be as follows:

First, planning control of any detailed kind would cease to apply. Any building that complied with very basic anti-pollution, health, and safety standards and that was not over a stated maximum height (that "did not threaten to frighten the horses in the streets") would be permissible, for any lawful purpose. IDCs and ODPs would not be required.

Second, the Community Land Act (itself a powerful obstacle to progress and in any case due for repeal) would be put effectively into reverse. Public authorities which owned land would be required, within a specific time, to dispose of it to private bidders, by auction in the open market. New developments in the area would be free from rent control.

Third, entrepreneurs who moved into this land would be granted exemption from Development Land Tax (without prejudice to the general case for lightening and simplifying the general burden of that tax) and perhaps exemption from rates, in whole or in part.

Fourth, businesses in the areas in question should be given a guarantee that tax law (affecting investment, depreciation, and so on) would not be changed to their disadvantage. And they should be entitled to an undertaking from the Crown that they would not be liable to any future proposal for nationalization. Marathon Shipbuilders were given such an undertaking on the Clyde, so that it is not without precedent. No government grants or subsidies would be payable to any enterprise within the area.

Fifth, certain other legal obligations or threats should be declared not to operate within the area: price control and pay policy, for example. There are other pieces of legislation that could be stated not to apply—such as some or all of the provisions of the Employment Protection Act.

Sixth, all these conditions would be guaranteed for a stated and substantial number of years.

MANAGING AN ENTERPRISE ZONE

How, finally would this kind of scheme be administered? It would be agreeable to believe that it could be managed by or through the existing framework of local government. Certainly it would be necessary to ensure an effective role for elected representatives of local people. But quite a lot of today's problems arise from the difficulty in securing a common view between overlapping or adjacent local authorities.

So, although I can sympathise with those (like Mr. Horace Cutler) who would hope to avoid this need, it would, I believe, be necessary to establish a new model of authority, as others have suggested, with *some* of the qualities of a new town corporation. As long ago as 1962, Godfrey Hodgson argued the case in *Crossbow* for the establishment of this kind of Old Town Renewal Agency—to be available as a kind of standard kit for those communities that wished to apply for it.

Certainly there would have to be differences from the standard New Town prototype. Most important is the fact that my kind of agency would not primarily be acquiring property for the public sector but disposing of it for private development. There is no reason why private capital should not have a part in financing the agency. In order to build the right kind of link with existing inhabitants of the area, it might be possible (as Godfrey Hodgson originally suggested) to arrange for them to be given a share in the action: a right to an equity stake in the new authority, perhaps? or a right to require the agency to buy up one's property—for those who did not like what was in prospect?

NO BIG BROTHER

Some people, of course, will be all too ready to be alarmed by these proposals, or even to misrepresent them. Let me try to offer re-assurance.

The good people of the Isle of Dogs, for example, where I am speaking tonight, should not take fright at the prospect of some new big brother organization being thrust upon them. My proposal (which will certainly require a great deal more analysis) is intended simply to offer the *chance* of a new, more hopeful way forward.

There are many who would like to see many of the elements which I suggest applied throughout the economy, forthwith. I can see their point. But in the present state of political argument, is it not suitable to carve out an opportunity for demonstrating on our own doorstep, that they will work?

If that happens, I hope we shall find communities queuing up to apply for Enterprise Zone Status. We shall have gone a long way towards winning the debate. Meanwhile my proposals are not intended to be a politically exclusive idea but an experiment that could fire the imagination of people in all parties or in none. I believe it would be worthwhile ensuring that part of any Enterprise Zone could be available to non-commerical groups, who wished, for example, to establish experimental workers' co-operatives—Mondrago fashion or any other. If the Tribune Group or the Socialist Workers' Party wanted part of an Enterprise Zone to themselves—well, why not?

ALL SYSTEMS GO?

But no one surely can doubt the need for dramatic change from the present position? In present circumstances, the enterprise—be it large or small—that wishes to move into these areas all too often feels reluctant even to start the bureaucratic battle of finding a way through. Despite the best intentions of many people, the prospect for the entrepreneur seems to be one of depressing hostility. Is it not worth taking some risks, departing from precedent, to replace this with an environment that is positively hospitable and inviting to enterprise? Why not try to make all systems go, for a change?

If the stormy waters of the North Sea can expect to attract £25,000 million of investment over the next ten years, because of the prospect of profit that is there, it should surely be possible for the same prospect to attract the same kind of skill and capital to work in partnership with the people of our great cities.

"THE GREY MEN"

Of course, the grey men whose job it is to consider the "administrative difficulties" of any new idea would be ready enough to start manufacturing the small print that could stop the initiative in its tracks. It might be argued, for example, that proposals of this kind would conflict with Treaty obligations to the European Community or in other directions. I suspect that these authorities would give a tolerant response if the model that I have in mind looked like offering a positive breakthrough to a more dynamic future for our society, and theirs as well. For it is high time for somebody, somewhere, to adopt a more dramatic and hopeful approach.

Winston Churchill, in 1940, was told that the idea of compensation for war damage was quite unthinkable. He was not prepared to take "no" for an answer. And the outlines of an entirely beneficent scheme were drawn up within three weeks.

No one can be sure whether my suggested approach would work or not (and I emphasise that it is a personal suggestion).

But it is about time we were prepared to make some fresh starts.

NOTES

1. John Burrows, *Royal Town Planning Institute Journal*, January 1978.

Enterprise Zones: Pioneering in the Inner City

Stuart M. Butler

FOCUSING THE NEW THINKING: THE ENTERPRISE ZONE

Certain broad conclusions come from the recent rethinking on the city and from the studies related to it. They may be summarized as follows:

a. Major injections of government money, either for housing projects or for commercial purposes, may not only be wasteful but may even lead to a deterioration of the situation. Projects with limited outside support, and drawing heavily from local inventiveness and effort, are relatively successful.

b. The greatest economic problem of the inner city is the poor birthrate of businesses—and especially small businesses. Small firms are the most effective creators of jobs in the economy, and provide the type of jobs most suitable to the inner city. They bring together local entrepreneurial talent and the young, unskilled workforce, and they play a crucial social role in the community. However, studies show that these types of enterprise either shun, or are shunned by, government agencies and the larger commercial lending institutions. The best way of encouraging this sector is thus to remove obstacles in the path of the entrepreneur in the cities and to give these individuals the kind of business climate that will provide the incentive to take risks.

c. Neighborhood residents have shown themselves eager to put their own time, effort, and limited resources into housing rehabilitation if given genuine encouragement to do so. Rather than funding new projects, governments would achieve more if they created a climate in which essentially self-help projects would be more likely to succeed.

THE FREEPORT CONCEPT

This line of thinking has been taken to its logical conclusion in proposals put forward in Britain during the last three years, and more recently in legislation introduced in the United States. The first significant elements of a plan were first suggested in 1977 by Professor Peter Hall, an urban planning expert at Reading University in England. He outlined a concept he referred to as a "Freeport," an idea which he felt would be ideally suited to the needs of the depressed inner city. According to Hall, the Freeport would be

> an essay in non-plan. Small, selected areas of inner cities would be simply thrown open to all kinds of initiative, with minimum control. In other words, we would aim to recreate the Hong Kong of the 1950s and 1960s inside inner Liverpool or inner Glasgow.[1]

The Hall plan would involve three central elements.

a. The "encouragement of entrepreneurship and capital." The specified areas would be free of national exchange and customs control, and foreign capital and business would be welcomed. All goods could be imported and sold free of duty, including sales taxes. Similar areas, known as free trade zones, exist in Hong Kong, Taiwan, and elsewhere. Hall's plan would set them up in the heart of declining cities.
b. The areas "would be based on fairly shameless free enterprise." They would be "free of . . . taxes, social services, industrial and other regulations. Bureaucracy would be kept to an absolute minimum. So would personal and corporate taxation. Trade unions would be allowed, as in Hong Kong, but there would be no closed shops. Wages would find their own level."
c. Residence in the area would be based on free choice. Existing residents would be free to leave or to stay under the new system of deregulation, low taxation, and low social benefits.

THE ENTERPRISE ZONE

The Freeport idea offered by Professor Hall encouraged several British politicians to look carefully for a policy based on similar foundations. This led ultimately to the concept known as the Enterprise Zone, first put forward publicly in a speech in 1978, by the then Conservative opposition spokesman on economics (and now chancellor of the exchequer) Sir Geoffrey Howe.[2]

Sir Geoffrey's Enterprise Zone plan differed somewhat from the Hall approach. Professor Hall saw his Freeport as an "extremely drastic last-ditch solution," which could be tried "only on a very small scale" in areas that were "largely abandoned and denuded of people." Thus it was seen mainly as an idea suitable for areas where we would be starting with a clean slate—areas where a pioneer society could be established.

Sir Geoffrey viewed the Hall plan as an extremely important "yardstick against which to judge more modest proposals." His Enterprise Zone approach, however, was designed to apply not only to areas almost totally lacking in population, but to the depressed inner cities in general. In depopulated areas, he conceded, the Freeport idea might well be implemented as part of the Enterprise Zone.

A further conceptual difference between the two approaches was that Sir Geoffrey also saw the zones as experimental areas:

> The idea would be to set up test market areas or laboratories in which to enable fresh policies to prime the pump of prosperity, and to establish their potential for doing so elsewhere.

He even saw the possibility of Enterprise Zones becoming testing areas for alternative social arrangements, where radical political groups might have the opportunity to demonstrate the effectiveness—or otherwise—of their views:

> My proposals are not intended to be a politically exclusive idea but an experiment that could fire the imagination of people in all parties or in none. I believe it would be worthwhile ensuring that part of any Enterprise Zone could be available to non-commercial groups who wished, for example, to establish experimental workers' cooperatives . . . . If the . . . Socialist Workers' Party wanted part of an Enterprise Zone to themselves—well, why not?

The basic features of an Enterprise Zone, as outlined by Sir Geoffrey Howe in 1978, would be as follows:

a. An area of a square mile or so in the most depressed part of a city would be selected, and designated as an Enterprise Zone.

b. Planning controls of any detailed kind would cease to apply within the zone. Any building that complied with very basic anti-pollution, health and safety standards, and was for a legal purpose, would be permitted.

c. City councils owning vacant land, or abandoned property, would be required to dispose of it to private bidders by auction in the open market.

d. New developments in the zone would be free from rent control.

e. Entrepreneurs who moved into the zone would be granted a reduction or exemption from property taxes, and there would be a reduction in capital gains tax on development.

f. Businesses in the zones would be guaranteed that public laws affecting investment, depreciation, etc. would not be changed to their disadvantage. But no special government grants or subsidies would be payable to any enterprise in the zone.
g. Wage and price controls would not apply in the zone.
h. All the above conditions would be guaranteed for a stated and "substantial" number of years.

BRITISH LEGISLATION

Other than discussion in the media, there was no movement on the Enterprise Zone idea until the Conservatives took office after the general election of May 1979. In the months that followed detailed consideration was given to the exact measures that would be applied within any initial group of Enterprise Zones.

In March 1980 these measures were announced, together with a list of the cities under consideration as possible sites. The proposed measures were broadly in line with the strategy laid out by Sir Geoffrey two years earlier. Since wage and price controls had been abolished in the meantime there was no item dealing with them, and since the government was already examining means of reducing the impact of rent control throughout the country, and ways of selling government-owned land and housing, these were not included.

The central features of the program to be implemented by the end of 1980 include a 100 percent reduction on all industrial and commercial property within the designated zones. Revenue lost by a city council as a result of this will be reimbursed by the Treasury. There will be a reduction in capital gains tax levied on developments within the zones, and a 100 percent capital allowance against corporate income tax for commercial and industrial buildings. A drastically simplified system of zoning will apply, and developments will need only to comply with that plan, not with any local ordinances. Planning applications will be simplified and dealt with as speedily as possible. The designation of Enterprise Zone status will last for a minimum of ten years but will be renewable.

Two elements not included in Sir Geoffrey's 1978 speech were included in the March 1980 announcement. Within the zones, government statistical inquiries will be kept to the bare minimum, removing much of the form filling routinely demanded of business. Furthermore, the government intends to speed up the processing of requests for customs warehousing in the zones. This does not go anywhere near as far as Professor Hall's Freeport, but it does signify an appreciation by the government of the need to stimulate foreign trade within the depressed areas as a means of creating jobs.

Within four months of the announcement by the government of the broad geographic areas under consideration, twenty-four district councils and London boroughs had made formal requests to be included as sites: many of these came from cities controlled by the opposition Labour Party. In July the prime minister, Mrs. Thatcher, announced that seven sites had been selected and that detailed discussions would commence with the cities involved, to ensure that the zones would be operational by the end of the year. These sites include a part of the depressed shipbuilding town of Newcastle, an area in the port of Liverpool, part of riot-torn Belfast in Northern Ireland, and the declining dockland district of east London (where, incidently, Sir Geoffrey made his 1978 speech first outlining the idea).

ENTERPRISE ZONES IN THE UNITED STATES

The Enterprise Zone concept was first introduced to the United States early in 1979 by The Heritage Foundation[3]. In view of the different political structure and body of laws in the United States, several modifications have been made to the original idea in Heritage Foundation publications and Heritage-sponsored articles.[4] Further, some new extensions of the proposal, not in the original British plan, have been put forward for discussion.

The following are the most important developments put forward by the Foundation as a basis for Enterprise Zones in the United States.

A. SUSPENSION OF MINIMUM WAGE LAWS

Overwhelming evidence has been provided to demonstrate that minimum wage laws create unemployment among the young and unskilled by pricing them out of the labor market. In the depressed central cities, where unemployment rates are well above the national average, suspending minimum wage rates within an Enterprise Zone would open up new opportunities for many who are currently unemployable.

One would have to be very naive not to appreciate that there is considerable opposition to the suspension of minimum wage laws, both from those who sincerely believe that they protect workers and do not create unemployment, and from others who are motivated more from self-interest (such as employees who fear competition from lower-paid workers). Two possible compromises might defuse at least part of this opposition. A youth minimum wage—lower than the standard minimum—could be instituted in the Enterprise Zones. This would have the effect of opening the door to employment for a specific segment of the population which necessarily commands a lower wage because of inexperience and lack of skills, yet it would confine the market impact on wages to a narrow group of workers. But even this modest change could have a very beneficial effect in the central cities, where the young constitute a high proportion of the available labor force.

An alternative relaxation of the minimum wage would be some kind of subsidy or tax credit for those hiring labor in the zones; such credits have been used before in this country and others. This would have the effect of reducing the cost of labor to the employer without depressing wage rates, and so might remove some of the more emotional opposition to suspending minimum wage. This is not a particularly attractive alternative, given that it opens up the possibility of large-scale manipulation of the labor market by the government through various forms of employment subsidies. On the other hand, it may be that outright suspension of the minimum wage might be less effective than is often supposed, due to the disincentive effects arising from the welfare system.

Some adjustment in the base cost of labor in the inner cities is essential, however, if the areas are to recover. The combination of low labor skills, and obstacles to enterprise in the central cities, makes it uneconomic to employ a high proportion of residents at the legal wage rate. And furthermore, the denial of a job at even a very low wage rate means the denial of an opportunity to enter the labor market, and with it the chance to gain the experience and skills needed to achieve more acceptable income in the future. It is this mobility that has largely been eradicated in the cities.

B. A TURNOVER TRIGGER POINT

One reservation expressed against the Enterprise Zone concept is that it might provide a loophole whereby major corporations could establish small outlets in the zones and then use these locations as a form of "urban offshore island" through which nationwide revenues could be channeled to obtain a substantial tax break, without any beneficial effect on the local community.

Since the thrust of the incentives within the Enterprise Zone is toward the start-up, labor, and real estate costs of new and smaller businesses, it is likely that the attractiveness of the areas to well-established companies would be marginal. A time cut-off for the tax suspension would also discourage companies from using the zones for purely tax-saving purposes. But a very effective way of preventing the misuse of an Enterprise Zone by a major corporation, and of targeting the incentives more accurately to new and small companies, would be to institute a turnover trigger system (with or without a time limit). Below the trigger point a business would enjoy all the tax incentives specified in the zone. But when the turnover moved past the trigger point, the business would become subject to an increasing portion of taxes on the excess.[5] Thus, when a small company began its operations in an Enterprise Zone it would have all the applicable benefits. As it grew and became more profitable, it would begin to bear a tax burden more in line with firms outside the zone. If a large company moved into the zone it would still obtain the tax break on the amount of turnover specified in the trigger level; but the larger the business, the less significant that would be in relation to its total tax load and costs of operation. So the incentive for a large, established concern to move to the Enterprise Zone simply to gain the tax savings would be much less.

The turnover trigger has other advantages over the simpler time limit, if the Enterprise Zone is seen principally as a means of giving depressed areas an economic "shot in the arm" by allowing temporary tax and regulatory suspensions. In the first place, the trigger concentrates the breaks on the new, small businesses—precisely the sector which must be encouraged if the inner cities are to be revived. It also means that successful companies begin to contribute to city finances as soon as they become viable, rather than at the end of some arbitrary time period. Also, the trigger point could be made appropriate to the area. For highly depressed, crime-ridden districts, where insurance and other costs are relatively heavy, a more generous turnover trigger could be used, reflecting the state of the area. Finally, phasing in taxes on the basis of turnover would also reduce the objection that Enterprise Zones would be damaging to companies outside the zone, who would have to compete with firms facing lower tax burdens. If this did happen, and an Enterprise Zone firm began to grow at the expense of neighbors outside the area, it would begin to lose the tax advantage that gave it the edge.[6]

C. FREE TRADE ZONES

Although the British plan does speed up the applications procedure for customs warehousing it will not set up free trade zones of the kind seen in Hong Kong and elsewhere. There are about 400 such zones around the world, and they have shown themselves to be very effective sources of employment for local labor.[7]

Within a free trade zone duties on imported goods and components are not paid until the product leaves the zone for the domestic market and are not paid at all if the product is re-exported. Capital normally tied up in customs bonds is thus available for other purposes. So the zones are very attractive sites for warehousing and trans-shipping facilities. Furthermore, if components are imported into the free trade zone and then assembled into a final product for sale in the domestic market, duty is not payable on the value added within the zone. So free trade zones also become attractive to foreign companies selling in the domestic market, since by establishing assembly plants within the zone the total customs liability may be reduced. The country receiving the goods has the benefit of the employment generated for its nationals. Such foreign investment in assembly plants has been a significant feature of free trade zones. In Hong Kong, for instance, it has been estimated that over 60,000 jobs have been created by foreign investment.

There are about forty free trade zones in the United States (the term "foreign trade zone" is used here), including sites in New York, Kansas City, and the recently established Volkswagen plant at New Stanton in Pennsylvania. Until the spring of 1980, duty was payable not only on imported components in the United States, but also on the American labor, overhead expenses, and profit involved in processing for the American market. Hence the only real benefit to a company using a foreign trade zone arose from customs deferment. Fortunately, the Department of Commerce revised its regulations this spring, and now the value added within the zone is not liable to duty—in line with the situation elsewhere in the world.

The designation of free trade zone status, wherever practicable, to Enterprise Zones is an important new dimension to the idea. It would attract new kinds of business into the inner cities (warehousing and assembling), and it would lead to an inflow of foreign capital. This would add to the capital available in the area, and create new types of industry, rather than creating businesses which might be in competition with firms elsewhere in the city. Furthermore, the type of labor required in assembly factories tends to be unskilled or semiskilled: precisely the kind of labor that is readily available in the central cities.

D. INNOVATIVE ACTION ON HOUSING

The original British Enterprise Zone idea rightly laid the greatest emphasis on job creation. While this is clearly the key to urban revitalization, the approach embodied in the Enterprise Zone concept also suggests ways in which shattered inner city housing might be rehabilitated.

The overriding philosophy behind the great renewal projects of the 1960s was that areas could be improved by tearing down old buildings and replacing them with new ones. Yet a visit to many such projects now shows that the buildings which were showpieces of the 1960s are often well on the way to becoming the slums of the 1980s. As Jane Jacobs has shown, the only effective way of restoring the social and economic health of a declining neighborhood is to encourage the rehabilitation of old, but sound, buildings alongside very modest new projects. This is just as true of residential properties as it is of commercial ones.

There are a number of ways in which rehabilitation can be induced. In the first place, rent control must be phased out in the inner cities, to allow property owners to gain sufficient revenue to maintain and improve their buildings, and to make investment in rental property once again economic. The immediate problem associated with this action would be its impact on low-income households. This problem could be largely eradicated by the expansion of a modified form of Section 8 housing assistance within the Enterprise Zones. This would, of course, be a subsidy to the low-income tenant, but it would be a selective and direct subsidy in line with the existing public policy goal of making it possible for low-income families to live in the inner cities in decent housing. Unlike the present policy of rent control in many cities, it would not involve a compulsory transfer of income from landlords to tenants (irrespective of the income of either) and it would not be a futile attempt to accomplish a policy goal by trying to abolish the law of supply and demand. One danger, of course, is that the possibility of well-maintained housing subsidized rates might encourage a flow of low-income families into the Enterprise Zone, but this could be prevented by relating the Section 8-style support to length of residence in the area.

Reducing property tax and increasing the capital gains deduction on property appreciation within an Enterprise Zone would stimulate rehabilitation by improving the returns available from residential buildings. It would also be useful to experiment with sweeping homesteading programs within the Enterprise Zones. Cities could write off the outstanding tax liability on abandoned buildings and offer them under such a program. In most cases the tax loss would only be a paper loss since the chances of recovering the outstanding tax is near-zero, and the city would be able to raise revenues on the properties when they had become renovated. An expanded program of homesteading would have the added advantage that it would attract young middle-income people back into the depressed areas.

Similarly innovative strategies could be applied to commercial property. Simplification of zoning in the Enterprise Zones would allow change of use, which would enable new businesses to start in low-cost buildings—even in buildings that were previously for residential purposes. In areas where considerable demolition has taken place, the use of temporary buildings might be encouraged, to enable companies to acquire inexpensive facilities which could later be replaced with more substantial structures when funds permitted. Similarly, new businesses could be assisted by an extensive program of shopsteading—the business equivalent of homesteading.

E. EXPERIMENTATION

In the early discussion of the Enterprise Zone concept by Sir Geoffrey Howe, the suggestion was put forward that Enterprise Zones could become laboratories for policy innovations as well as the application of tested approaches. In the final British plan this aspect was not given prominence, but it is nevertheless a logical extension of the concept.

At the heart of the Enterprise Zone idea is the notion that the best solution to the urban problem lies in mobilizing the trial-and-error process of private enterprise, so that the most appropriate combination of businesses for the area will evolve. It would be totally in keeping with this approach for a form of trial-and-error process to be applied to the realm of public policy.

If there is a genuine difference of opinion about the effects of repealing the minimum wage laws, for example, let the laws be suspended in one or two Enterprise Zones for a test period. A youth minimum wage might be introduced in another zone for the same period. The results could then be compared with the employment patterns in other areas. A similar approach could be taken to regulation. Certain OSHA regulations, building codes, etc., aimed primarily at large corporations or non-urban areas, could be modified or suspended in selected zones on a test basis. Again the results could be compared with other areas.

Enterprise Zones would also be very suitable areas in which to test innovative policies such as the negative income tax. As with many new ideas there is not total agreement on the probable effects of the negative tax, and so there is justifiable hesitation at the prospect of applying the approach to the whole tax system. But the Enterprise Zone offers the opportunity to examine the consequences of the policy on a small scale. In addition, the zones would be in areas where most conventional policies have proved ineffective, and thus would be ideal locations to test more radical approaches without dismantling programs which were already effective.

Testing the negative income tax in an Enterprise Zone would be particularly valuable, since its supporters argue that it is not only a particularly efficient form of welfare, but that it also provides the incentive for people to accept even low-paid jobs and move out of the poverty trap. If so, it could have a highly beneficial effect in the inner cities, where policymakers are faced with the apparent dilemma that they must provide adequate support to the unemployed and low-income households, and yet by doing so much of the incentive to take a job is removed.

LEGISLATION IN AMERICA

Soon after the Enterprise Zone concept was introduced in the United States early in 1979, a bill embodying many of the original British elements was introduced in the Illinois legislature. To the surprise of the sponsors it gained very wide support and passed the lower house with little discussion. It narrowly failed to win the necessary three-fifths majority in the Senate only after strong opposition was expressed by the City Council of Chicago.

The Illinois bill could only deal with aspects of the Enterprise Zone proposal which could be implemented at the state level, such as property tax changes and the suspension of the state minimum wage. It was not possible, of course, to make changes in the national minimum wage or federal tax rates. A version of the bill will be introduced once again in the full session of the legislature in Illinois in 1981, and it is very probable that similar bills will be introduced in a number of other states.

The Enterprise Zone has also attracted strong support in Congress, where the lead has been given by Representative Jack Kemp of New York. His first version of the Enterprise Zone, presented to Congress in May 1980 (H.R. 7240), received considerable attention. Very significantly, a great deal of support came from groups and individuals on the liberal side of the political spectrum, hardly a faction normally associated with the conservative Kemp. The breadth of interest in Kemp's proposal gives an indication of just how far thinking on the city has moved in the last decade.

Liberal support for the Kemp proposal was not limited to words. When a second version of the bill was introduced in June (H.R. 7563)[8] its chief cosponsor was Democrat Robert Garcia of the South Bronx. The Urban Jobs and Enterprise Zone Act has since become the focus of discussion regarding inner city policy. Support for the measure became a plank in the Republican Party's campaign platform, and many Democrats have voiced their belief that the Enterprise Zone approach is the most exciting proposal that has come forward in recent years to deal with the problems of the inner city.

The Kemp-Garcia bill has been put forward mainly as a basis for discussion at the present time. As with any radical measure, detailed argument is needed to develop a workable law, and a revised version will be placed before Congress in the 1981 session. But it is clear that the center of discussion on the cities has moved decisively since the Kemp-Garcia bill was introduced.

RELATED ISSUES

Reduced to its essential foundations, the Enterprise Zone aims to stimulate businesses—especially small enterprises—in depressed central-city neighborhoods by encouraging entrepreneurs to take the risk of setting up a business by removing unnecessary obstacles and reducing taxes. It seeks to establish an entrepreneurial *climate* in the neighborhoods, rather than embark on a policy of selecting particular firms which would then receive government aid. By removing these tax and regulatory obstacles the cost and complexity of doing business in these areas would be reduced, making it more likely that entrepreneurs with limited capital, borrowing power, and business know-how would be able to go into business.

Encouraging the first-time businessman is an important feature of the concept, both from the point of view of job creation, and because of the need to open opportunities for local business talent. The inner cities were traditionally districts where people obtained their first job or business experience. When they became successful many left, but their places were filled by other workers and entrepreneurs. In some areas, such as the South Bronx, the new entrants were generally immigrants. It is this process of upward mobility that has ended in the declining inner cities and which the Enterprise Zone seeks to recreate.

Given the radical approach embodied in the idea, it is hardly surprising that several objections have been leveled against it. The following are the most common questions raised.

RELOCATION

It is sometimes argued that the Enterprise Zone merely robs Peter to pay Paul. In other words, suspending regulations and tax laws may well cause an area to thrive, but it would do so only by causing an influx of firms currently located in other parts of the country, leading to a loss of tax revenue elsewhere. If there was a movement of firms into the zone from other parts of the same depressed city, it is pointed out, there could be damaging financial consequences for the city. What is the point of reviving the South Bronx, the argument goes, if it just causes the decline of Brooklyn?

Plausible though this argument is from a theoretical point of view, it is far less likely to be a problem in practice. While it must of course be admitted that *some* businesses will relocate, studies suggest that these would not constitute a high proportion of the total new companies. David Birch's studies, for instance, indicate that the alleged movement of firms to the Sunbelt is not a movement at all, but is a reflection of different birthrates of companies in different areas of the country—giving the impression of relocation. As Birch concludes:

> Virtually no firms migrate from one area to another in the sense of hiring a moving van and relocating their operations. The oft-cited move of textiles and shoes from New England to the South represented a rare fluke in the 1950s, not an example of a significant process today.[9]

Even within a city, Birch argues, less than one-quarter of the job changes within the central district can be attributed to the movement of businesses either inward or outward. Differences between the birth and death rates of companies, and business expansions and contractions, on the other hand, were responsible for three-quarters of the changes.[10]

There are good reasons why this is so. Uprooting existing facilities in order to locate a business elsewhere is a costly and risky decision. Besides the immediate cost of the physical movement there is the possibility that goodwill and an established market might be lost, and it may be necessary to retrain new workers. For this to be worthwhile the incentives would have to be substantial. The incentives would certainly be powerful in an Enterprise Zone, but they would relate mainly to start-up costs (particularly if some form of turnover trigger existed), rather than to the long-term costs of doing business. The incentive for a well established company to move would be far less powerful.

BORDER EFFECTS

A related argument to the relocation issue involves the possible economic damage that might be inflicted on businesses in the neighborhoods immediately adjacent to an Enterprise Zone. If a firm is in the next block to an Enterprise Zone, might it not be put out of business by firms enjoying tax breaks for which it is not eligible?

Once again this is likely to be far more of a problem in theory than in practice. If companies are currently not located in a district it is because costs outweigh the benefits. If we reduce these costs by tax and regulation changes, we do not necessarily end up with total costs for a business that are substantially lower than those of the surrounding area, and so we do not necessarily give zone firms a decisive competitive edge over their neighbors.

Even if companies within an Enterprise Zone clearly had an impact on the same markets as firms just outside the zone, there are other factors which should be taken into account in assessing the overall border effects. Decay is often a spreading phenomenon: block follows block down the economic spiral. A business on the edge of a very depressed area may well be surviving now, but it is invariably next in line for closure. But if the depressed area experiences economic revival due to an Enterprise Zone, this upturn is also beneficial to neighboring areas. The new income stream generated by new employment would not be spent only in the zone; there would be an overflow into the nearby districts. Similarly the improvement in real estate values and potential for investment would also not be confined to the zone. One might reflect that it would be surprising to find a retailer or manufacturer who would prefer to see his neighboring blocks going downhill rather than uphill.

THE COST OF ENTERPRISE ZONES

Another argument occasionally put forward is that Enterprise Zones would impose a heavy cost on already hard-pressed cities and would mean a significant reduction in federal revenues because of tax suspensions and reduction.

This objection misses several very important points. In the first place, the amount of revenue actually lost by the city is likely to be very small. Enterprise Zones would be areas with little existing commerce and many abandoned buildings. Suspending taxes on abandoned buildings, heaps of rubble, and non-existent businesses involves no loss. The only loss, other than that from tax-paying businesses and properties in the area, would arise in the case of businesses relocating; and that is not likely to be substantial. It should also be noted that the existence of Enterprise Zones would lead to savings for the city. Local welfare and protection costs are likely to decline as new employment is generated and communities become stronger and more viable. In addition, workers hired in the zones would become contributors to city revenues through sales tax on their expenditures and, in some cases, city income taxes on their earnings.

The argument that the Enterprise Zones would be expensive to the federal Treasury is based on a very common confusion. If the result of reducing a tax rate is to stimulate more business, it is a misuse of language to say that there is a loss because a lower rate applies to those new businesses. Had the original rates applied the businesses would not have been in existence and would not have paid *any* tax. So there is a tax *gain* when new businesses are brought into existence by the tax cut. The only real loss is on the lower taxes now paid by businesses already in existence (and even here there may be no net loss if business expands sufficiently). In the case of Enterprise Zones, the number of preexisting businesses covered by the tax changes is likely to be small, as is the number of tax-paying businesses that would move into the area. If the zones are a very effective stimulus to new business and job creation, as supporters believe, it is quite likely that the increase in tax revenues due to the existence of new firms and new individual taxpayers would more than offset any reduction in revenues from existing companies and employees.

WILL ENTERPRISE ZONES WORK?

The bottom-line question which must be asked of any plan to revive the inner cities is, simply, will it work? In the case of Enterprise Zones, will tax reductions, drastically streamlined regulation, and other changes actually bring about a flowering of enterprise in the centeral cities?

Some writers have argued that tax incentives are not an effective way of luring business into a district.[11] Such skeptics point out that major corporations are influenced in their location decisions by a host of factors—availability of resources and appropriate labor, transportation facilities, nearness of markets, etc. The tax climate is only one consideration among many: if it were the only factor there would be a stampede of companies to low-tax states.

While there is truth in the general contention, one should look very carefully at the evidence before drawing false conclusions about the probable effectiveness of the Enterprise Zone concept. It has been stated earlier that the zone is not intended to be a magnet for companies that would otherwise locate elsewhere. Indeed, relocation effects are seen as a danger, not a benefit. So the argument that major companies will not tend to switch their operations from another area into an Enterprise Zone is not a flaw. The real question is whether the zones would be a stimulus to *new* and *small* firms.

Smaller, more competitive companies are more influenced by cost considerations than the larger companies. Property taxes and labor costs generally constitute a higher proportion of total costs for small firms, and the burden of bureaucratic red tape falls more heavily on companies without the resources to have specialist staff to deal with the agencies. So the cost-related incentives and simplification of regulation in the Enterprise Zone are likely to be effective in the case of the small sector—exactly the type of business which the zone would try to reach. Needless to say, as discussed earlier, there would be some inducement for these firms to relocate, but for the most part the effect of the incentives would be to encourage new business ventures.

Critics go on to argue, however, that while tax-related incentives might have some influence in the case of smaller companies as such, new companies normally have little or no tax liability in the first few months, or even years, of their operation. For these firms the most significant problem is a lack of capital, and an inability to borrow for inner-city ventures. There is no point in giving tax breaks or any other kind of indirect assistance, some would contend, if entrepreneurs in redlined areas cannot find the money to get into business in the first place.

This objection overlooks some important elements in the Enterprise Zone approach. In the first place, the result of the package of measures involved in the idea would be to reduce the start-up costs of businesses, and hence the total amount of capital necessary. Property tax, labor costs, social security etc. apply on the first day of operation: reducing these costs also reduces the borrowing needs of the company. Although the business tax reductions may not be a saving in the early days of a company, moreover, any lending institution would know that Enterprise Zone designation would improve the cash flow of firms in the neighborhood, and hence the chances of loans being repaid in full. Jack Kemp has often referred to the Enterprise Zone as "greenlining" the inner city, and that is indeed what the concept would do.

It would indicate to lenders and investors (private individuals as well as financial institutions) that the chances of a company succeeding in a depressed neighborhood had been raised, and the likelihood of a basically sound business being crushed by taxes and regulation had been substantially diminished.

CONCLUSION

The Enterprise Zone concept marks a radical departure in thinking on the inner-city problem. But unlike most radical ideas, enthusiasm for it is not limited to one narrow political group or lobby. The proposal has drawn support from a wide range of individuals and organizations who are rarely in agreement on any aspect of public policy.

Fiscal conservatives appreciate that the Enterprise Zone approach is not just another bureaucratic program designed to throw tax dollars at the inner cities. The idea is fundamentally anti-bureaucratic; it clears away guidelines and regulations rather than creating them. Furthermore, it does not involve the expenditure of billions of dollars in grants and loans in the hope that something just may spring out of the rubble. The "expenditure" is limited to tax revenue forgone—and for the most part forgone only on businesses that would not exist were it not for the tax concession. Even if one mistakenly believes this to be a cost to government, it is a cost that can only occur by virtue of successful revitalization, not failure.

But the Enterprise Zone also appeals to those who have been directly involved for many years in central-city projects—the urban liberals and the minorities. Many such people have grown frustrated, disillusioned, and tired of the ineffectiveness of large government projects, which never seem able to deal with local conditions. The Enterprise Zone, in contrast, seeks to stimulate local projects and commercial risk taking by removing financial and regulatory obstacles. It aims, in other words, to provide a climate that will make it more likely that community initiatives and businesses will succeed. It will not guarantee success, but it will reduce the number of needless failures.

There is another reason for the widespread enthusiasm voiced for the Enterprise Zone. Although the original proposal came from Europe, the Enterprise Zone is essentially a very American approach to the inner-city problem. The citizens of other countries generally look to their governments to deal with the growing pains of society. Local suggestions have to be channeled and filtered through an elaborate network of officialdom before a decision can be made—right or wrong—and a project undertaken. But throughout the short history of this country a rather different tradition has been evident. Unexpected local problems and crises have generally been dealt with at the local level, by a combination of individual initiative and community resolve. This apparently haphazard approach has allowed unconventional but effective solutions to be applied to problems, and has caused the evolution of peculiarly American institutions and customs to deal with peculiarly American situations.

The Enterprise Zone is strongly within this tradition. It is a recognition both that at least part of the urban crisis is due to government, and that success is more likely if the residents of a community are given a real chance to rebuild the commerce and housing of their neighborhood with a minimum of taxes and red tape. The Enterprise Zone imposes no blueprint and stifles no local idea. What it does do is to declare the blighted inner cities open neighborhoods, devoid of as many regulations and tax costs as possible, and to invite what may be called Urban Pioneering—the same kind of local projects and enterprise that once built countless successful communities across the continent.

NOTES

1. Speech to the Royal Town Planning Institute, June 15, 1977.
2. Speech to the Bow Group, London, June 26, 1978. For a summary and analysis of Sir Geoffrey Howe's version of the Enterprise Zone and the Freeport idea offered by Professor Hall, see Stuart Butler, "Enterprise Zones: A Solution to the Urban Crisis?" (Washington, D.C.: The Heritage Foundation, 1979).
3. See Note 2.
4. See Stuart Butler, "Enterprise Zones: A Real Solution to Urban Decay," *Lincoln Review*, Winter 1980; "Urban Renewal: A Modest Proposal," *Policy Review* 13, Summer 1980.
5. Because some types of businesses, such as food retailing, normally have much lower profit/turnover ratios than others, different trigger points might be applied to different sectors.
6. It should be remembered, of course, that there are certain costs that would be heavier inside the zone—crime, insurance, etc. The tax breaks are designed to offset these costs, but it should not be assumed that an Enterprise Zone firm will actually face lower total costs than one in an adjacent neighborhood.
7. For a survey of free trade zones around the world, see *The Journal of Commerce*, Oct. 22, 1979, section 4.
8. For an analysis of this bill see Stuart Butler, "The Urban Jobs and Enterprise Zone Act" (The Heritage Foundation, 1980).
9. David L. Birch, *The Job Generation Process* (unpublished, MIT, 1979) p. 4.
10. Birch, *Economic Change in Cities*. Birch used 1969–72 data for the following cities: Charlotte, Dayton, Houston, New Haven, Rochester, and Worcester. The figures differed little between cities.
11. For a review of several of these studies see Bennett Harrison and Sandra Kanter, "The Political Economy of States' Job Creation Business Incentive," *AIP Journal*, October 1978.

KEMP-GARCIA ACT: An Initial Evaluation

George Sternlieb

INTRODUCTION

The essentials of the Kemp-Garcia Urban Jobs and Enterprise Zone Act are as follows:[1]

I. Enterprise Jobs Zone:

A. Unemployment and Poverty Requirements:

1. the average unemployment for the past 24 months must be greater than or equal to twice the national average and 30 percent or more of the families living in the areas must be at or below 85 percent the Bureau of Labor Statistics lower living standard; or
2. the average unemployment rate for the past 24 months must be greater than or equal to three times the national average; or
3. 50 percent of the families within the zone are at or below 85 percent of the Bureau of Labor Statistics lower living standard.

B. Area Requirements:

1. the area must be defined by a continuous boundary; and

2. the population of the area must be at least 4,000.

   Any local unit of government may apply for one or more Enterprise Jobs Zones within its jurisdiction, if (a) the area under consideration for zone designation meets the above requirements; (b) the local government will agree to reduce its effective property-tax rate within the zone by 20 percent over a four-year period. The tax reduction will remain in existence for the life of the zone.

II. Tax Incentives:

A. For individuals or businesses who own real estate in the zone:

1. a 20 percent reduction in local property taxes.

B. For resident homeowners in the zone:

1. an increase in the capital-gains deduction from 60 percent to 80 percent; the capital gain is exempt from the minimum tax.

C. For employees who work in the zone:

1. if employee is less than 21 years old, a 90 percent reduction in employer and employee social-security taxes.

D. For businesses 50 percent of whose employees live and work in the zone:

1. a 15 percent reduction in corporate tax rates;
2. 3-year straight-line depreciation for all property (except land) up to $500,000 in value;
3. loss carry-forward is extended to ten years;
4. may use the cash method of accounting if the business' gross income does not exceed $1.5 million.

E. For individuals or corporations which (1) own property (except land) used by the taxpayer to conduct business in the zone; or (2) own an interest in a business as defined in (D) above:

1. an increase in the capital-gains deduction from 60 percent to 80 percent for individuals;
2. a reduction in capital gains from 28 percent to 15 percent for corporations;
3. such capital gain is exempt from the minimum tax for individuals and corporations.

THE URBAN ECONOMIC DYNAMIC

The issue of the high level of unemployment, particularly among youth, and its linkage with a variety of other socioeconomic variables has come increasingly to the fore in public thinking over the last generation. The United States, unlike most Western European countries does not enjoy the two principal buffer elements that have enabled the latter—at least from a statistical point of view—to adjust to the changing nature of the increasingly postindustrial economy that dominates advanced technologies. Western European countries have the buffer of substantial protection for small-scale agriculture. Thus the proportion of population involved in that activity in such countries as West Germany or France is higher than the equivalent in the United States. This higher proportion has been achieved by a variety of protective mechanisms specifically directed toward the maintenance of relatively small-scale agricultural pursuits. The price of this higher ratio has been a relative lack of efficiency in agricultural production; it is paid by the general consuming public through higher prices for their basic foodstuffs. The United States, in contrast, has rationalized its agriculture and thus, despite the greatest level of agriculture throughout the world, has a relatively small portion of the work force absorbed in its basic production. American consumers are better fed at lower prices than consumers anywhere else.

The price paid here, however, is the high degree of dislocation associated with the vast migration from agricultural employment that has taken place in the United States. Some observers have commented that the migration off the land in our country is without precedent in its speed and scale. Much of this migration has been achieved in a most positive fashion—the income characteristics of the former agricultural workers and residents for the larger part have increased substantially, and with it their standard of living has increased.

It has, however, left a residual of marginally employed individuals. They and their children tend to be concentrated in so-called "pockets of poverty"—many of them in our major cities. In this very process the United States has moved from an underrecorded level of de facto unemployment, or in many cases marginal jobs with relatively low incomes, to our present high number of visibly poor people.

Thus increases in uemployment—particularly unemployment among youth—although of very real importance and an appropriate area of concern, in part are reflective not so much of a changed functional reality but rather of a change in areal location and statistical measurement. The contrast with the Soviet Union—where nearly a third of the people still work on the land—is evident. Much of this labor force literally is warehoused in redundant agricultural employment.

A second factor that differentiates the U.S. circumstance from that of equivalently developed countries in Western Europe is the fact that the United States has, practically uniquely, internalized its marginally employed. With the possible exception of some seasonal agricultural workers brought in from other countries, the United States does not have the equivalent of the so-called guest worker. When employment turns down in such countries such as Germany, Switzerland, or France, in general it is very slow to affect citizens of the several countries in question. It may have, however, a much more immediate impact on Yugoslavian or Algerian or Spanish or Turkish employment figures as the so-called guest workers find that their services in the developed countries are brought to an end and they are forced to return to their native land. More than 10 percent of the labor forces in each of the former countries comes from abroad and has residence rights only when employed. In the United States, on the contrary, the marginally employed, particularly in industry, are Americans. When they lose their jobs or are laid off, they remain to be counted—to be cared for—and to be very properly issues of major national concern.

The linkage of unemployment and low incomes with a variety of other variables, costly not only to the individuals specifically and directly impacted by them, but also to the nation as a whole, is examined in more detail later in this chapter. Suffice it to say that there are enormous costs in terms of the degeneration of the nation's capital stock (particularly on housing) and the entire quality of life—as well as the drastic weight on the specific individuals who must pay the immediate price.

Within this context it should be noted that the United States has lagged in the provision of incentive strategies for ensuring a flow of entreprenuerial activity into impacted areas. West Germany has been a leader in this regard, providing a variety of tax incentives and capital funding, as well as very substantial apprenticeship allowances, to minimize unemployment costs and dislocation. In the United States, on the other hand, there has been little in the way of redress for impacted areas other than efforts at rectifying housing and physical blight conditions (as, for example, urban slum clearance and the urban-renewal program as a whole) until the development of approaches to coping with depressed regions, such as the Area Redevelopment Administration, whose focus was at first rural but then increasingly urban.

Thus the United States has unique responsibilities to its urban poor and the impacted areas within which they reside but has, as yet, lagged in meeting them.

The seeming failure of urban renewal to rectify central-city ills lies in the weakness of positive tools embodied in the program. Essentially, at most it provided a cleaning out of barriers to new development, that is, land assemblage and, in some cases, clearance and write-down. An implicit assumption, however, was that the enabling activity was sufficient unto itself—and that entreprenuers would seek out the available areas. The weaknesses of the program in terms of providing incentive packaging were such as to limit its effectiveness.

The depressed-region approach was much more sweeping and, particularly in the case of the Appalachia Redevelopment effort, has much more substantial claims to success. The successor agency to the Area Redevelopment Administration—the Economic Development Administration, or EDA—while continuing its assistance to depressed regions, now has a much broader scope of services. In more recent years the Urban Development Action Grant program (UDAG), with its very sharp focus and its stress on private/public partnerships and on leveraging public dollars, has met with good acceptance and considerable promise for the future.

However, efforts at "picking up the bottom"—bringing genuine economic revitalization to lagging areas and the people within them—should be viewed within the context of a United States suddenly grown fearful of its overall economic vitality. Within this context the whole issue of supply-side economics has come to the center. The virtual permanence, for example, of the investment tax credit since 1978 and the proposals to increase its level, as in H.R. 3477, mark just the beginning of a tide of efforts to stimulate capital investment and ensure the nation's future.

There should be no conflict between the development of these overall economic regenerative activities and the issue of impacted areas. The sheer waste and costliness of the latter need little comment here.

It should further be noted that the changing demographics of the United States, the shift from the baby-boom generation that has stretched our new-job-creating capacity to the utmost, to the baby-bust replacement, suggests that the United States may well become labor short in the near future. The number of children from five to seventeen years of age declined by 2.7 million between 1970 and 1976, and this is the group that will move front and center as the next wave of newcomers to the labor market. The gap between this future need and the poor employment experience of teenagers that is the complement of 35 percent unemployment rates is evident, as is the waste involved in bypassing areas whose infrastructure we cannot afford to duplicate. Moreover, these are national challenges, not merely those of one or another group.

Thus a wave of targeted tax and other forms of fiscal packages have been proposed to rectify the balance. These included an administration proposal, part of the 1978 Urban Policy Statement, for an additional 5 percent tax credit for machinery and equipment purchased by businesses located in areas of distress. In addition, a variety of efforts have been offered geared specifically to impacted areas.[2]

STRATEGY OF THE ANALYSIS

The Kemp-Garcia proposal is one of the most sweeping to be advanced. Its mechanisms as earlier cited are quite comprehensive. The operating mechanics involved are practically unique in their present form—which permits them as of right within qualifying areas rather than (as holds true for most other action-oriented efforts) requiring specific application.

The targets of the Kemp-Garcia initiative are most important ones for the United States as a whole. The issues at hand are not the objectives of the program but rather its efficiency, its capacity to deliver most effectively regenerative results on areas and individuals that otherwise will remain blotches not only on the national conscience but on the economy as a whole. Given the realities of limited resources, it is essential that the details of the program be analyzed and placed within the context of alternative devices, particularly the EDA and UDAG initiatives.

The paper that follows analyzes the specifics of S2823's language.[3] Efforts are then undertaken to analyze the impact of the bill, as written, within a reasonable cost/benefit context. As indicated above, there are at least two other major ranges of activity under the EDA and UDAG banners that have somewhat similar targets. It is therefore important that the Kemp-Garcia initiative be viewed in terms of its potential for either complementing, replacing, or perhaps being redundant to the former strategies.

The analyses are undertaken within a relatively brief time span and are further limited, as will be noted in more detail, by some internal contradictions within the legislation as drafted, as well as data availability for making the program operative. The bill is in the process of being modified. Thus the paper prepared here should be viewed more as one that attempts to raise issues of definition and administrative procedure than as a definitive full-blown costing effort, although efforts at defining some ball-park parameters on the latter element are incorporated.

THE KEMP-GARCIA INCENTIVES

Rectifying high unemployment levels and poverty is a very important target for society as a whole. How effective are the measures brought to bear within the bill? There is a basic differentiation between the Kemp-Garcia incentives and those of EDA and UDAG. The latter are essentially front-end capital grants. They provide immediate funding, either for infrastructure or very specifically for new development. Kemp-Garcia, as will be noted in more detail later, provides much more in the way of flows-of-funds reductions in the ordinary costs of doing business.

The assumption implicit within the program as projected is that these operating subsidy elements are adequate to 1) maintain employment within the impacted areas at the very least; or 2) to increase the level of activity of extant employers; or 3) both of the above. They should also bring new employers and new facilities to the scene that can take advantage of the explicit and implicit operating subsidies. The subsidies proposed do not provide initial capital but rather reduce the expenses of doing business as well as the tax bite.

A very strong thrust—both at the beginning of the bill, as earlier noted, and repeated in more detail in the section under incentives—is the concept of local support through property-tax reduction as a complement to the other forms of subsidies that are offered. As mentioned earlier, admittance and continuance within the program is conditional on this element.

REQUIRED REAL-PROPERTY TAX REDUCTION

The bill states bluntly that there shall be a permanent reduction applicable to the property and the private jobs in the enterprise zone of not less than 20 percent in the effective real-property tax rate. Note that this must be implemented within the first four real-property tax years and thus in many cases may precede the development of new ratables that might offset the impact of a reduced tax. The issues of dislocation—that is, of the reduction in tax rates within the private jobs and enterprise zones in turn requiring tax increases elsewhere in the interim—is not discussed. Further, there is no reference to the possibility that increased business within the tax zone will in turn generate increases in required municipal expenditures, both for human services—police, fire, and the like—as well as infrastructure—increased sewer, water, and so on. The real-property tax reduction applies not to a specific additional amenity but rather, following the phrasing of the bill, to the zone as a whole. Whereas the concept of local responsibility and cost sharing is to be applauded, its implementation may well be self-defeating.

On a practical base this will mean communities either speculating that the declaration of an enterprise zone will immediately bring new capital dollars, assessment base, and other forms of tax income into the zone or that there will be a general tax-rate increase. The probable sequence of events will be to wait on a developer to come into sight with an appropriate proposal before making the declaration. This will reduce the marketability of the concept. It involves issues of timing, that is, clearing the red tape for declaration of an enterprise zone while trying to keep the potential developer interested, which may well work against the program.

It will further probably discourage communities from being interested in relatively small-scale initial ventures. Such ventures will involve a triggering of tax reduction for an entire area with little in the way of immediate recompense.

Although the legislative discussion on the bill presumed that in many areas that might lend themselves to enterprise zone status tax collections are relatively low, this may not necessarily be the case, particularly in some of the older industrial areas that are moving downhill but whose taxes are still reasonably current. This has become increasingly the case as communities move into programs shortening the allowable periods of tax delinquency. There is no reference to the limitations, constitutionally imposed in a number of states, on local communities deviating from full equivalent taxation and assessment policies. These again may serve as barriers to the appropriate initiation of the incentive areas.

The foreign trade zone designation: Clearing the encumbrances that sometimes surround such designations, particularly for impacted areas, certainly makes excellent sense. Whether such designations should be limited in number in order to minimize regulatory costs and consequences requires more profound discussion than can be given here but certainly should be looked into. Currently, for example, the developer of a major foreign trade zone in New Jersey has required a ten-year period of exclusivity within the state as a condition of its financing. Experience with the functioning of such areas as Brooklyn's Bush Terminal has indicated their positive—if limited—job-generating aspects.

FURTHER TAX INCENTIVES: SOCIAL-SECURITY TAXES

In the guise of providing a job growth incentive program, a very major, far from resolved issue is swept to the sidelines—the appropriate funding of social-security payments. Thus the 90 percent reduction for employees under the age of twenty-one or 50 percent for employees over the age of twenty-one is to be secured from general revenues. I would raise some question here whether in all political practicality this is not requiring the shooting of an elephant in order to make mouse stew. In any case, this permits a 90 percent reduction of the current social-security payment by both employee and employer respectively, assuming that the employee is under twenty-one, and 50 percent for those over twenty-one. As I read the bill, this applies to all individuals within the district; it does not apply specifically to new employees or to new employers; and it is not restricted to net additions to the activity of the district but rather is available to all automatically. Its relationship, for example, to minimum wages is not discussed—that is, assuming that there is a net of 6.7 percent reduction in social-security imposts on the wages of an individual, can that individual be paid 6.7 percent less than the minimum wage, yielding a net post-social security equivalent to full minimum wage with full social security? The bill is silent on this point.

For those above minimum-wage status, it is unclear whether the reduction in social-security taxes nominally on the employee results in a generalized reduction of wage costs to the employer or an additional incentive to employees at higher wage levels. Thus the incentive to the employer may be viewed either as strictly limited to the reduction in social-security tax payments required of him (or her) directly, or that same figure plus some fraction of wage savings secured by employee willingness to settle for slightly smaller face wages in the light of the social-security reductions.

In any case, there is nothing in the bill as written that necessarily confers any of these benefits as a result of new activities, as against simply a bonus for being in an impacted area in the first place. Secondly, because social-security base pay by 1982 will go up to above the $30,000 level, this may well reward individuals who by any present standards are well out of the poverty level.

There is substantial leakage, and perhaps necessarily so, in terms of the ties between the incentives given activities within the private sector of enterprise zones and the residents thereof. Qualified businesses, that is, those entitled to the tax incentives, are simply those in which 50 percent or more of the employees are local residents, or residents within the zone. Thus the incentives are quite broad, and the spillage of subsidy may be quite extraordinary; the social-security tax saving of a middle-level executive earning $25,000 a year may be nearly triple that of the factory hand at $9,000 a year.

Much of the incidence of unemployment is linked to youth. In recognition of that fact as indicated above, there is a differentiation in the level of social-security subsidy that differentiates between workers under the age of twenty-one and those of greater maturity. Assuming a social-security incidence of 6.7 percent and an average salary of $9,000, the dollar reduction from the employers' payment sector would be $542.70. Even if this is doubled—assuming a commensurate reduction in the salary level of more youthful employees—the resulting incentive of $1,083.40 is relatively modest.

Assuming an annual salary of $9,000 circa 1982 when the social-security payments will be 6.7 percent, a 90 percent reduction would yield $542.70, or an effective 6.02 percentage reduction in the wage bill. For senior workers the 50 percent would yield $301.15, or a reduction of 3.5 percent. Whereas certainly it can provide some level of incentive for hiring more youthful individuals, when contrasted with the training requirements and not uncommonly the long learning curve to full productivity, it seems like relatively weak medicine for a most fateful disease.

To the executives of such a facility, the savings are far greater. Indeed, for someone over the maximum level of incidence—as of 1982, $31,800—a 50 percent reduction would yield a saving in excess of $1,000 a year. In essence, therefore, the incentive is somewhere on the order of 5 to 10 percent a year of payroll. The lower figure assumes savings merely on the part of the employer, whereas the higher one assumes an equivalent reduction of wage levels to be paid to employees. In this regard it should be noted that earlier ventures by the federal government in apprenticeship-training allowances and the like were far more significant—not uncommonly yielding incentives on the order of 50 or more percent.

Again the point should be stressed that this subsidy is not one merely made available to new additions to the zones' work force but rather[4] all employment, including that presently within the zone. The actual costs to the general fisc for new increased employment therefore depend on the ratio between new employees—or employment saved—and the scale of the base labor force. Both of these elements are modified by the age character of the work force.

Assuming that the newcomers represent a net new addition of about 25 percent to the base labor force, this would yield a cost of reduced social-security taxes of approximately five times the nominal subsidy, that is, something in excess of $5,000 for additional persons under the age of twenty-one. There is, therefore, important incentive in further defining the rewards mechanisms and, if at all possible, making them specific to additional employment. If this definition is forthcoming, it can either reduce the costs of such individuals to the Treasury or provide a much more substantial bonus/incentive—and probably much more success for the program as a whole.

REDUCTIONS IN CAPITAL-GAIN TAX RATES AND DEPRECIATION PROVISIONS

The rules relating to corporations are far from clear. They can be read as indicating approximate halving of capital-gains taxes for the sale of "qualified property,'' regardless of whether it continues to be located within the private jobs and enterprise zones, so long as at the time of the sale it ''is used predominately by the taxpayer within the zone.'' One can envision a variety of tax-evasion mechanisms emerging from this language.

The inclusion of capital-gains reduction is relatively unique in terms of incentive packaging. It halves the maximum capital-gain tax to be paid for any business or facility of a business that qualifies under the program. This proposal must be viewed in conjunction with Section 231 on accelerated depreciation. The incentive package is very striking and of considerable substance here. In essence, we permit an unusually fast write-off, include the full investment-tax credit, and then permit a sale of the assets or holding entity in question under a privileged capital-gains approach. If this is viewed in common with the tax-rate reduction under Section 221, in a large number of cases where there are meaningful capital improvements minimal or no income taxes would be paid.

It should be noted in this context that the rapid depreciation potential is somewhat offset by the tax-rate reductions also incorporated in the program. That is, there is less in the way of tax-payment impact on nominal income under the reduced tax-rate scheme, and therefore the depreciation provisions are less meaningful.

Nothing in the format would limit the tax cover secured by the rapid depreciation to corporations or business entities solely conducting their operations within the enterprise zone. Thus there could be a spillover effect of redundant tax cover on other income-producing areas or activities of the individual or corporate entrepreneur. This spillover could also take the form of reporting the bulk of profits in a multi-plant operation as having been generated within the enterprise zone. This is a procedure whose equivalent has been widely rumored for multinational corporations with facilities in tax havens.

For the moment, however, what is presented here is an enormously sweeping measure of tax subsidy for capital improvements. The scale of the improvements in question obviously will determine the governmental fiscal implications that are involved (and it should be noted that there are indications of a relatively broad revision of general tax-depreciation policy for production facilities nationally).

There is no differentiation made between the various forms of capital improvements (as, for example, the differentiation in the so-called 10–5–3 proposals). In essence, however, the federal government would be paying somewhere in the order of 35–40 percent of the capital improvements through forgone taxes. Assuming a somewhat arbitrary \$10,000 of depreciable plant and equipment per worker and a normal write-off of 10 percent (see Exhibit 1), the bonus without income-tax considerations is somewhere on the order of \$3,800. There is very substantial variance here depending on the tax status of the total operation, the flows of nominal profits that can be offset by the depreciation provisions, and so on. The provision, therefore, may be much more significant to already successful firms, which require tax cover for extant earnings and which are assured of this need, rather than newcomers to the scene, for whom its virtues may be much more conjectural. The point is so important that it must be expressed again even at the risk of redundancy: The incentive mechanisms under the Kemp-Garcia initiative are not limited to "new" jobs or "new" enterprises but rather are specific to the areal construct of an appropriately designated zone. Their targeting, while implicit in the characteristics of the residents of the zone and the requirement for 50 percent of the employees or more from these specific zones, is limited. Whether the beneficiaries are necessarily the very same individuals of low income and/or unemployment characteristics is not spelled out. Although there is a heavy probability of this being at least partially the case, it is far from exclusively true.

EXHIBIT 1

ENTERPRISE ZONE: HYPOTHETICAL DEPRECIATION BONUS
(without including Income Tax)

	Normal Depreciation (@ 10% Straightline)	Enterprise Zone (1/3 Depreciation each Yr.)	Nominal Marginal Cash Available	Interest Compounded Annually @ 10%
Yr. 1	$1000	$3,333	$2,333	$ 233
2	1000	3,333	4,666	490
3	1000	3,333	7,490	749
4	1000		6,750	675
5	1000		5,670	567
6	1000		4,560	456
7	1000		3,450	345
8	1000		2,340	234
9	1000		1,230	123
10	1000		-	-
			Total	$3,872

Note: Assumes a capital investment of $10,000; a normal write-off of 10 percent a year; a rate of return on excess capital of 10 percent; and does not take into account income taxes to be paid on interest earnings. These are rough calculations and do not take into account lag factors. The latter, however, would not substantially alter the conclusions.

Source: Rutgers University Center for Urban Policy Research.

These elements—together with certain facilitating mechanisms, such as optional cash method of accounting for certain small businesses as well as very generous carry-over provisions for operating losses—are the sum of the incentive mechanisms that are embodied.

The basic differentiation of the mechanisms from those operative under UDAG and EDA is the fact that under Kemp-Garcia the incentives are all operating subsidies rather than front-end funding elements. As such they tend to be of more importance to ongoing operations than to newcomers—unless the latter have independent resources of substance with which to get into business.

The set of subsidies is very complex. Their impact and costs may be clarified by the use of an example. Exhibit 2 gives a very rough model of a hypothetical but not atypical tool shop that provides some insights into the working of the mechanisms. It is an attempt to assemble a modular business of a scale commensurate with the focus of the program. Its characteristics essentially represent a blending of industry operating results.[5]

THE MODEL COMPANY

Employment—The company has 50 basic production/clerical employees at an average income of $9,000 per year. In addition, it has 10 executives/salespersons at $20,000 a year. Seventeen of the former workers are under twenty-one; none of the latter are.

Capital Investment—There is a capital investment of $10,000 per employee.

Rents and Taxes—Rents are 3 percent of sales, taxes are 25 percent of the rent.

Sales—Sales are $30,000 per worker.

Profits—Before depreciation, profits are 10 percent of sales.

The company, as indicated in the left-hand side of Exhibit 2, thus has sales of $1,800,000. Its labor costs are $650,000. The nominal social security and employer payments at 6.7 percent (the figure for 1982) are about $43,550. Real-estate taxes are based on rents equaling 3 percent of sales, or $54,000, with the tax element of this approximately a quarter, thus yielding $13,500. Profits before taxes and depreciation at 10 percent of sales would be $180,000. Normal depreciation, arbitrarily held as an average of 10 percent for plant, furniture, tools, and so on, and assuming further $10,000 of capital investment per employee, would be $60,000—that is, 10 percent of $600,000.

If this investment is deducted from the profits before taxes and depreciation, it yields a taxable income of $120,000. Income taxes have been computed at the current rate and amount to about $35,950. The post-tax income

EXHIBIT 2

MODEL MACHINE SHOP: FINANCIAL PARAMETERS WITH AND WITHOUT KEMP-GARCIA

Without Kemp-Garcia		With Kemp-Garcia		Savings
Sales $1,800.00				
Labor Costs 50 @ $9,000 [17 under age 21]	= $450,000			
10 @ $20,000 [all over age 21]	= 200,000			
Total Labor Costs	$650,000	Total Labor Costs	$650,000[1]	
Nominal Social Security Employer Payments @ 6.7%	43,550	Actual Social Security Employer Payments	17,674	$25,876
Real-Estate Taxes [3% of sales = Rent 25% of rent = R.E. Taxes]	13,500	Real Estate Taxes [Reduced 20%]	10,800	2,700
Profits before Taxes and Depreciation [10% of sales]	180,000	Profits before Taxes and Depreciation [the sum of the previous profits plus savings]	208,576	
Depreciation [average, of plant furniture, tools, etc. 10% assuming $10,000 capital investment per worker]	60,000	Depreciation [⅓ of $600,000]	200,000	
Taxable Income	$120,000	Taxable Income	$ 8,576	
Income Tax		Income Tax 14%	1,200	34,750
17% $25,000		Post Tax Income [PTI]	$ 7,376	
20% 25,000		Cash Flow [PTI + Depreciation]	$207,376	$63,326
30% 25,000				
40% 25,000				
46% 20,000	35,950			
Post Tax Income	$ 84,050			
Cash Flow [PTI + Depreciation]	$144,050			

[1] Assuming workers keep their share of the rebated social security taxes.

Source: Rutgers University Center for Urban Policy Research.

thus is equal to $84,050 with a cash flow (i.e., adding depreciation back in) of $144,050.

On the right-hand side of the Exhibit 2, the results are shown for the same operation given the Kemp-Garcia elements. Social-security payments are reduced by approximately $25,876. Real-estate taxes, reduced by 20 percent, yield a saving of $2,700. Thus profits before taxes and depreciation of $208,576, are the sum of the pre-Kemp-Garcia profits of $180,000 plus the savings accruing through Kemp-Garcia.

The major change takes place as a function of depreciation. Under Kemp-Garcia there is a three-year straight-line write-off. Assuming the capital investment of $600,000, this write-off would yield about $200,000. Thus the taxable income of the enterprise is reduced to a relatively trivial $8,576. This element in conjunction with a reduced income-tax rate yields a savings in income taxes paid of nearly $35,000. Whereas the nominal post-tax income of the post-Kemp-Garcia operating statement is only $7,376, its cash flow—a much more meaningful figure—is approximately $207,376, or more than $60,000 higher than the same company without the Kemp-Garcia exemptions.

Although certainly there is an enormous level of variation between various types of businesses, in the capital investment ratio to sales, to number of employees, and the like, the model exemplifies the key elements. The labor-cost-saving from the employers' point of view is approximately 4 percent of total labor costs. The real-estate tax saving is relatively slight, both in absolute terms—$2,700—and also as a percentage of the rent—5 percent. The major shift, both in absolute and proportionate terms, is in the elements that accrue to the impact of alternate forms of depreciation. Taxes are reduced by fully $34,750, and, as already indicated, the cash flow from the company is increased by about 44 percent.

As exemplified by the model, there are some elements of redundancy in the several forms of incentive that are embodied within the bill. The lowering of income-tax rates, for example, actually reduces the impact of the depreciation tax cover, at least in the years in which this is available; the real-estate tax saving is relatively trivial, representing as it does less than 1½ percent of the net cash flow generated by the operation. Whereas certainly rents—and therefore real-estate taxes—will vary by types of industry (they will be several times as high for a general-merchandise retail operation, for example), the saving is not meaningful, assuming that it is limited to the 20 percent of taxes required by the bill.

ENTERPRISE ZONE DESIGNATION

The acceptance of a zone as appropriate to the program depends on the inclusion of real property-tax reduction. It should be noted in this context that in some cases this change will involve not merely legislative action on the part of a city council or local legislature but rather constitutional or legislative changes at the state level. Although it may be the intention of the sponsors to provide such important incentives as to make this a worthwhile step for states, the time/procedural constraints may be quite substantial.

DURATION OF THE PROGRAM

The program is specifically defined as lasting for a minimum of ten calendar years. Although certainly, if substantial capital improvement is to be made, significant write-off period and stability of incentive is essential, the limitation of a minimum of ten years may be overly generous in some cases and, to the degree that the minimum also becomes the maximum, less so in others. Note further that in a sense the local jurisdiction has (in Section B2) essentially a one-way "put," that is, a capacity to terminate the program by simply "not substantially complying with the real property tax reduction."

I would suggest that the concept of local property-tax relief be endorsed but would hesitate to make it essential. If, for example, there are significant tax reductions in one subset of a jurisdiction, this will raise tax rates for the community as a whole, given constant expenditures, much less increased municipal costs. Politically, this may become very deleterious as well as being negative to the economy of the whole jurisdiction. This will be particularly evident in the former case if success is achieved reasonably quickly.

AREA REQUIREMENTS

The minimal size of area as defined by the program is one that has a population of at least 4,000 persons. This area is approximately the size of the average census tract. Although the point will be made more sharply below, the only data available for such small units typically is that provided by the decennial census under the tract reporting requirements. Whereas indeed the issue of pockets of poverty in both EDA and UDAG has taken cognizance of the issues of subsets of municipalities, counties, and the like, there are potentially significant problems of administering such small areas—even assuming the possibilities of data accumulation appropriate for their inclusion and maintenance within the program.

UNEMPLOYMENT AND POVERTY REQUIREMENTS

There are three alternative entry standards established for the program:

1. The first of these combines both an unemployment criterion (twice the average national rate for a twenty-four–month period) as well as a poverty threshold (30 percent or more of the families living below the poverty level).

The difficulties of using these formulae are examined below.

2. The second is an average rate of unemployment at least three times that of the nation.

3. The third is an area in which 50 percent or more of the families are below the poverty level.

1. *Unemployment.* In an appendix to this paper, detail is provided on the limited availability of unemployment data by areal partition. In essence, since President Johnson was astonished to discover that there was no unemployment data for the Watts area immediately after the riots in that subregion of Los Angeles, there has been a continuous demand for much greater levels of availability, consistency, and detailing, both in terms of persons and areal constructs, for this essential variable. Unfortunately, relatively little has been done in this regard.

Reliable and valid unemployment statistics are available nationally, for the ten largest states and for the NYC, LA-LB SMSAs, as well as the 202 largest SMSAs. These statistics are collected by the Bureau of the Census in the *Current Population Survey*. At the remaining state and substate levels unemployment statistics are estimates generated by individual State Employment Security Agencies using the Bureau of Labor Statistics (BLS) "Handbook" methodology in the case of counties within SMSAs or multi-county labor-market areas (LMAs) and subcounty areas, through a system of apportionment. These state unemployment statistics include an adjustment based on the *Current Population Survey*.

The formula for unemployment as stated in the proposed legislation, that is, the average rate for the most-recent twenty-four months for which data were available, is unclear. Is the average of each of the monthly tabulations available? Or is it the average of the two terminal points, that is, the sum of the rates at the beginning and the close of any twenty-four–month period divided by two? The latter would permit inclusion of communities hit by a sudden work stoppage;—the former would apply to more chronic situations. The same strictures hold for the average national rate of unemployment to which local incidence is to be compared.

There is substantial controversy surrounding the use of data from individual state employment and unemployment offices as well as its comparability from jurisdiction to jurisdiction. At this writing, however, it is the only material that would be reasonably up to date on this key variable.

It should be further noted that considerable criticisms have been leveled at the unemployment figure as defined currently by the Bureau of Labor Statistics for the United States. Stated at its simplest, the denominator for determining unemployment is currently the sum of those who are employed plus those who are unemployed but are looking for work within a reasonable period from the time of the survey. (The sum of these two elements is referred to as the labor force.) The numerator is those individuals who, on the basis of the BLS survey, were actively seeking employment in the four weeks prior to their responses.[6]

Crucial to the subject at hand, however, is the fact that the so-called disenchanted potential job seekers simply are not counted either in the numerator or in the denominator of the fraction that we call unemployment. These individuals are principally those who simply have given up searching for employment. There are significant variations regionally, in central cities versus the suburbs, and between central cities in the scale of the phenomenon of labor-force participation (the proportion of people in the labor force to total individuals of an appropriate age/status to potentially be in the labor force). The complement of labor-force participation rate—that is, nonparticipation—is a very significant variable. It is most heavy in its weight in deeply impacted, long-term high-unemployment areas, particularly among youth—among whom there is a significant degree of turning away from active search for employment. The formula brought to bear here suffers from a failure to recognize this key variable.

Further information on underemployment—that is, jobs at a lower status than should be held by individuals of specific capacities or skills—or partial employment, and the scale of these phenomena are reported by the National Commission on Employment and Unemployment Statistics.

2. *Poverty Status.* The definition of poverty status as used by the Census Bureau in 1970 was developed by the Social Security Administration. It took into account such factors as family size, number of children, and farm-nonfarm residence, as well as the amount of income. Poverty level was based on an "economy" food plan designed by the Department of Agriculture for "emergency or temporary use when funds are low." The definition assumed that a family should not have to spend more than a third of its income for food. A family was classified as in poverty status if its total money income amounted to less than three times the cost of an "economy" food plan. This approach has since been revised to reflect a broader market basket/cost of living approach, which is reflected by the Kemp-Garcia bill.

The definition of poverty level for the purposes of inclusion into the private jobs and enterprise zones is 85 percent of the average lower living standard income level as determined annually by the Secretary of Labor and published by the Bureau of Labor Statistics. Its specification within the bill seems to have been made without reference to data availability.

It should be noted in this regard that budgets pertain only to urban families with relatively limited specified characteristics. No budgets are available for rural families.[8] There are a variety of reports on a more current basis that do provide information on poverty status by region. Principal among them is the Department of Commerce's "Money, Income and

Poverty Status of Families in the United States." The report for 1978 was issued in November 1979. The areal partitions, however, are limited to 25 regions. An additional source is *Quarterly Labor Force Developments*, which provides trends in employment and unemployment based on the *Current Population Survey* and which further details poverty-area residents. Again the partitions are limited to the sum of metropolitan areas in which 20 percent or more of the residents had incomes below the poverty threshold as specified in the 1970 census. This tends to lag the calendar by only a matter of months. The precise linkage between the two definitions is somewhat obscure. The Lower Living Standard Budget is presently made available for 44 regions. This is soon to be reduced to 25 SMSAs. Within those regions incomes would have to be determined. This is presently estimated for communities for inclusion within the CETA program on a somewhat rough-and-ready basis. At best, however, the data are limited. More defined estimates tend to have a significant time lag. For example, income data for communities for 1977 were just published by the Bureau of the Census in June 1980. Thus there are significant limitations on the utility of such material in small areas unless major efforts at increasing the frequency, coverage, and accuracy with which it is secured are undertaken. It should be noted in this context that although the nominal definition (as in Section 3 of the bill) refers to the materials determined annually by the Secretary of Labor and published by the Bureau of Labor Statistics, Section 4 indicates that determination will be made by the Secretary of Commerce on the basis of data submitted by the applying government and after the secretary further determines that "such data is reasonably accurate." This may permit a much greater diversity of locally gathered statistical material. The phrasing, however, is imprecise as to whether this is the case and if so what would be permissible.

DATA AVAILABILITY AND PROGRAM ADMINISTRATION

It is data availability, nor merely its specification within legislation, that ultimately determines the administrative realities of the bill in question. If, realistically, the unit of consideration is to be one of 4,000 persons, the unit will be the equivalent of U.S. Census units. The realities of survey research and statistical significance are that they are not linked to the size of the universe, but rather to the scale of the sample. Virtually as large a sample is required to define unemployment within an area of 4,000 persons as one of 40,000. The same holds true for income and poverty characteristics. Unless the sponsors of the bill are willing to accept the enormous costs that are involved in order to secure the basic counts and measures that are presently incorporated within it, I would strongly endorse modifications of the trigger mechanisms to make them compatible with the limitations of presently secured data—and, rather than requiring a whole new set of surveys, follow those presently in use under the UDAG or EDA programs.[9]

The opportunity of launching the program based on the 1980 census-tract material should not be overlooked. It would permit percision targeting of entry standards. For the purposes of securing a handhold on the levels of incidence of acceptance into the program, we have reanalyzed census-tract data for one sample state—New Jersey. in 1970. This is the latest available data—pending publication of the 1980 results—which provide detail down to areas of approximately 4,000 persons. Because the unemployment levels required under Kemp-Garcia are comparative rather than absolute, that is, showing local incidence of unemployment versus that of the nation, the changing overall national ambience of unemployment is not as important for projective purposes as would otherwise be the case.

There are some 1,510 census tracts of New Jersey for which data were available for 1970 (this includes nineteen out of twenty-one counties and incorporates all of the urban areas as well as the bulk of the rural areas of the state). Only seventeen of these tracts had employment levels double that of the state, as well as at the same time having 30 percent of their individual families below the poverty level as defined circa 1970. In turn, this involves a population of slightly less than 60,000 in a tracted universe of 6.8 million—or slightly less than 1 percent.

If the second approach is utilized, that is, unemployment level triple that of the nation, once again using the individual tracts versus the state as a whole as a microcosm of the nation yields about sixteen tracts with 42,000 persons.

Utilizing the third approach, that is, 50 percent of the families below poverty level—and once again with the 1970 definition of poverty level—no census tracts whatsoever are found.

If definitions 1 and 2 are combined, the net result is twenty-three tracts, or one and one-half percent of the state. (A number of those in definition 2 are subsumed under definition 1.) This indicates the gap between unemployment and poverty. The former partakes both of structural and transient characteristics; the latter tends to be related much more to structural elements alone.

Implicit in the program is a linkage of the demographic characteristics of a specific geographic area and the bringing of jobs directly into the same area. The issues of whether mixed land uses—that is, mixing of industrial and residential activities—is either possible in terms of physical space or is desirable in terms of living conditions and overall efficiency is not approached.

It is difficult to clearly conceptualize and project the kinds of areas that would be subject to the program as presently formulated. One of them, however, would be an effort to bring back the classic mixed residential and industrial areas that once clustered around the hearts of some of our older industrial communities, along the order of a Somerville or East Cambridge in Massachusetts or the Ironbound area of Newark, N.J. Whether this is either feasible or desirable within the context of late-twentieth-century business and living standards remains an open question.

In such areas as the South Bronx or some of the zones of abandonment in Chicago, clearly there is a juncture of space and all too much poverty of residents, which could provide both the juridical and physical settings. Even in these zones of disaster, however, there is a considerable shortage of *contiguous* space for new industrial development.

One can easily envision a situation in which the traditional employment areas are at some distance, that is, noncontiguous to the residence places of impacted workers. Under Kemp-Garcia it might prove very difficult to subsidize the job area, but rather there would be a requirement for the generation of new facilities within the residential zone.

This is one of the implicit weaknesses of programs by right as opposed to those which have a discretionary overview, such as UDAG or the bulk of the EDA measures. Whereas the trade-off may be worthwhile, it certainly is not without some measure of costs and practicality.

It should be further noted that there is no functional termination date for an area's eligibility—and when does an area become ineligible? Is there a grace period for programs that are planned but not implemented for areas that once met standards but then improved?

In a later section of this paper, the qualifying standards of Kemp-Garcia are viewed within the context of other similarly targeted programs. It is worthwhile here, however, to briefly view the collection of blight syndromes that would be obtained, assuming the criteria were to be utilized as presently is proposed. Exhibit 3 incorporates data for New Jersey based on the 1970 census for 405 suburban New Jersey municipalities in terms of the correlation of socioeconomic and housing characteristics with the proportion unemployed. Note first that unemployment has a tight linkage (as would be expected) with the percentage of people below the poverty level—indeed, that linkage has the highest coefficient of all the socioeconomic characteristics. To this degree using both elements is somewhat redundant.

The other socioeconomic characteristics that are highly linked with poverty are median income and years of school completed (negatively linked); and lower-status types of employment (positively linked).

That unemployment is far from a strictly minority-group problem is in-

EXHIBIT 3

CORRELATION OF SOCIOECONOMIC AND HOUSING CHARACTERISTICS WITH PERCENT UNEMPLOYED, 405 SUBURBAN NEW JERSEY MUNICIPALITIES, 1970

Variable	PEARSON CORRELATION Coefficient	Significance Level p<
SOCIOECONOMIC CHARACTERISTICS		
% Below Poverty Level	.521	.001
Median Income	-.515	.001
Years of School Completed	-.476	.001
%Employed, Operatives	.415	.001
%Employed, Service Workers	.340	.001
%Total Popluation Black	.253	.001
% Moved in Pre-1950	.227	.001
% Employed, Craftspersons	.211	.001
% 65 Years and Over	.094	.03
HOUSING CHARACTERISTICS		
% Renter-Occupied Units Black	.532	.001
Median Value, Owner-Occupied Units	-.454	.001
% Units with 1.01 or More Persons Per Room	.451	.001
% Units Lacking Complete Plumbing	.427	.001
Median Gross Rent	-.408	.001
Median Number of Rooms Per Unit	-.361	.001
% Owner-Occupied Units Black	.358	.001
Median Number of Bedrooms Per Unit	-.329	.001
% Total Units Black Occupied	.293	.001
% Owner-Occupied Units	-.248	.001
% Units Built Pre-1950	.169	.001
% Units Built 1960–70	-.104	.020

Source: Rutgers University Center for Urban Policy Research

dicated by the strong but far-from-overwhelming linkage with the percent of the total population that is black—only .253.

Regarding housing characteristics, the variables associated with unemployment are similarly clear-cut. Black renter-occupied units have the highest level of correlation, as do low-value owner-occupied units. Overcrowding, inadequate housing (as shown by units lacking complete plumbing), and low rents are precisely the elements that would be anticipated as poverty indicators. Thus, on a community basis there is significant potency to the unemployment criterion—and it is certainly a significant multiplier. A variety of scars within our society can be healed if the unemployment incidence can be rectified.

Appropriately gauged full-employment measures have a payoff far greater than simply to those who have newly secured jobs. Full employment is important to the community as a whole and its capital stock, as seen in the housing variables associated with it.

In Exhibits 4 and 5 are shown equivalent data for the same 1,509 census tracts earlier referred to, for nineteen of the twenty-one New Jersey counties. The variables are shown initially in terms of their linkages with unemployment rates, rather than with the percent of families below the poverty level. The strong correlation of these elements is evident. The level of social dislocation indicated by the female-headed household incidence, the proportion separated or divorced, as well as the impacts of lack of schooling, are most definite. It will take strong incentives to bring this population into the productive labor force.

EXHIBIT 4

CORRELATION OF PERSONAL AND FAMILY CHARACTERISTICS WITH PERCENT UNEMPLOYED, NEW JERSEY CENSUS TRACTS, 1970

Variable	Pearson Correlation Coefficient	Significance Level P <
% Families with Female Head	.59	.001
% Families with Children under 18 with Female Head	.59	.001
% Persons Married	-.42	.001
% Persons Separated or	.55	.001
Divorced	.55	.001
Median Years of Education	-.52	.001
% of High School Graduates	-.54	.001

Source: Rutgers University Center for Urban Policy Research

EXHIBIT 5

CORRELATION OF PERSONAL AND FAMILY CHARACTERISTICS WITH PERCENT OF FAMILIES BELOW THE POVERTY LEVEL, NEW JERSEY CENSUS TRACTS, 1970

Variable	Pearson Correlation Coefficient	Significance Level P<
% Families with Female Head	.80	.001
% Families with Children under 18 with Female Head	.83	.001
% Persons Married	-.62	.001
% Persons Separated or Divorced	.73	.001
Median Years of Education	-.61	.001
% of High School Graduates	-.62	.001

Source: Rutgers University Center for Urban Policy Research

Thus, regardless of whether communities as a whole or individual census tracts are analyzed, unemployment tends to be related to a variety of other social trauma. The precise cause-and-effect relationships of these elements can be left to the logician; the cycle must be broken. The return, therefore, of appropriate successful investment strategies can yield a very high multiplier; the problem of achieving the success, however, is far from trivial.

Clearly, the syndrome at work here of familial disruption and poor schooling is very powerful. The cures that are going to be required to turn the process around must be equally potent.

SUMMARY AND CONCLUSION

TARGETING

In a previous paper members of the Center for Urban Policy Research summarized the admission standards for the UDAG program together with several of the EDA programs.[10] The criteria that they both embody represent a blending of a variety of socioeconomic variables based on available direct data or proven analogs. Elements of age of housing, for example (to denote infrastructure need), together with the income and welfare characteristics of the residents, are brought together in formulas that represent the substantial learning that has taken place over a period of a generation of program activity. All programs that seek to address the problems of people and places must define the relative characteristics of the distress elements.

As discussed in the earlier paper[11] there are at least a dozen other approaches to measurement of the same trauma; they differ in ultimate results scarcely at all.

The Kemp-Garcia proposal is at one and the same time both simpler and more complex. It is simpler because of its straightforward emphasis on unemployment and poverty. It is more complex, however, because it insists on a variety of measurement requirements that simply do not exist in forms or details appropriate for the program.

There is, however, a unique opportunity to utilize the 1980 census, at least as a launch platform for the program. This would permit precision targeting to relatively small areas (areas of 4,000 or more persons), which is called for in the program. Our analysis of 1970 New Jersey tract data permits some insight into the proportion of areas that would qualify under the standards within the bill. They are extremely limited. For example, in New Jersey the qualifying tracts would represent barely 1.5 percent of the state. This is in substantial contrast to both UDAG and EDA, which allow 40 percent or more of the urban population of the United States to qualify.

The issues of comparability are more complex, however. Both UDAG and EDA have a substantial measure of selectivity in their funding. Application may be made, but even if the areas under question meet the standards of the program, funds are relatively scarce, and discretion in terms of the feasibility and desirability of the particular initiative is used as a sorting mechanism. The Kemp-Garcia method, on the other hand, nominally does not require any subjective consideration on the part of the federal government. It is rather the offering of a variety of subsidies as an implicit entitlement on meeting the simple statistical requirements of the program. (However, again it should be noted that these requirements are only "simple" if the data are available—or if the criteria are changed to meet the limitations of our present statistical webs.)

The comparability of the realities of the Kemp-Garcia standards with those of the two earlier-mentioned programs is indicated in the Exhibit 6 which shows appropriate data on 30 major cities for incomes/budget requirements as well as unemployment data. These findings basically corroborate the significance placed on both criteria in all of the programs at hand. The accentuated qualifications called for by Kemp-Garcia would be of most importance within subsets of municipalities, that is, districts within municipalities. For actual qualifications we must wait for the 1980 census, the 1970 results earlier discussed indicated a relatively small coverage.

HOW POTENT ARE THE INCENTIVES?

In my own estimation the present elements of the Kemp-Garcia initiative are perhaps the most substantial that have ever been offered in terms of fos-

EXHIBIT 6

ELIGIBILITY STANDINGS FOR THIRTY UDAG CITIES UNDER THE KEMP-GARCIA URBAN JOBS AND ENTERPRISE ZONES ACT

City[1]	Unemployment Rate Average for 1977 and 1978[2]	85% of Poverty Level[4]	Percentage of Families Below the Poverty Level[5]	Eligibility Under Kemp-Garcia Urban Jobs and Enterprise Zones Act — Criteria: A[6]	B[7]	C[8]
			Data are unavailable	(see notes)		
Newark	13.95	$10,950				
St. Louis	7.05	10,710				
Cleveland	7.75	10,710				
Buffalo	11.15	10,950				
Detroit	9.9(1977)	10,710				
New York	9.45	11,010				
Boston	8.4	11,580				
Chicago	7.4(1977)	10,960				
New Orleans	7.45	10,170				
Cincinnati	6.85	10,710				
Pittsburgh	7.8	10,950				
Philadelphia	9.2	10,950				
Baltimore	8.15	10,850				
Birmingham	7.05	10,170				
Rochester	7.9	10,950				
Louisville	5.5(1977)	10,170				
Atlanta	8.35	10,170				
San Francisco	7.55	11,820				
Los Angeles	8.35	11,390				
Akron	7.2	10,710				
Kansas City	5.95	10,710				
Minneapolis	4.35	10,870				
Milwaukee	N.A.	10,790				
Seattle	7.15	11,827[9]				
Miami	9.15	10,170				
Tampa	7.0	10,170				
Sacramento	8.75	11,250				
Norfolk	6.45	N.A.				
Columbus	5.8	10,710				
Denver	6.65	11,250				
United States[3] =	6.5					
Two Times =	13.0					
Three Times =	19.5					

EXHIBIT 6 (*Continued*)

Notes:

1. Cities ranked under UDAG as needy jurisdictions with populations above 250,000.
2. Unemployment rates are for civil jurisdictions and represent the average unemployment rate for 1977 and 1978. The data were obtained from "*C.E.T.A. Area Employment and Unemployment*" Jan.-Dec. 1977 and Jan.-Dec. 1978., Bureau of Labor Statistics, U.S. Department of Labor, Mar. 1978 and Mar. 1979.
3. National unemployment rates are based on the *Current Population Survey.*
4. "Poverty," as defined in the Kemp-Garcia Urban Jobs and Enterprise Zones Act, is 85 percent of the Bureau of Labor Statistics' "average lower living standard income level" (lower budget) for autumn 1979. Poverty thresholds for cities were obtained from the U.S. Department of Labor, Office of Information, "News" (USDL: 80-357), June 2, 1980. The data were originally made available for C.E.T.A. prime sponsors and were estimated for prime sponsor jurisdictions. A less-detailed listing of the average lower budget for regions and the twenty-four largest SMSAs is available in "Autumn 1979 Urban Family Budgets and Comparative Indexes for Selected Urban Areas," U.S. Department of Labor, Bureau of Labor Statistics, "News" (USDL: 80-278), Apr. 30, 1980.
5. Reliable data on the percentage of families that fall below B.L.S. living standards are unavailable at the substate level. The availability of national and state estimates, based on the *Current Population Survey*, depend on user request to the Employment Policy Division of the Congressional Budget Office.
6. Possible eligibility for Newark under criterion "A", depending on the percentage of families below the poverty level.
7. None are eligible.
8. Eligibility is unknown. Data on the percentage of families below the poverty level are required.
9. The 85 percent threshold for Seattle was derived from the lower living standard income level for the Seattle SMSA apearing in "Autumn 1979 Urban Family Budgets and Comparative Idexes for Selected Urban Areas," U.S. Department of Labor, "News" (USDL: 80–278).

tering operations of companies in impacted areas. The prime elements center on the concessions involving depreciation and income-tax policy rather than the social-security reductions and the real-estate tax exemptions.

If we take the last first, it is not at all uncommon for states (which are empowered to do so by their constitutions and/or legislatures) to offer completely tax-free facilities. Indeed, so common is this practice as to raise some question whether it represents truly an incentive or rather merely a windfall to entrepreneurs.[12]

The social-security tax reductions are less striking than earlier efforts that have been fostered from time to time as apprenticeship allowances and the like. Much more significant, however, is the *multiplier* that is given to them. Earlier precedents simply covered new workers of various characteristics (for example, youth unemployed). The current proposal, however, would cover all employees of a firm within the incentive zone, assuming that the firm qualifies. Thus the cost per new employee may be several times the nominal specific social-security write-down that is called for in the bill. (See page 51 and following.)

It is within the sphere of depreciation that the most significant incentives are incorporated. As demonstrated on pages 51 and following, this represents a practically unique scale of incentives. It is only matched by some of the fast write-offs given exotic equipment for the production of defense armaments. There certainly would be a significant effort on the part of a number of companies to qualify for such capacities. It should be noted, moreover, that there is no limit on the investment per worker. One can easily envision a tank farm or its equivalent that would maximize writeoff but yield relatively little in the way of employment.

So significant is the depreciation write-off as to dwarf the very substantial lowering of income-tax rates and capital-gains assessments in the program, which are far from trivial in and of themselves. The disadvantaged worker, however, may be viewed by the potential employer more as a necessary encumbrance to qualify for the tax advantages implicit in the program rather than as a vital working part of the firm. And jobs as ritual rather than as real impetus are corrosive to the spirit and discipline of the very individuals that need to be aided.

There is little in the way of safeguards within the program on the issue of marginality, that is, of extant workers receiving the benefits of new workers and reducing the targeting—and increasing the costs. There is no addressing the issue of "musical chairs"—moving from a declining area that does not meet the enterprise zone requirements into one that does, simply to take advantage of the benefits available in the latter.

The very sweep of the subsidies built into the program and the limited number of areas that qualify, based on 1970 data at least, suggest a strong possibility of the creation of tax havens with much in the way of capital investment—and perhaps much less striking advances in net growth of employment.

In this regard, the program in question compares particularly unfavorably with UDAG. In the latter program, there is an evaluation of a specific business, its impact not only on the specifics of the area in which it is located but on the broader environment as well. Again, let me repeat: the Kemp-Garcia initiative does not have this review, but rather is essentially an entitlement situation.

COSTS

The total costs of the incentives are impossible to evaluate. The very fact that they are not addressed necessarily to new workers but rather to extant ones as well means that the marginal costs per new employee may vary substantially. Incorporated within the earlier analysis is a simplified model example of the total tax implications. Clearly, the level of forgone revenue through reduced income taxes depends on a number of vagaries, not least of them the types of businesses that are attracted. However, the program as now presented is too much a blank check in direct costs and too obscure in new benefits to inspire total acceptance.

In terms of the multipliers available under the UDAG program and some measure of early success being shown by newer EDA initiatives, I would have to rank the Kemp-Garcia program, as presently phrased and structured, as overly costly in terms of its results. There are, however, some strikingly important elements that could be useful in a more precise framework.

RECOMMENDATIONS

I would strongly suggest that the Kemp-Garcia initiative, in terms of a rapid write-off of allowable improvements within impacted areas, be reviewed for possible inclusion in both the EDA and UDAG programs as they presently stand. The three-year write-off is perhaps overly extreme. A five-year write-off certainly would be more than adequate and would serve to limit the temptation to resell the enterprise within a very short time span, which is now implicit within the program.

Rather than inventing a variety of new admission standards in any case, I would tend to move to the UDAG formula as presently constituted. If on further consideration, some form of subsidy should be available to hiring the long-term unemployed—particularly more youthful individuals—I would strongly suggest that this subsidy be made explicit rather than "going around the barn door" through reduction in social-security taxes—and causing the necessity to raise general revenues with which to replace them.

The elements of a hidden agenda in the program, however, should not take away from its very real virtues. It represents an initial draft of a systematic approach toward making the operations of companies within impacted areas less riskful (through fast write-off) and potentially more profitable (through a variety of incentive mechanisms). As such it represents a very important complement to the capital grants and front-end loading, which hitherto have been our major instrumentalities.

APPENDIX A

UNEMPLOYMENT AND POVERTY DATA

UNEMPLOYMENT DATA

Unemployment statistics are available for a range of geographical areas, from the level of the nation and the largest Standard Metropolitan Statistical Areas (SMSAs)[14] to areas with populations of 2,500 or less. However, the methods for the collection and dissemination of unemployment statistics are not uniform. The following describes some of the dimensions along which unemployment statistics may vary at each geographical level (see Exhibit 7).

1. *The Nation*—Unemployment data are collected by the Bureau of the Census in the *Current Population Survey* (CPS), and are then analyzed and published by the Bureau of Labor Statistics (BLS). Covering all states and the District of Columbia, the survey seeks to elicit information on the socioeconomic characteristics of the sampled households. The time reference of the survey is the week in which the twelfth day of the month falls.

To obtain information on the incidence of unemployment the survey asks respondents about their employment situation. Individuals are considered unemployed if:

- they did not work during the survey week;
- they made specific efforts to find a job within the previous four weeks; and
- they were available for work during the survey week.

The unemployed category is also applied to those who did not work but who were available for work and

- were waiting to be called back to a job from which they had been laid off; or
- were waiting to report to a new wage or salary job within thirty days.

The design and size of the sample survey allow for a reliable estimate of the national unemployment rate. The sample is a multistage stratified probability sample of households, with primary sampling units (PSUs) representing all SMSAs, special non-SMSAs with large populations, and non-SMSA counties that are usually combined for purposes of increasing diversity and facilitating interviewer contact. The PSUs are stratified according to homogeneous socioeconomic characteristics, with the larger SMSAs and other large non-SMSA areas forming individual strata. Approximately one out of every 1,500 households is sampled within each stratum, yielding a current sample size of about 67,000 households.

National unemployment data are published monthly by the BLS in *Employment and Earnings*. There is a two-month lag period in publishing current data.

2. *Ten Largest States*—(California, Florida, Illinois, Massachusetts, Michigan, New Jersey, New York, Ohio, Pennsylvania, Texas)—Estimates of unemployment are taken directly from the CPS. The data are published monthly in *Employment and Earnings*.

EXHIBIT 7

SOURCES AND SCOPE OF UNEMPLOYMENT DATA AVAILABLE BY AREA[1]

Area	Method	Time Reference	Geographic Categoration of the Unemployed	Frequency of Collection	Frequency of Publication	Place of Publication
1) National	Current Population Survey (CPS)	The four weeks preceding the week in which the twelfth day of the month falls (FW-12)	County of Residence (CR)	Monthly (M)	Monthly (M)	"Employment and Earnings"[2] (EE)
2) Ten largest states	CPS	FW-12	CR	M	M	EE
3) The remaining states	Handbook (70-step) adjusted by CPS	FW-12	CR	M	M	EE
4) New York, and Los Angeles–Long Beach SMSAs	CPS	FW-12	CR	M	M	EE
5) 214 largest SMSAs	Handbook (70-step) adjusted by CPS	FW-12	CR	M	M	EE
6) Remaining SMSAs	Handbook (70-step) adjusted by CPS	FW-12	CR	M	M	EE
7) Non-SMSA LMAs and counties not part of LMAs	Handbook (36-step) adjusted by CPS	FW-12	CR	M		

EXHIBIT 7 (*Continued*)

SOURCES AND SCOPE OF UNEMPLOYMENT DATA AVAILABLE BY AREA[1]

Area	Method	Time Reference	Geographic Categoration of the Unemployed	Frequency of Collection	Frequency of Publication	Place of Publication
8) Counties within LMAs or within multicounty LMAs[2]	-Experienced unemployed based on county share of U.I.[2] claimants in LMA -Entrants and reentrants proportionate to census age cohorts	FW-12	CR	DEPENDS ON USER NEED AND PROGRAM REQUIREMENTS		
9) Subcounty areas (cities and other areas)	-Unemployed proportionate to share of county's U.I. claimants, and/or proportionate to census share of county unemployment or population	FW-12	subcounty area of residence if known			

[1] The diagram is a modified and expanded version of Table 15-1, "Method and Major Source of Data for Estimates of Employment and Unemployment by Area, 1978," appearing in National Commission on Employment and Unemployment Statistics, *Counting The Labor Force*, (Washington D.C.: The Commission, 1979, pp. 246–247).

[2]See text.

3. *The Remaining States*—The sample size of the CPS is not sufficient to provide reliable unemployment data for the remaining states and other local areas. As a result, unemployment estimates are obtained by state employment-security agencies using the "handbook" methodology, which estimates unemployment on the basis of the number of unemployment-insurance claimants.

Under the technical direction of the Bureau of Labor Statistics, the handbook method comprises a set of adjustment procedures that estimates the state unemployment rate by adding various catagories of the unemployed to the state count of insured claimants. In all instances, the time reference and definition of unemployment is the same as the CPS, except that the CPS does not count the involuntarily, partially employed as unemployed. The unemployed are geographically categorized according to their county of residence. The estimate for the experienced unemployed is produced by adding to the number of claimants 1) those who have exhausted their benefits, 2) the unemployed who have been disqualified from receiving benefits, 3) the late filers, those who are eligible but have not yet filed a claim, and 4) the unemployed who were working in noncovered establishments.

The unemployment estimate for entrants and reentrants into the labor force is obtained on the basis of the relationship of state employment to the size of the state's fourteen- to nineteen-year-old and twenty-years-and-over age cohorts, which is reported in the decennial census.

In order to improve the comparability of unemployment statistics across states (many of which differ with respect to the legal and administrative structure that implements the federal legislation governing unemployment insurance), the BLS requires adjustments to the handbook estimates to bring them more into line with the estimates provided by the CPS. A monthly adjustment is made to the handbook estimate using the ratio of a six-month average of the CPS estimate to a six-month average of the handbook estimate. Each year state unemployment is adjusted to the state annual averages obtained by the CPS.

Two versions of the handbook method are the "70-step" method and an abbreviated "36-step" method. The "70-step" method is used in estimating unemployment in all states except for the ten largest, which use the CPS.

Unemployment data for the states are reported monthly and are published in the BLS *Employment and Earnings*.

4. *New York and Los Angeles–Long Beach SMSA*—The unemployment estimates for these two largest SMSAs are taken directly from the CPS and are published in *Employment and Earnings*.

5. *Remaining SMSAs*—Unemployment data for the remaining SMSAs are estimated by state employment-security agencies using the "70-step" handbook method. Data for 214 of the largest SMSAs are published monthly in *Employment and Earnings*.

6. *Non-SMSA Labor Market Areas (LMAs)*[15] *and Non-LMA Counties*—The abbreviated ("36-step") handbook method is used in estimating unemployment at this geographic level. Adjustments are made according to the CPS-based estimates for the state.

Unemployment data are collected monthly, but the publication of unemployment data for areas below the SMSA level depends on user need and program requirements. For example, the Comprehensive Employment and Training Act (CETA) of 1978 authorizes the collection of unemployment data for areas of substantial unemployment, which are areas with a population of at least 10,000 located within a prime sponsor area (a unit of local government with a population of at least 100,000), and which have an unemployment rate of 6.5 percent or more for three consecutive months. These data are published annually by the BLS in *CETA Area Employment and Unemployment*. Also, Defense Manpower Policy No. 4B, which gives preference for federal procurements to firms located within areas of substantial unemployment, requires monthly estimates of unemployment for cities with a population of at least 50,000.

7. *Counties within LMAs or within Multicounty LMAs*—Unemployment data at this level are gathered by disaggregating the LMA's unemployment. The estimate of unemployment among the experienced unemployed is allocated to the county on the basis of the county's share of unemployment-insurance claimants. The estimate of entrant and reentrant unemployment is related to the census count of the county's share of fourteen- to nineteen-year old and twenty-years-or-over age cohorts.

These data are reported and published according to user need and program requirements.

8. *Subcounty Areas (Cities and Other Subcounty Areas)*—Areas with a population of 2,500 or more are allocated their share of the non-LMA county's unemployment on the basis of their proportion of unemployment-insurance claimants residing in the county. When such data are unavailable, unemployment is prorated according to the area's share of county unemployment at the time of the decennial census.

Areas with a population of 2,500 or less are allocated unemployment on the basis of their share of the county population at the time of the decennial census.

Unemployment data are reported and made available according to user need and program requirements.

POVERTY DATA

The Bureau of Labor Statistics, on the basis of the *Current Population Survey*, provides the average thresholds for lower, intermediate, and higher living standards for the Northeast, Southern, and Western Regions, for the twenty-four largest SMSAs, and for Anchorage, Alaska. The data appear annually in the Bureau of Labor Statistics' "Urban Family Budgets and Comparative Indexes for Selected Urban Areas."

Data on the average lower budget are provided at a finer geographic level for CETA program prime sponsors, which are defined as units of local government with a population of 100,000 or more. These data are approximations and are released by the U.S. Department of Labor for use in determining the eligibility of CETA participants.

According to informants at both the Bureau of Labor Statistics[16] and the Employment Policy Section of the Congressional Budget Office,[17] reliable data on the percentage of families falling below the average lower budget are not available at the substate level. National and state estimates are available on user request to the Employment Policy Section of the Congressional Budget Office.

An individual in Congressman Garcia's office[18] reported that the drafters of the legislation were not aware of a source of information for the percentage of families falling below 85 percent of the BLS lower budget.

APPENDIX B

URBAN JOBS AND ENTERPRISE ZONE ACT OF 1980

§2823 - *Be it enacted by the Senate and House of Representatives of the United States of America in Congress assembled,*

Section I. SHORT TITLE: AMENDMENT OF 1954 CODE.

(a) Short Title—This Act may be cited as the "Urban Jobs and Enterprise Zone Act of 1980".

(b) Amendment of 1954 Code—Except as otherwise expressly provided, whenever in this Act an amendment or repeal is expressed in terms of an amendment to, or repeal of, a section or other provision, the reference shall be considered to be made to a section or other provision of the Internal Revenue Code of 1954.

TITLE I—DESIGNATION OF PRIVATE JOBS AND ENTERPRISE ZONES

Sec. 101. Designation of Zones.

(a) General Rule—Chapter 80 (relating to general rules) is amended by adding at the end thereof the following new subchapter:

"Subchapter C—Designation of Private Jobs and Enterprise Zones."

Sec. 7871. Designation.

"(a) General Rule—For purposes of this title, the term "private jobs and enterprise zone" means any area in the United States which is designated by one or more local governments for purposes of this section if—

"(1) the Secretary of Commerce approves such designation, and

(2) the government (or governments) making such designation provide assurances satisfactory to the Secretary of Commerce that the real property tax reduction described in subsection (d) will be made with respect to real property located in such area. The Secretary of Commerce may not approve any designation under paragraph (1) unless an application therfore is submitted in such manner and in such form, and contains such information, as the Secretary of Commerce shall by regulations prescribe. A designation under this subsection may be made by a State government on behalf of one or more local governments with the consent of such local government or governments.

(b) Period for which designation is in effect.

(1) In general—any designation of an area as a private jobs and enterprise zone shall apply—

"(A) for purposes of subtitle A. to all taxable years ending during the first 10 calendar years beginning after the date on which the Secretary of Commerce approves such designation, and

"(B) for purposes of Chapter 21, to all calendar months during such taxable years unless the Secretary of Commerce revokes such designation under paragraph (2).

"(2) Revocation of Designation—The Secretary of Commerce may revoke any designation of an area if the Secretary of Commerce determines that the government (or governments) which designated such area are not substantially complying with the real property tax reduction described in subsection (d). Any such revocation shall take effect under rules similar to the rules of paragraph (1).

"(C) Area Requirement—

"(1) In general—The Secretary of Commerce may approve the designation of any area under subsection (a) only if—

"(A) the area is within the jurisdiction of the government (or governments) designating such area.

"(B) the boundary of the area is continuous.

"(C) the area—

"(1) has a population of at least 4,000 or

"(ii) is an Indian reservation (as determined by the Secretary of the Interior), and

"(D) the area meets the requirements of paragraph (2).

"(2) Unemployment and Poverty Requirements—For purposes of paragraph (1), an area meets the requirements of this paragraph if such area meets the requirements of 1 or more of the following subparagraphs:

"(A) An area meets the requirements of this subparagraph if—

"(i) the average rate of unemployment in such area for the most recent 24-month period for which data are available was at least twice the average national rate of unemployment for such 24-month period and

"(ii) 30 percent or more of the families living in such area were below the poverty level.

"(B) An area meets the requirements of this subparagraph if the average rate of unemployment in such area for the most recent 24-month period for which data are available was at least 3 times the average national rate of unemployment for such 24-month period.

"(C) An area meets the requirements of this subparagraph if 50 percent or more of the families living in such area are below the poverty level.

"(3) Poverty Level—For purposes of this subsection, the term 'poverty level' means 85 percent of the average lower living standard income level determined annually by the Secretary of Labor and published by the Bureau of Labor Statistics.

"(4) Determinations made by Secretary of Commerce—Determinations under this subsection shall be made by the Secretary of Commerce on the basis of data submitted by the government (or governments) designating the area if the Secretary determines that such data is reasonably accurate.

"(D) Required Real Property Tax Reduction.

"(1) In general—the real property tax reduction described in this subsection is a permanent reduction applicable to property in the private jobs and enterprise zone of not less than 20 percent in the effective real property tax rate (determined as of the submission of the application)

"(a) Any such reduction shall be made not less rapidly than ratably over the first 4 real property tax years beginning after the date on which the Secretary of Commerce approves the designation under subsection (a).

"(2) Effective Tax Rate—For purposes of paragraph (1) the effective real property tax rate is the rate of the real property tax multiplied by the percentage of assessed value which is subject to such rate."

(b) The table of subchapters for chapter 80 is amended by adding at the end thereof the following new item:

"SUBCHAPTER C DESIGNATION OF PRIVATE JOBS AND ENTERPRISE ZONES."

(c) Property Tax Reduction to be disregarded for tax effort purposes—for the purpose of determining the eligibility of a State or local government for assistance or benefits under any law of the United States, and for the purpose of determining the amount or extent of any such assistance or benefits, any reduction in real property taxes made for purpose of obtaining or maintaining the designation of a private jobs and enterprise zone under Section 7871 of the Internal Revenue Code of 1954 shall be disregarded.

Sec. 102. SENSE OF CONGRESS WITH RESPECT TO DESIGNATIONS OF FOREIGN TRADE ZONES.

It is the sense of the Congress that in the case of any application for designation of an area in an Urban Jobs and Enterprise Zone as a foreign-trade zone.

(l) the Foreign-Trade Zone Board should expedite the application process as much as possible;

(2) in evaluating such application, the Board should take into account not only current economic development within the Urban Jobs and Enterprise Zone but also future development to be expected from the incentives offered by this Act; and

(3) the Board should provide technical assistance to the applicants.

TITLE II—TAX INCENTIVES

Subtitle A—Social-Security Tax Reduction

Sec. 201. Reduction in Social Security Payroll Taxes.

(a) General Rule—Subchapter C of Chapter 21 (relating to social security payroll taxes) is amended by redesignating section 3126 as section 3127 and by inserting after section 3125 the following new section:

"Sec. 3126. Reduction in Employee and Employer Taxes for Employees in Private Jobs and Enterprise Zones.

"(a) In general—if an employee is an eligible employee for any payroll period, each rate of tax specified in Section 3101 or 3111 shall, for wages paid for such payroll period, be reduced by—

"(1) 90 percent if such employee has not attained the age of 21 before the close of such payroll period, or

"(2) 50 percent if such employee has attained the age of 21 before the close of such payroll period.

"(b) Eligible Employee—for purposes of subsection (a), an employee is an eligible employee for any payroll period if at least 50 percent of the services performed by such employee during such period for the employer are performed within one or more private jobs and enterprise zones."

(b)Clerical Amendment—The table of sections for subchapter C of Chapter 21 is amended by striking out the item relating to section 3126 and inserting in lieu thereof the following:

"Sec. 3126. Reduction in Employee and Employer Taxes for Employees in Private Jobs and Enterprise Zones.

"Sec. 3127. Short Title."

Sec. 202. Reduction in Social Security Tax Not to Affect Benefits.

The reduction in rates of tax under section 3101 or 3111 of the Internal Revenue Code of 1954 because of the application of section 3126 of such Code shall not affect the eligibility of any individual for benefits under the Social Security Act nor the amount or extent of such benefits.

Sec. 203. Reduction of Social Security Tax Collections to be Made Up From General Revenues.

There is hereby appropriated to the trust funds established under sections 201 and 1817 of the Social Security Act amounts equivalent to the amounts by which the amount of taxes received under sections 3101 and 3111 of the Internal Revenue Code of 1954 are reduced by the application of section 3126 of such Code. The Secretary of the Treasury shall transfer amounts appropriated under this section to the appropriate trust funds in the appropriate amounts. The Secretary shall make such transfers on a quarterly basis and on the basis of estimates made by him of such amounts, with appropriate adjustment for inadequate or excessive previous transfers due to errors of estimate.

Subtitle B—Reduction in Capital Gain Tax Rates

Sec. 211. Corporations.

(a) General Rule—Subsection (a) of section 1201 (relating to alternative tax for corporations) is amended by striking out paragraphs (1) and (2) and inserting in lieu thereof the following:

"(1) a tax computed on the taxable income reduced by the amount of the net capital gain, at the rates and in the manner as if this subsection had not been enacted,

"(2) a tax of 15 percent of the lesser of—

"(A) the net capital gain, or

"the net capital gain determined by only taking into account sales or exchanges of qualified property, plus

"(3) a tax of 28 percent of the excess (if any) of—

"(A) the net capital gain for the taxable year, over

"(B) the amount of the net capital gain taken into account under paragraph (2)."

(b) Definition of Qualified Property—Section 1201 is amended by redesignating subsection (d) as subsection (e) and by inserting after subsection (c) the following new subsection:

"(d) Definition of Qualified Property—For purposes of this section—

"(1) In General—The term 'qualified property' means—

"(A) any tangible personal property which was used predominantly by the taxpayer in a private jobs and enterprise zone in the active conduct of a trade or business,

"(B) any real property located in such a zone which—

"(i) was used predominantly by the taxpayer in the active conduct of a trade or business, or

"(ii) is sold or exchanged by an individual whose principal residence (as of the date of the sale or exchange) is in such zone, and

"(C) any interest in a corporation, partnership, or other entity if, for the most recent taxable year of such entity ending before the date of the sale or exchange, such entity was a qualified business.

"(2) Qualified Business—A person shall be treated as a qualified business for any taxable year if—

"(A) such person is actively engaged in the conduct of a trade or business during such taxable year,

"(B) at least 50 percent of the employees of such person during such taxable year are qualified employees, and

"(C) in the absence of extenuating circumstances (as shown to the satisfaction of the Secretary), at least 50 percent of the average daily number of qualified employees of such person, for each taxable year after the first taxable year in which the person is actively engaged in the conduct of a trade or business in the private jobs and enterprise zone, are residents of a private jobs and enterprise zone.

"(3) Qualified Employees—An employee shall be treated as a qualified employee for any taxable year if substantially all the service performed by such employee for the employer during such taxable year are—

"(A) performed in 1 or more private jobs and enterprise zones, and

"(B) performed in a trade or business of the employer,

"(4) Property remains qualified after zone designation ceases to apply—

"A) In General—The treatment of property as qualified property under paragraph (1) shall not terminate when the designation of the private jobs and enterprise zone in which the property is located or used ceases to apply.

"(B) Exceptions—Subparagraph (A) shall not apply after the first sale or exchange of property occurring after the designation ceases to apply to the zone."

Sec. 212. Taxpayers Other Than Corporations.

Subsection (a) of section 1202 (relating to deduction for capital gains) is amended to read as follows:

"(a) Deduction Allowed.

"(1) In General—If for any taxable year a taxpayer other than a corporation has a net capital gain, there shall be allowed as a deduction from gross income an amount equal to the sum of—

"(a) 80 perent of the lesser of —

"(i) the net capital gain, or

"(ii) the net capital gain determined by only taking into account sales or exchanges of qualified property (as defined in section 1201(d)), plus

"(B) 60 percent of the excess (if any) of —

"(i) the net capital gain, over

"(ii) the amount of the net capital gain taken into account under subparagraph (A).

"(2) Property remains qualified after zone designation ceases to apply.

"(A) In General—The treatment of property as qualified property under paragraph (1) shall not terminate when the designation of the private jobs and enterprise zone in which the property is located or used ceases to apply.

"(B) Exceptions. Subparagraph (A) shall not apply after the first sale or exchange of property occurring after the designation of the private jobs and enterprise zone in which the property is located or used ceases to apply.

Sec. 213. Minimum Tax.

Paragraph (9) of section 57(a) (relating to tax preference for capital gains) is amended by adding at the end thereof the following new subparagraph:

"(E) Sales of certain property not taken into account—For purposes of this paragraph, sales or exchanges of qualified property (as defined in section 1201(d) shall not be taken into account."

Subtitle C—Corporate Rate Reduction

Sec. 221. Rate Reduction.

Section 11 (relating to tax imposed on corporations) is amended by redesignating subsections (c) and (d) as subsections (d) and (e), respectively, and by inserting after subsection (b) the following new subsection:

"c) Reduction in Rate of Tax for Corporations which are Qualified Businesses—If any corporation is qualified business (as defined in section 1201(d) (2) for any taxable year, the amount of the tax imposed by subsection (a) on the taxable income of such corporation shall (in lieu of the amount determined under subsection (b)) be the sum of—

"(1) 14 percent of so much of the taxable income as does not exceed $25,000,

"(2) 17 percent of so much of the taxable income as exceeds $25,000 but does not exceed $50,000,

"(3) 25 percent of so much of the taxable income as exceeds $50,000 but does not exceed $75,000,

"(4) 34 percent of so much of the taxable income as exceeds $75,000 but does not exceed $100,000 plus

"(5) 39 percent of so much of the taxable income as exceeds $100,000."

Subtitle D—Other Incentives

Sec. 231 Accelerated Depreciation.

(a) Three-Year Straight Line Method—Section 167 (relating to depreciation) is amended by redesignating subsection (r) as subsection (s) and by inserting after subsection (q) the following new subsection:

"(r) Rapid Depreciation for Certain Small Businesses.

"(1) In General—In the case of any taxpayer who is a qualified business (within the meaning of section 1201(d)(2) for any taxable year, the taxpayer may elect to compute the depreciation deduction under this section with respect to any property placed in service during such taxable year in a private jobs and enterprise zone by using the straight line method with a useful life of 3 years.

"(2) Limitation. The aggregate bases of property placed in service during any taxable year to which an election under paragraph (1) applies shall not exceed $500,000."

(b) Full Investment Credit Allowed—Subsection (c) of section 46 (relating to qualified investment) is amended by adding at the end thereof the following new paragraph:

"(7) Special rule for private jobs and enterprise zone property. Notwithstanding the second sentence of paragraph (2), the useful life, for purposes of this subpart, of any property with respect to which an election is made under section 167(r) shall be determined without regard to that election."

Sec. 232. Optional Cash Method of Accounting for Certain Small Businesses.

(a) General Rule—Section 446 (relating to general rule for methods of accounting) is amended by adding at the end thereof the following new subsection:

"(f) Optional Cash Method.

"(1) In General—Any taxpayer who is a qualified business (as defined in section 1201 (d) (2)) or any taxable year may elect to compute taxable income—

(A) under the cash receipt and disbursements method of accounting, and

"(B) without any requirement to use inventories under section 471.

"(2) Gross Receipts Limitation. Paragraph (1) shall not apply for any taxable year with respect to any taxpayer if for any prior taxable year the gross receipts of such taxpayer exceeded $1,500,000.

"(3) Election. An election under paragraph (1) may be made by any taxpayer without the consent of the Secretary for the taxpayer's first taxable year for which the taxpayer is a qualified business."

Sec. 233. Extension of Net Operation Loss Carryovers.

(a) General Rule—Paragraph (1) of section 172(b) (relating to net operating loss carrybacks and carryovers) is amended by adding at the end thereof the following new subparagraph:

"(J) In the case of any taxpayer which is qualified business (as defined in section 1201(d)(2)) for any taxable year, any net operating loss for such taxable year shall be a net operating loss carryover to each of the 10 taxable years following the taxable year of such loss."

(b) Technical Amendment. Subparagraph (B) of section 172(b) is amended by striking out "(F)" and inserting in lieu thereof "(F), and (J)."

TITLE III—EFFECTIVE DATE

Sec. 301. Effective Dates.

The amendments made by this Act—

(1) insofar as they relate to subtitle A of the Internal Revenue Code of 1954, shall apply to taxable years beginning after December 31, 1980.

(2) insofar as they relate to Chapter 21 of such Code, shall apply to wages paid after December 31, 1980, and

(3) insofar as they relate to subtitle F of such Code, shall apply from January 1, 1981, through December 31, 1990.

NOTES

1. See *Congressional Record* - Senate S 7006, June 13, 1980.
2. I am deeply indebted to the Northeast-Midwest Institute's *Targeted Tax Credit Alternatives*, by Mary Fitzpatrick, for information on this point. For a full recital see the document.
3. As reproduced in the *Congressional Record—Senate* for June 13, 1980, page S7007 and following; see Appendix B.
4. At least as the legislation presently is shown on page S7007 of the *Congressional Record—Senate*, June 13, 1980.

5. See Financial Research Associates, *Financial Studies of the Small Business*, 3d ed., 1979.

6. Extensive analysis of the limitations of these definitions as well as other important factors bearing on additional definitional matters is available in *Counting the Labor Force, Preliminary Draft Report* of the National Commission on Employment and Unemployment Statistics (Washington, D.C., 1979).

7. Ibid.

8. See the *Monthly Labor Review*, January 1980, "Family Budgets", page 44 and following.

9. For a full description of 15 trigger mechanisms either in use or proposed for targeting, see G. Sternlieb et al., *Measuring Urban Distress* (New Brunswick, N.J.: Rutgers University Center for Urban Policy Research, 1980).

10. Ibid.

11. Ibid.

12. See B. Harrison, "The Political Economy of State Job Creation Business Incentives," in Sternlieb and Hughes, *Revitalizing the Northeast* (New Brunswick, N.J.: Rutgers University Center for Urban Policy Research, 1978).

13. Useful sources on the procedures for collecting unemployment statistics and on the scope of their availability include: U.S. National Commission on Employment and Unemployment Statistics, *Data Collection, Processing and Presentation: National and Local* (Washington, D.C.: U.S. Government Printing Office, 1980); U.S. National Commission on Employment and Unemployment Statistics, *Counting the Labor Force* (Washington, D.C.: The Commission, 1979).

14. An SMSA, except in New England, is essentially a county or group of contiguous counties that contain at least one city of 50,000 inhabitants or more, or "twin cities" with a combined population of at least 50,000. Contiguous counties are included in the SMSA if they are metropolitan in character and are socioeconomically linked to the central city. In New England, SMSAs consist of towns and cities rather than counties.

15. Labor Market Areas (LMAs) are geographic areas in which there is a concentration of economic activity or of labor demand. The assumption is that in these areas workers can change their jobs without necessarily changing their residence. Major LMAs normally contain a central city with a population of 50,000 or more and in most cases have the same boundaries as those for SMSAs.

16. William Warden, analyst at the Bureau of Labor Statistics (telephone conversation on July 22, 1980).

17. Maureen McLaughlin, analyst working on employment policy at the Congressional Budget Office (telephone conversation on July 22, 1980).

18. Paul Bardick, attorney with the staff of Congressman Garcia (telephone conversation on July 22, 1980).

A National Development Bank: Survey and Discussion of the Literature on Capital Shortages and Employment Changes in Distressed Areas

George Richard Meadows
and
John Mitrisin

INTRODUCTION AND SUMMARY OF FINDINGS AND RECOMMENDATIONS

INTRODUCTION

In March 1978, after years of discussion inside and outside of government, the Carter Administration proposed that a National Development Bank (NDB) be established to stimulate private investment and the rate of private job creation in distressed areas. At the time the NDB proposal was introduced, its importance was underscored by Assistant Secretary of the Treasury Altman's statement that "this legislation is one of the Administration's highest priorities; it is crucial, and perhaps the linchpin of our urban and regional strategy."[1] To many, the NDB approach was attractive because it addresses directly the problem of disinvestment—a pervasive reality in all declining areas. Moreover, the proposal reflected the Administration's desire to rely primarily on private institutions and the reduction of unemployment through the creation of long-term private jobs. Finally, the proposal appeared to offer a new, innovative approach to touch old problems with a relatively small budgetary commitment.

The details of the Administration's National Development Bank proposal—goals, policy tools, organization, and the eligibility criteria for jurisdictions and firms—are spelled out later in this chapter. The NDB combines five separate financial incentives: equity grants of up to 15 percent of the capital costs of a project, loan guarantees of up to 75 percent, interest subsidies on the guaranteed loans, interest subsidies on unguaranteed taxable development bonds, and a secondary facility to buy long-term private development loans made to firms in distressed areas. These incentives are aimed at inducing businesses to remain in, expand, or locate in distressed areas. The NDB proposal contains two crucial implicit assumptions: (1) that significant capital shortages exist in the distressed area, and (2) that private enterprises will modify their locational decisions in favor of distressed areas if financing costs are significantly reduced. The purpose of this chapter is to review the professional literature on these two assumptions and to discuss and evaluate the development bank proposal in light of the existing evidence.

SUMMARY OF FINDINGS—CAPITAL SHORTAGES

The literature defining and measuring capital market imperfections and the identification of distressed areas is reviewed below. At the outset, the distinction is made between two largely separate literatures on macro and micro capital shortages. This chapter concentrates almost entirely on the micro concern of the availability of capital to specific borrowers. In an overview of micro-level capital market imperfections, the following capital shortages are noted by several observers:

1. a lack of funding for large-scale redevelopment projects in central cities,
2. a lack of long-term expansion capital for small to medium-sized firms,
3. a lack of new product development finance for small to medium-sized firms, and
4. limited access to capital markets by minority borrowers, especially those in central cities.

Michelson's 1978 useful taxonomy of capital market imperfections is presented below to provide a general theoretical overview of the problem. Michelson notes that private capital markets may fail to allocate capital to its highest return because of:

1. ignorance of available alternatives,
2. the failure to incorporate social benefits and costs,
3. the presence of institutional constraints external to the direct market participants, and
4. below-potential performance caused by inefficient organization of productive factors.

The empirical evidence on capital gaps and financial market imperfections (see below) yields the following generalizations:

1. Several studies confirm the existence of significant differentials in the cost of accessing capital markets by size class of firm. Capital costs are inversely related to firm size and market power.
2. Investigations of lending practices of commercial banks confirm regional differentials in interest rates and in capital availability. Borrowers, especially smaller, higher-risk enterprises, face difficulties in concentrated banking markets. This problem appears to be greatest in rural areas.
3. The evidence regarding capital shortages in the venture capital market is mixed. Many knowledgeable observers perceive widespread problems in the availability of venture capital finance, whereas the most comprehensive empirical investigation of this market (Charles River Associates 1976), concluded that no significant market imperfections exist.
4. When viewed from the perspective of capital parity with nonminorities, two studies agree that minority-owned enterprises suffer a massive capital shortage. By one estimate (Knight and Dorsey 1976), achieving financial parity would require an additional annual investment of $7.3 billion for twenty years.
5. The generalized increased reliance on external (to the firm) funding during the 1970s has intensified the capital market barriers facing small firms, especially those seeking long-term financing.

Later in this chapter, recent work on the related concern of the identification of distressed areas is examined. The complexity of the concept *distressed area* is richly illustrated by the significant differences in both approaches taken and results obtained on this question. Clearly, there is no single unambiguous index of distress available to policymakers at present, nor is it obvious that additional research on this subject will produce clear-cut choices given the present state of the art.

SUMMARY OF FINDINGS—LOCATION DECISIONS

In the post-World War II period several important population shifts have occurred. The magnitude of these population changes has been such that significant employments shifts have also resulted. Briefly summarized, the following major changes have been observed:

1. Since 1970 the trend of increasing urbanization in the United States has reversed. Not only have central cities populations declined in absolute terms, but the fraction of the total population in SMSAs has also started to drop.
2. Population losses during the 1970s were confined to the large SMSAs (over 1 million), whereas the small SMSAs continued to grow.
3. Employment shifts have closely paralleled population shifts.
4. Although regional employment shifts have been substantial—especially from the Northeast and Midwest to the South—actual interstate migration of firms accounts for a very small fraction of annual net employment change.

The primary reason for interstate variation in the rate of employment change is differences in the birth and expansion rates of firms.

The review of the literature on firm mobility below is largely restricted to studies of intrametropolitan moves because this includes the overwhelming fraction of all firm moves. Because of data limitations, much of this research is further constrained to manufacturing-plant location changes only. Several recent intrametropolitan studies confirm the following observations:

1. Firm mobility rates are high, especially among small firms.
2. Manufacturing employment continues a decentralizing trend to locations outside of central cities, although a decline in the rate of firm births is more important than migration in explaining the lagging employment patterns of central cities. This finding suggests that the "incubator" role of central cities is waning.
3. The presence of agglomeration effects is suggested by the high concentrations of specific industries in individual analysis zones. This helps explain why central-city locations are still favorable to many firms.
4. There is some evidence that firms do respond to favorable intrametropolitan differentials in cost factors, such as access to transportation, land availability and cost, local tax rates, and access to a good supply of labor.

Theoretical and empirical investigation of firm location has been carried out by Roger Schmenner (1972, 1977, 1978) of the Harvard Business School. Schmenner argues for an "evolutionary" theory of firm behavior in choosing new plant sites, namely, that firms change locations only when compelled to, and then usually prefer to remain near the original location to maintain their labor force and supplier networks. Moreover, Schmenner argues that existing research on firm behavior is highly consistent with his theoretical arguments. Although Schmenner's firm-level empirical analysis centers largely on only one city (Cincinnati), nevertheless his findings and their implications for public policy are quite provocative. Schmenner urges that efforts designed to retain manufacturing employment in central cities take the following forms:

1. Public policy should focus on small mover firms, especially those on the margin of existence—either just beginning or about to fail. Larger, more-established firms have traditionally had little impact on changes in local employment levels.
2. Most firms move because their space requirements have changed. Once the decision to move is made, the search time for a new site is usually just a few months. To be competitive, cities need to be able to react quickly and decisively. Efforts in this direction may yield substantial benefits in retained employment.
3. State and local fiscal incentives, especially property-tax reductions and

industrial revenue bonds, have not been shown to be cost effective, although part of the problem may stem from a lack of information and understanding regarding their availability.
4. Public policy should focus on retaining and assisting the expansion of existing firms rather than emphasizing attempts to lure out-of-area plants.

Additional insight into central-city business conditions is provided by the results of three recent surveys. These investigations (reviewed below), tend to confirm many of the findings of other studies. For example, a majority of firms indicated that they would remain in the city because it was uneconomic to move and non–central-city firms showed little inclination to relocate in the city. The most comprehensive of these surveys (Joint Economic Committee 1979) yields several interesting observations:

1. Perceptions of a city's overall business climate are highly correlated with stated intentions to expand, relocate, or curtail operations.
2. Firms in the 25-to-499-employee size class are the most likely to expand operations and employment in the near future.
3. By industrial classification, manufacturing firms are least likely to expand operations and employment in central cities, whereas financial-sector firms are the most likely to expand.
4. Respondents indicated that the overall "quality of life" of a community is often more important to business-location decisions than narrowly defined "business cost" factors.

This review of the literature on the determinants of firm location is concluded with a summary of studies of the efficacy of state-local fiscal incentives to promote economic development. Although these fiscal incentives are common to most states and many localities, the empirical literature is almost uniformly critical of these measures. Some observers believe that the only reason why these incentive systems persist is that jurisdictions fear their business image will decline relative to other states and communities if they discontinue the programs. Thus, although the elimination of these programs would probably be in the public interest, it is unlikely that these programs will be removed because of the strategic position of the participants.

IMPLICATIONS FOR PUBLIC POLICY

Later in this chapter the key assumptions underpinning the National Development Bank proposal—that significant capital shortages exist in distressed areas, that firms will respond in a desirable way to the battery of NDB incentives, and that the net economic response will justify the expenditure—are discussed in light of the empirical literature cited above and several excellent critical studies of the NDB concept. The searching and comprehensive analysis of development financing innovations by Belden

Daniels and Michael Kieschnick (1978) of Harvard's Department of City and Regional Planning was especially helpful in all phases of this report. Their report, done for EDA, is required reading for anyone who wants to become fully informed on this subject. Another very useful and wide-ranging document is the papers and proceedings of a conference on Mobilizing Capital for Economic Development, edited by Peter Bearse.

The literature on the existence and implications of private capital shortages reduces to three points of view: (1) that private capital markets work as well as can be expected and therefore public intervention is neither required nor desired, (2) that significant capital market imperfections do exist, especially in distressed areas, and that public intervention is desirable, and (3) that capital market imperfections do exist but that the social and economic problems of distressed areas are so profound that changes in the cost of finance cannot be expected to have a significant impact. Little evidence in support of the first position is found. Even those investigators who deny private-market imperfections generally acknowledge that the inclusion of social benefits and costs may frequently dictate a different allocation than the private market outcome. Clearly, the second position is that taken by the Administration and most other proponents of an NDB, although there is widespread disagreement about the specific form the intervention should take. The third view is the least orthodox, but in many ways it is the most compelling. Daniels (1978) and Daniels and Kieschnick (1978) argue forcefully that capital costs are almost never a principal reason why firms select a particular location. Capital costs are usually a small fraction of total costs and, as a result, financial incentives can be expected to produce only a negligible effect on firm profits. Moreover, if the NDB directs its activities toward larger, more-established corporations, there is an increased likelihood that the principal outcome will be the substitution of public for private capital. Perhaps the most serious disagreement between the Administration's NDB proposal and the literature reviewed in this chapter centers on the question of which firms the NDB should attempt to assist. The Administration's apparent preference for larger, more-mature employers runs counter to the consensus in the literature that both the greatest need for expansion capital and the greatest potential for significant gains in employment opportunities are to be found among smaller firms.

Another section of the chapter is devoted to a discussion of other means of achieving NDB objectives of employment and income gains in distressed areas. The Economic Development Administration, the Farmers Home Administration, and the Small Business Administration all have development loan programs for borrowers in distressed areas. These programs could be expanded to perform some of the functions contemplated for the NDB. Alternatively, however, one could certainly argue that the reverse—consolidating these various development loan programs in the NDB—would be more efficient. Another option, especially for firms in serious financial trouble and for very large scale projects, is the enactment of special legislation. This approach, especially if combined with expanded development programs in HUD, EDA, FmHA, and SBA, might be an attractive alternative to the NDB provided the legislative process proved to be sufficiently responsive to be effective.

This chapter is concluded with a brief discussion of three alternative proposals of how a development bank might work. Differences between the Administration's NDB and the alternatives encompass several issues: equity financing, venture capital, area and firm targeting, a backstop facility for municipal bonds, and the active role of the NDB as a coordinator and packager of development activities. Equity participation and venture capital funding (especially for high-technology firms) are not included in the Administration's proposal. Both options are shown to present difficulties for an NDB because of the likelihood of higher default rates and questions of how the bank's equity position could be protected without undue involvement in daily firm operations. The issue of targeting the bank's activities is shown to be closely related to the question of how much political and financial risk the bank is willing to assume. Political risk is minimized by spreading the available funding as widely as possible, whereas financial risk is minimized by lending to well-established, mature firms. The literature reviewed in this chapter suggests that the decision to minimize one or both of these risks may substantially reduce the potential effectiveness of the NDB. There are no easy choices here.

ADMINISTRATION NDB PROGRAM

INTRODUCTION

The National Development Bank (NDB) was the centerpiece of President Jimmy Carter's urban program announced in March 1978. In addition to the NDB, the program included renewal of the Comprehensive Employment and Training Act, employment and investment tax credits, incentives for states to aid urban areas, supplementary fiscal assistance, and labor-intensive public works.

The Administration's legislative proposal for the NDB was submitted later in the 95th Congress (June 20, 1978, HR13230 and S3233) and received only two days of hearings before the House Banking, Finance and Urban Affairs Committee.

Additional action was expected in the 96th Congress, particularly because President Carter's 1980 budget, submitted in January 1979, called for a National Development Bank "to provide grants, loan guarantees, interest rate subsidies and other financial assistance to business willing to locate and remain in economically depressed areas."[2] The bank would "stimulate private investment and increase private sector employment in rural areas experiencing lagging growth and persistence of increasing unemployment."[3] It would form the nucleus for the consolidation of new and existing federal economic-development programs run by the Departments of Agriculture, Commerce, and Housing and Urban Development.

The tools of the bank as outlined in the 1980 budget are nearly identical to those proposed in June 1978. They include:

- capital grants to firms of up to 15% of the capital costs of a project, with a $3 million limit on any single project;
- guarantees of private loans for job-producing plant and equipment: up to 75% of the long-term debt with a maximum of $15 million on a specific project;
- interest subsidies for the long-term debt guaranteed by the Bank, which could bring a firm's cost of funds on the guaranteed loan to a rate as low as 2.5%
- a 40% interest subsidy for up to $20 million of taxable development bonds to finance the capital costs of a project as an alternative to the guarantee; and
- a financial intermediary to buy long-term private loans made to businesses in distressed areas to encourage the flow of capital in those areas.[4]

The projected budget authority for the bank for fiscal year 1979 through 1981 is $6.3 billion, and outlays are estimated at $2.5 billion for the same period.

The National Development Bank proposal considered in this and the following sections is the one submitted to Congress in June 1978, in HR13230.

GOALS AND STRATEGIES

The overall goal of the NDB as proposed by the Administration is to halt or slow the chronic long-term economic decline and erosion of private-sector jobs in distressed metropolitan and nonmetropolitan areas and to improve the fiscal base of local governmental units through increased tax revenues. This goal would be achieved by increasing private investment and private opportunities in qualified distressed areas. This would be done through various types of federal credit assistance, which would allocate private capital to eligible firms for the acquisition, construction, or rehabilitation of physical facilities in eligible distressed areas. The strategy of the NDB program is to provide incentives that would be sufficient to influence firms to remain, expand, or locate in designated distressed areas. The bank would concentrate on reducing the cost of capital to eligible firms. It would not become involved in the other factors that influence locational decisions discussed later.

TOOLS

Five basic tools would be used by the bank:

1. grants
2. loan guarantees
3. interest subsidies on guaranteed loans
4. interest subsidies on taxable development bonds
5. a secondary market for qualified loans

Grants could be made for up to 15 percent of a project's capital costs. They could be used for land acquisition, site preparation, rehabilitation, or equipment and machinery, but not for working capital. The maximum grant per applicant would be $3 million.

The loan guarantees could be for up to 75 percent of the cost of a project, with a maximum guarantee of $15 million per project.

An interest-rate subsidy on federally guaranteed loans could be used to bring the interest charged the private borrower down to 2.5 percent, with the federal government paying the difference.

Interest subsidies on taxable development bonds would permit the bank to provide an interest subsidy on taxable industrial development bonds.The subsidy would be 35 percent of interest costs in fiscal years 1979 and 1980 and 40 percent in the following years. This is part of another legislative proposal that would raise the ceiling on tax-exempt industrial revenue bonds from $5 to $20 million in eligible areas. This proposal would give those using industrial revenue bonds the option of either going the tax-exempt or the interest-subsidy route.

The secondary market facility would permit the bank to purchase and then resell to the Federal Financing Bank, an arm of the Treasury, two types of private loans. The first would be the unguaranteed portion of project financing advanced to firms using the NDB loan guarantee. The second would be private loans made to small and medium-sized firms in designated areas. In order to participate in the secondary market facility, the private lending institution must pledge collateral to secure the loan purchased by the NDB.

ORGANIZATION

The Board of Directors of the NDB would be composed of the Secretaries of Commerce, Housing and Urban Development, and Treasury. The bank would be located in Washington. The legislation gives local development authorities an important role in deciding the projects funded by the bank. All projects, except the activities of the secondary market, would have to be submitted and approved by the local development authority. Local development authorities would set priorities and would monitor projects after they were approved.

ELIGIBLE AREAS

In order to receive assistance firms would have to expand or locate in designated distressed areas. In order to be eligible, an area's per capita income at the time could not be 125 percent or more of the national average. In addition, it would have to meet three of the four following criteria covering the last five years:

1. an unemployment rate above the national average.
2. population growth below the national average.
3. a growth rate in total employment below the national average.
4. an increase in absolute dollars in per capita income less than the national average.

Areas with 10,000 or more persons would apply directly to the bank. Areas with fewer than 10,000 would have to combine with other eligible areas to receive assistance. Cities of 50,000 or more that were not eligible could obtain assistance if they had pockets of poverty. Under these eligibility criteria, the Administration considered dividing local jurisdictions into two groups, those within and those outside standard metropolitan statistical areas. Different national averages would be used for each group.

ELIGIBLE FIRMS

Eligible firms would include manufacturing and nonmanufacturing establishments that serve metropolitan, regional, or national markets. Approval would be based on the employment and income impact of the firms as well as their financial soundness. In order to determine the soundness, a private market test would be used. The test would use a standard financial analysis approach to determine if a project could provide the jobs and income projected at a level of risk similar to that associated with unsubsidized private-sector financing for comparable projects. The kinds of projects envisioned, according to Treasury Department testimony, are assistance to a manufacturer in a midwestern city to renovate a plant employing 6,000 persons, funds for an industrial park in a New England city that would employ 1,200, the renovation of a produce market in a western city that would employ 1,100 new persons, and help to a city acquiring a 52-acre vacant riverside plant that would be leased or sold to firms using it as an offshore drilling base.[5]

ECONOMIC ASSUMPTIONS

A basic assumption associated with the NDB proposal is that firms need assistance because capital market imperfections exist that are deleterious to distressed areas as defined in the legislation. These imperfections, it is believed, make it difficult for large firms or large projects employing several hundred persons to obtain credit. The Administration argues that, through the use of NDB financing tools, the cost of funds used and the amount needed to invest in such large projects in distressed areas can be substantially lowered.[6] The NDB programs, it is asserted, will not only reduce the amount of capital needed through the grant program but will also help overcome higher costs of operation because the NDB subsidies will partially offset other higher costs associated with distressed areas.[7]

Capital financing subsidies, it is argued, have been the traditional and appropriate means of government assistance to private business in distressed areas. The bank would not attempt to deal with many of the other factors that influence the costs or locational decisions of firms or to provide assistance to small businesses or venture capital for high-risk new-technology firms.

CAPITAL SHORTAGES AND DISTRESSED AREAS

INTRODUCTION

The current national debate on stimulating economic development in distressed areas, especially in urban centers, has focused attention on private capital (finance) flows in these regions. Most commentators assert that serious capital shortages exist in these areas and that these shortages play a crucial role in the now-familiar downward spiral of businesses unable or unwilling to expand in distressed areas. This leads in turn to reductions in employment opportunities, higher unemployment levels, reduced incomes, declines in the real-property tax base, and higher property taxes on those remaining in the area. Moreover, it is apparent that all of these forces combine and reinforce each other in a circular and cumulative fashion, thus deepening the economic decline. Private capital flows affect this process at the very beginning—at the level of individual firms making decisions about how much and where to produce.

The purpose of this section is to survey the existing literature on the set of concerns broadly referred to as capital shortages. Many different types of capital market problems have been identified, although careful empirical investigations of these problems are severely limited. Nevertheless, both theoretical and empirical studies are reviewed in an attempt to deduce what, if any, favorable impact a National Development Bank might have on these problems.

CAPITAL SHORTAGES—OVERVIEW

Discussions of capital shortages diverge broadly into two separate issues—first, the macro concern of whether the nation's supply of aggregate savings is adequate to maintain a high rate of gross private domestic investment and, second, the micro concern of how private capital is allocated among competing users. These two questions also tend to have different temporal and spatial contexts—discussions of the first have focused on capital needs over a period of several years (frequently a decade) but without any regard to the location of investment, whereas discussions of the second usually center on the present functioning of financial institutions and often include an evaluation of how financial practices affect specific geographic areas, industries, and size classes of firms.

The macro capital-shortage debate surfaced in the early 1970s when the New York Stock Exchange (1974) released a study that projected a substantial gap between combined investment needs of business, households, and the government from 1974 to 1985 and projected aggregate savings during the same period. The Exchange study concluded that immediate steps should be taken to amend the federal tax code (reduce corporate income taxes, liberalize depreciation allowances and the taxation of capital gains, and eliminate the double taxation of dividends to increase the flow of business and individual savings). An exellent overview of this debate and a summary of the findings of three other major studies (Bosworth, Duessenberry, and Carron 1975, Dennis 1975, and Sinai and Brinner 1975) precipitated by the New York Stock Exchange report is contained in Shaul (1977). No further attention will be given to this macro debate because it lies outside the primary purpose of this review.

The second literature on capital shortages is much more diverse than the first, and it may be helpful initially to attempt an overview of the many elements in this discussion. Recall again that this micro-oriented view of the functioning of private capital markets takes as given the amount of finance available in any time period and addresses the manner in which this fund of finance is allocated to different sectors of the economy.

The literature suggesting that small businesses are denied equal access to private financial markets dates back at least to 1958 when the Federal Reserve System issued its report on Financing Small Business (1958). The opinion that small businesses have special problems in obtaining financing is still popular today. In the 1960s attention was focused on capital shortages encountered by minority entrepreneurs, especially those concentrated in urban ghettoes. At the very least it might be expected that minority entrepreneurs would face the same financing difficulties common to most small businesses, but, as Garvin (1971) indicates, the problem may be much broader:

> The capital gap in the inner city is all pervasive, extending to consumer, home mortgage and business credit. It is aggravated by a high incidence of crime against business and the availability of crime insurance at several multitudes of standard rates, if at all. The cost of doing business is further increased by usurious interest rates and losses on credit customers. (p. 445).

The more recent literature on capital shortages has lengthened the list of specific problems. At a recent round table discussion on Urban Development Banking sponsored by the Brookings Institution (1977), James Rouse, perhaps one of the most successful private developers in central cities, argues that a crucial capital gap at present is related to the need to undertake large "community-scale" redevelopment as against the "urban renewal project scale." Rouse's point is that private financing is simply unavailable—due to the perception of risk—to permit revitalization at a level where it is most likely to be successful. At the same round table discussion Ed Hamilton, a well-known fiscal consultant, identified capital gaps in four areas:

> 1. There is a lack of venture capital or other expansion capital to enterprises between the sizes of $25 to $250 million in annual sales. This problem is especially acute in high-technology, capital-intensive industries in the Northeastern States but is also a general problem. Often the only way for these firms to expand is by outright purchase and "the purchase mechanism tends to exacerbate the trend to the Sunbelt." (p. 27)
> 2. There is a lack of venture capital for service or industrial firms with an after-tax profit of less than 25 percent during the first five years of operation.
> 3. There are great problems of capital access for minorities, especially those in depressed areas.
> 4. There is a capital shortage in rural areas. (pp. 27–28)

In recent hearings before the Subcommittee on Fiscal and Governmental Policy of the Joint Economic Committee (1978), James Howell, economist of The First National Bank of Boston, offered the following observations on the role of capital and business expansion in the city:

> Our research at The First National Bank of Boston suggests there are two distinct capital gaps. The first gap is the nonavailability of long term senior debt financing for small-to-medium sized business firms. These are very successful firms that do not have access to the bond market because of a lack of identity. Since they are small, the insurance companies show very little interest in financing them because of the costs involved in packaging and servicing their loans. Moreover, they are nonbankable because the banks themselves do not like to engage in term lending—10 to 15 year loans. That is the first gap.
>
> The second gap is the role of venture capitalists in new business startups. The ven-

ture capitalist often finds himself in a situation where he is frozen into his venture or new startup because of a loss of the new issue market. The ability of the venture capitalist to continue to recycle his money and to engage in new startups is hampered by his inability to take the new firm public. Thus the inability of the new issue market to take him out of the first round funding is the second capital gap. (p. 155)

In the most thorough review to date of the functioning of private capital markets and their implications for the New England region, Katzman and Daniels (1976) document capital shortages in six separate financial areas. Katzman and Daniels define a capital shortage as:

> a gap . . . which can be remedied by an institutional innovation that perfects the capital market. To the extent that interest rate differentials reflect real transaction costs or risks, then differential returns on capital may not imply that capital shortages (and simultaneously surpluses) exist. To the extent that interest rate differentials result from monopoly power or from governmental regulations that prohibit profitable transactions, such as interest rate ceilings, imperfections and gaps can be said to exist. (pp. 16–17)

Briefly summarized, Katzman and Daniels identify the following specific capital shortages in New England:

1. In small to medium-sized firms—the most efficient incubators of new products—finance for new product development must come largely from venture capital companies. Yet, "unfortunately, the history of venture capital companies, and the nature of their function, suggests that they are not equipped to fill this gap." (page 26)
2. There is a general shortage of equity funds for the start-up of new firms. Traditionally, finance for this purpose has come from three sources: individual investors, investment bankers specializing in new issues, and venture capital firms. All three are severely limited now. Direct investment by private investors has fallen in importance (Baty, 1964). The new issues market has essentially collapsed since 1969, and this in turn has resulted in venture capital firms being locked into old investments. This "lock-in" has turned venture capitalists to firms with better track records than most new enterprises.
3. Some firms, especially small firms in locales where banking competition is limited, have to pay higher than market interest rates for working-capital loans.
4. Finance for medium- and long-term expansion is generally more expensive for small to medium-sized firms because of the high fixed cost of public offering and the requirement that they pay a high-risk premium because they are confined by information costs to small geographic financial markets. Moreover, industrial revenue bonds are not easily used by smaller firms because they lack a nationally recognized credit rating.
5. Low-income municipalities, especially those on the periphery of the New England region, have very limited access to organized municipal-bond markets for needed infrastructure rehabilitation because they are not rated by bond-rating agencies.

THE THEORY OF CAPITAL MARKET IMPERFECTIONS

Discussions of the functioning of private capital markets often begin with a general characterization of just how highly efficient this market is. Some would say that it comes close to the theoretician's ideal of a perfectly competitive market—a homogeneous good (finance) being traded between well-informed "price-taking" market participants. How can the long list of capital shortages presented above be reconciled with this characterization of the generally "perfect" capital market? To put the question differently: is urban distress the correlate of private market perfection? (Bearse, 1979) The purpose of this section is to integrate these apparently conflicting observations into a coherent overview of the functioning of private capital markets.

The most general theoretical perspective on private capital flows and their implications for economic development in urban communities is that provided by Michelson (1978). Michelson begins with the observation that private investment decisions often have two separate sets of benefits and costs—those internal to the firm in question, that is having an impact on the firm's welfare, and those external to the firm. External benefits or costs do not influence the accounting statements of the firm and may have a monetary or nonmonetary form in their impact on those affected. In a competitive framework, firms will have no choice but to make decisions on the basis of net internal benefits to the firm. Thus, even if market activity is very efficient in allocating capital on the basis of internal criteria, clearly there is no guarantee that the same set of decisions would have been made if the criteria of net social (external) benefit had been employed. Michelson combines this argument with two other instances when the assumptions of perfectly competitive markets are not met—participants do not have full information, and productive factors are not organized in the most efficient manner—to arrive at four separate types of private market failure.

1. Capital is not allocated to its highest private (internal) return because of ignorance of available opportunities.
2. Capital is misallocated because of the failure to incorporate social (external) benefits and costs.
3. Investors are unable to make what would have been desirable investments (from both private and social perspectives) because of external constraints.
4. Capital "fails to produce the return it would, without additional cost, through a change in some legal form such as ownership control." (Michelson, 1978)

Michelson suggests that land-acqusition problems in central cities may be a common example of the third type of market failure, and that the fourth problem exists when production processes are not as efficient as they could be because workers lack incentives to become more efficient. As Daniels (1978) points out, Michelson's insights are important because they highlight the importance of distinguishing between two separate problems in capital markets—"misperceptions . . . where investors fail to see an opportunity to make a return on investment and misallocations, where they are failing to incorporate social costs." (page 8) However, it is also true that misallocations may be the result of a host of other constraining factors, such as government regulations that restrict the flow of finance to certain categories of borrowers, severe general credit restrictions due to restrictive monetary policies by the Federal Reserve, and imperfections in markets for other inputs in production. The possibilities for less-than-ideal capital market allocations are indeed broad. The empirical literature on these problems is examined next.

EMPIRICAL EVIDENCE OF CAPITAL MARKET IMPERFECTIONS

The most detailed summary of the available evidence of capital market failures is provided in Daniels and Kieschnick (1978). They suggest that private capital markets may not perform efficiently for several different reasons:

> The allocation of risk may not be optimal with private markets achieving inadequate sharing and diversification of risk. Financial intermediation may take place in markets with oligopolistic or monopolistic elements. Investors may not have enough accurate information. Transaction costs may prevent all but the most advantageous trades. The suppliers of capital may be prejudiced against some ventures, for racial, political, sexual, or locational reasons. Finally, public regulations of capital markets may have unintended side effects which distort market outcomes. (page 44)

The evidence that an inadequate rate of interest obtains when private investors (especially small investors) are forced to bear the full risk associated with individual investment projects follows from the realization that both borrower's and lender's risk can be substantially reduced through pooling. Thus, if the social return of investment exceeds the return available to some private investors, the logic exists for public intervention to increase the flow of investment by changing "the financial risk faced by an investor." (page 47–48) A development bank would be one form public intervention could take.

Capital market exchanges always have some associated transaction and information costs. Daniels and Kieschnick show that these fixed costs of acquiring capital are much larger for small issues (firms) than for large blocks of capital. They cite data from the Securities and Exchange Commission for 1951 to 1955, which shows that fixed costs of acquiring debt finance (bonds, notes, and debentures) as a percentage of the proceeds exceeded 10 percent for issues of less than one million and was below 2 percent for issues greater than five million. Fixed costs as a percentage of proceeds exceeded 20 percent for equity issues of less than one million and fell to approximately 5 percent for common-stock issues exceeding five million. (p. 51) Other empirical investigations that confirm the existence of differentials in the cost of accessing capital markets by size of firm are Archer and Faerber (1966), Levenson (1962), and Sullivan (1978). Sullivan measures the "market power" of a firm by its size or its presence in a concentrated industry. Although he confirms that the cost of capital is clearly inversely related to the market power of a firm, he questions whether this differential should be regarded as a capital market failure.

> Although this study suggests that powerful firms can acquire capital at lower costs than non-powerful firms, it does not necessarily follow that these lower costs are evidence of capital market imperfections. Indeed recent research suggests the capital market is a highly efficient allocator of capital, i.e., it allocates capital based upon risk/return considerations in light of available information. The lower per dollar capital flotation costs to powerful firms seem to represent the high fixed costs (e.g., legal costs) in a public security sale and not unfair discrimination against non-powerful firms. And the lower expected dividend and price appreciation return demanded by suppliers of capital to invest in the securities of powerful firms seem to arise because the securities of powerful firms are less risky, i.e., less susceptible to non-diversifiable periodic revaluation in the secondary capital market. (p. 215)

Here again one encounters the question of whether internal or external (private or social) criteria should apply. Sullivan's point is that, by internal criteria, the market does what it is supposed to do. On the other hand, if one says that, as a matter of public policy, all firms should have access to capital markets at the same price, then clearly the market has failed and some corrective public intervention is called for.

Daniels and Kieschnick note that the market for business finance is not one highly integrated market, but rather it is segmented into "banking markets, commercial paper, public bond, private placement, and new issues equity." (p. 56) When any market is segmented, the likelihood is greater that actual market performance will deviate from that of the competitive ideal. They note that it is also possible for these markets to be geographically segmented, thus increasing the potential for violations of perfect competition. There is a substantial literature of financial market structures, but it is concentrated almost entirely on commercial banking. Daniels and Kieschnick divide their review of the literature into two separate inquiries: (1) interarea variations in interest rates and the degree of banking competition and (2) banking market concentration and the availability of capital. On the first point they note that, although many studies have confirmed the existence of interarea interest-rate differential between communities and regions (Jacobs 1971 and Straszheim 1971), the observed differentials were small and perhaps not as significant to the question of economic development as interarea variations in the availability of capital. Daniels and Kieschnick note that several studies—both urban (Gardner 1973 and Heggestad 1977) and rural (Fraser and Rose 1971, Chandross 1971, and McCall and Peterson 1977)—suggest "that banks in concentrated markets trade off potentially higher profits for reduced risk exposure." (p. 58) Although the studies cited do not address the economic development implications of this tendency toward a lower risk loan portfolio, Daniels and Kieschnick concluded:

> We expect the problem of bank concentration to be more important for small corporations in rural areas than in metropolitan areas, because there are a large number of isolated banking markets in rural areas and fewer alternative sources of finance." (pp. 61–62)

At the request of the Experimental Technology Incentives Program of the National Bureau of Standards, Charles River Associates (CRA 1976) undertook the most comprehensive investigation to date of market imperfections in the flow of funds from venture capitalists. On the question of whether significant market imperfections exist the report is unequivocal:

> We found no evidence of substantial market imperfections that restrict the flow of funds to small technology based firms. We found no evidence that small technology based firms paid higher rates of interest or returned their unaffiliated stockholders more than other small firms. We found no indication that suppliers of funds to small technology based firms earned higher profits than could be earned in listed securities. We found no elements of the structure of behavior in the venture capital industry which would enable firms in the business to charge higher rates or earn greater profits than necessary to compensate for the risks assumed. (pp. S-1, 2)

Nevertheless, CRA noted that their findings did not necessarily imply that the rate of private investment in new-technology firms is ideal from a social perspective. They note that if these firms generate significant positive external benefits (a point they do not address empirically), even a perfectly functioning capital market will not allocate enough capital to these undertakings. Moreover, CRA did find that "securities and tax regulations influence the rate of return required by suppliers of funds to small technology based firms" but also concluded "that attempts to increase the flow of funds by direct government investment in small technology based firms may tend to displace private funds rather than increase the total flow of funds."

In contrast to the strong conclusions in the CRA study, Daniels and Kieschnick point out that there may be much that we do not know about venture capital markets because of limitations in the CRA analysis. Specifically, Daniels and Kieschnick raise the following criticisms:

> 1. The sample of firms analyzed by CRA is not representative of the universe of small technology-based enterprises because they included only those firms involved in public offerings of securities, Daniels and Kieschnick note that this is equivalent to studying a problem by examining circumstances where the problem does not exist.
> 2. No analysis was made of the cost of capital obtained, nor was there any direct analysis of the rate of return to small corporations.
> 3. The period used by CRA for their analysis of sources of funds (1960–71) may have been significantly different from the most recent period.

In addition to these points, Daniels and Kieschnick point out that the CRA analysis "allows no conclusion on the geographical structure of the venture capital market." (p. 65) Daniels and Kieschnick are forced to conclude:

> Clearly we do not know enough about the structure of long-term capital markets for new and small corporations. We lack sufficient information about both long-term debt and equity. This area must be a high priority for further research. (p.66)

Although popular discussions of capital shortages, especially in urban areas, often focus on the problems minority borrowers encounter in capital markets, nevertheless, there is little detailed evidence on the magnitude of this presumed capital gap. Garvin (1971) in a *Journal of Finance* symposium on minority financial problems noted that, in 1968, minority-owned enterprises represented only 3.7 percent of all U.S. businesses, whereas minorities constituted 15 percent of the population—a gap of about 600,000 businesses. Moreover,

> There is a qualitative gap as well. Minority-owned businesses, on average, are half as large as other businesses in employment, sales and assets. We estimate that it would require in excess of $40 billion to raise the number of minority-owned businesses to the level representative of their share of the U.S. population and to change their industry distribution, location and size to conform with like characteristics of the total business community. (p. 448)

Garvin also notes the seriousness of what might be called the "discouraged entrepreneur" problem, that is, many minority persons may never attempt to start businesses because experience has taught them that finance will not be available. In a 1971 survey of black households in 33 cities, Garvin noted that only 5 percent of those surveyed were in business. Of the remainder, 37 percent had not considered going into business for themselves, whereas 58 percent had considered starting their own business. Of those having considered entering business, 72 percent cited lack of finance as the primary reason why they had not done so. This finding prevailed even among the high-income and better-educated portions of the sample.

In another more recent analysis of capital problems in minority business development, Knight and Dorsey (1976) examine the contribution of three separate institutions—banks, the Minority Enterprise Small Business Investment Company (MESBIC) program, and the Small Business Administration (SBA)—to the minority capital gap. Knight and Dorsey base their analysis on the premise that the objective of minority business development is the achievement of financial parity between the majority and minority populations. They estimate that achieving financial parity would require an annual capital investment of $7.3 billion—$2.04 billion in equity and $5.24 billion in debt—over a twenty-year period. Knight and Dorsey conclude that the total contribution of the three institutions they examine "appear to provide less than 10 percent of the yearly amount required to reach asset parity."

In an attempt to assess the net effect of the numerous capital market imperfections noted above, Daniels and Kieschnick examine sources of funds and profitability of manufacturing firms by asset size for two separate periods, 1958–71 and 1972–76. They note that the smallest size class (less than one million) firms do quite well in both time periods and even outperform all other classes in the 1972–76 period. They also analyze risk by comparing the variation in rates of return by asset class. In the 1958–71 time interval, the expected inverse relationship between size and risk prevailed, but during the 1972–76 period there was no significant relationship between asset size class and risk.

In their analysis of firm's sources of funds during the same two subperiods, Daniels and Kieschnick note the particular difficulties faced by the smallest corporations in the 1972–76 period.

> For the period 1972–76, the smallest corporations, on average, suffered an annual decrease in capital stock equal to nearly 7 percent of their annual change in total finance. This in contrast to the period 1958–71, when capital stock increases accounted for over 5 percent of annual financing requirements. The smallest corporation's dependence on internal funds increased from about 30 percent of annual financing to nearly 50 percent. Their use of long-term bank loans increased from 11 percent to 22 percent of annual financing, as their use of other long-term liabilities, principally bonds and leasing agreements, decreased from 17 percent to about 2 percent. . . . These comparisons dramatically show the difficulty small

> corporations faced in accessing long-term capital markets. This stands in sharp contrast to the annual rate of return on equity of 16.2 percent earned by the smallest size-class. Clearly these corporations were facing capital market barriers unjustified by their rate of return on equity. (p. 87–90)

Although the difference in circumstances between the smallest and largest manufacturing firms is clear-cut, Daniels and Kieschnick note that the position of intermediate-sized firms is more ambiguous. Their data suggest that these firms do not tend to be as profitable as smaller and larger firms. Nevertheless, the data suggest that they have had some difficulty "accessing equity and long-term capital markets, especially during the 1972–76 period."

In concluding their analysis of access to capital markets by firm size, Daniels and Kieschnick note:

> Thus our results indicate a justification for public intervention into private capital markets. For small corporations, capital is not being allocated on the basis of rate of return. The results indicate that long-term capital markets appear to be the logical point of intervention. What is not indicated by these results is the best form of intervention. Any intervention should take into account the fact that the severity of the misallocation appears to be a recent phenomenon, with access by small corporations to long-term capital markets dramatically decreasing in comparison to previous years, as well as in comparison to larger corporations.
>
> These results are valid when examining all manufacturing corporations by asset sizes. They may not be true for manufacturing corporations in particular geographic areas or industries. The average figures may obscure significant geographical differences in the performance, financial structure, and sources of funds. (pp. 92–93)

Research on the existence, nature, and size of capital gaps by region has been hampered by a lack of regional flow-of-funds data. One recent study by Shaul of the Academy for Contemporary Problems (1978) examined, again by less direct means, the availability of investment capital for the Great Lakes states. Shaul concluded that although capital availability had not been a special problem for the Great Lakes region, nevertheless concern was expressed about the region's "low rate of birth of new firms relative to growing parts of the country." (p. ii). Schaul suggests that this low birthrate of new firms is particularly vexing because of the large employment gains often associated with innovative, young companies. Schaul also notes that SBA activity has been low in the region relative to the nation and that an increased commitment by SBA "would probably strengthen small firms in the area." In addition to noting that SBA activity has been low in the region,

Schaul makes an interesting observation concerning investment in the region.

> To some extent the problem in the region appears to be lack of demand for investment funds by potential growth firms. In general, the birth of new firms is low relative to growing areas of the country. Greater encouragement and technical assistance could be helpful, and there are a number of ways to do this—organizing something similar to the Connecticut Product Development Corporation, expanding SBA activity, increasing the SBA-University cooperation program, or a development bank. (p. 44)

CAPITAL SHORTAGES—CONCLUSION

The National Development Bank proposal is based, in large part, on the premise that significant capital shortages exist in distressed areas. The several analyses of capital shortages surveyed here highlight a variety of financial problem areas to which an NDB could respond.

For example, small and medium-sized firms report difficulties in their search for long-term financing—in the form of either borrowing or equity—to use for either operating or capital expenses. The NDB proposal might be more responsive to these problems if it emphasized lengthening the term for which funding was available rather than concentrating on interest-rate subsidies. It could make a provision to lend for operating as well as land, plant, and equipment expenses. It could also concentrate its funding efforts on small and medium-sized rather than large firms.

Still, in declining regions, central cities, and minority neighborhoods, the low level of capital investment observed may reflect as much a lack of demand by entrepreneurs as a shortage of capital. The role of other factors in influencing firms' location decisions is reviewed below.

DISTRESSED AREAS—OVERVIEW

Although the President's Urban Policy Report calls specifically for the need to "provide for strong incentives to attract private investment to distressed communities," how these distressed areas are to be identified is not discussed in any detail. The President's Urban and Regional Policy Group (1977) did point out that urban distress is not limited to our nations' central cities: "Small cities as well as large are in distress. Urban distress can be found in every major area of the nation." (pp. 1–5).

As might be imagined, the literature on measuring relative economic hardship approaches this question at several different levels of geographic aggregation. The most careful analysis of the definition of a distressed region is found in Kraft, et al (1971). They point out that economic distress is usually thought of in terms of differential levels of unemployment and income and that it might be thought that both of these problems would tend to coexist in distressed areas. Unfortunately, as their research demonstrates, this is often not the case. Unemployment is often a cyclical phenomenon related to national swings in business activity, whereas community income levels are much more directly related to the underlying vitality of the regional economy.

Interesting work on measuring economic hardship among cities has been done recently by Nathan and Dommel (1977). They point out that even the term *city* is ambiguous. Should it mean only those cities with populations over 500,000, or should it mean the central cities surrounded by Standard Metropolitan Statistical Areas (SMSAs), or should it include all "urban places" as designated by the Bureau of the Census? There is no simple answer to this question. Nathan and Dommel select a point in the middle and include 397 cities with populations exceeding 50,000 in their analysis. They use three indicators—population decline, age of the housing stock, and the fraction of the population in poverty—to construct an "urban conditions index." They show that although the incidence of hardship is greatest among the very largest cities it clearly is not confined only to them. They conclude:

> Several lessons can be drawn from this analysis. It is important to recognize that the United States does not have what can be called a "national urban crisis." Many large cities are well off. Moreover, most city dwellers live in suburbs or relatively small cities. What we face, in short, is a situation in which some—though by no means all—central cities and a few large suburban cities are experiencing what can be called "urban crisis conditions." (p. 288)

In an earlier article, Nathan and Adams (1976) address the question of intrametropolitan differentials in economic hardship. In addition to the usual interarea comparisons the second perspective is essential because:

> Geographically dispersed central cities compete with one another only in a rather remote and long-term sense. In the short haul, each of them is much more intensively affected by whatever differences may exist in the severity of social and economic problems within its own boundaries in relation to its adjacent suburbs. In this context, what are needed are comparative data on the social and economic hardship of the central city in relation to its surrounding surburban areas. Where the city-to-suburb hardship ratio is high and no structural measures have been adopted to spread this burden, flight to the suburbs can be expected to accelerate and urban crisis conditions will deepen. (pp. 48–49)

Nathan and Adams combined six socioeconomic indicators—unemployment, age distribution of the population, education, income level, crowded housing, and poverty—into a composite index of urban hardship. Here again they noted that the greatest relative economic hardship is found among Northeastern cities, although there are some significant differences in the rankings obtained when the nature of the relative comparison was changed. The ten cities having the highest hardship ratings are shown below.

Index of Central-City Hardship Relative to the Balance of the SMSA	**Interarea Comparisons of Central-City Hardship**
Newark	Newark
Cleveland	St. Louis
Hartford	New Orleans
Baltimore	Gary
Chicago	Miami
St. Louis	Birmingham
Atlanta	Youngstown
Rochester	Baltimore
Gary	Cleveland
Dayton	Detroit

The differences between these two rankings suggest the ultimate importance of specific eligibility criteria included in any legislation directed at distressed urban centers.

Perhaps the most thorough discussion of measuring urban need is contained in a 1978 paper written by Peggy L. Cuciti of the Congressional Budget Office for the Subcommittee on the City, of the House Committee on Banking, Finance and Urban Affairs. Cuciti points out that "there is no single 'objective' standard of need," and she presents city rankings on three separate measures—social need, economic need, and fiscal need. After detailed discussions of the problems in measuring each of these dimensions, some interesting results of composite measures of social, economic, and fiscal needs are presented for 45 large cities. These composite calculations yield the surprising conclusion that only two cities—Newark and St. Louis—rank among the top ten in all three measures although a total of 17 different cities are included in the top ten of at least one of the three measures. Cuciti notes:

> It is more common for cities to rank high on two dimensions simultaneously. New York, Jersey City, Boston, and Philadelphia have both serious economic and fiscal problems. Cleveland and Buffalo combine relatively severe economic and

> social problems while social and fiscal beset Detroit, Baltimore, and Birmingham. (p. 52)

Six cities ranked among the top ten in only one dimension—Chicago and Pittsburgh, economic need; Gary, Miami, and New Orleans, social need; and Washington, D.C., fiscal need. Although these results are interesting and suggestive, it is troublesome to note that Cleveland is ranked only sixteenth in fiscal need. It is hard to escape the conclusion that ranking urban areas by "need" is an imprecise activity given the present state of the art.

Finally, at the most disaggregated level, there are significant variations in the degree of economic hardship within every major city. Thus, if it is desirable to target public programs to specific neighborhoods, a methodology for selecting those areas will be required. Cannon, Lachman, and Bernhard (1977) have suggested an index of "relative residential status" as a means for identifying neighborhoods that are prime targets for revitalization efforts. This index is distilled through factor analysis from a long list of socioeconomic variables. Meadows and Call (1978) suggest that neighborhoods be compared by gauging the relative performance of the private real-estate market.

Clearly, additional work remains to be done on the identification of distressed areas. The several studies reviewed here suggest that each definition is likely to generate a different list of places considered to be distressed areas. The problem of identification is likely to remain a difficult one, especially if there is a need to be highly discriminating in targeting National Development Bank funds.

EMPIRICAL EVIDENCE ON INDUSTRIAL LOCATION DECISIONS

INTRODUCTION

In this section a selective review of the literature on the determinants of firm-location decisions is presented. But before turning to the direct consideration of these locational studies, Daniels and Kieschnick's (1978) excellent review of another literature—recent trends in regional population and employment change—is presented. It will be shown that conclusions on population and employment shifts can be helpful in guiding our examination of the literature on firm mobility.

In the post–World War II period the United States has experienced significant changes in the urban/rural distribution of its population. Exhibit 8 (from Daniels and Kieschnick 1978) shows that the urban shares (SMSAs) of the total U.S. population rose from 1950 to 1970 but began to decline in the 1970s. Population in central cities rose from 1950 to 1970, although at a much slower rate than the surrounding ring of suburbs, but declined be-

EXHIBIT 8

POPULATION OF THE UNITED STATES BY PLACE OF RESIDENCE, 1950 TO 1976

	Population [in millions]				Percentage distribution			
Area	1950	1960	1970	1976	1950	1960	1970	1976
Standard Metropolitan Statistical Areas[1]	94.6	119.6	139.5	142.6	62.5	66.7	68.5	67.8
Central Cities	53.7	59.9	64.3	60.7	35.5	33.4	31.6	28.9
Outside Central Cities	40.9	59.6	75.2	81.8	27.0	33.2	37.0	38.9
Non-metropolitan Areas	56.7	59.7	63.8	67.8	37.5	33.3	31.5	32.2
Total	151.3	179.3	203.2	210.3	100.0	100.0	100.0	100.0

[1] Covers 243 SMSAs as defined in 1970 census publications.

Source: U.S. Department of Commerce, Bureau of the Census. *Statistical Abstract of the United States 1977*, Table 15, p. 16. From Daniels and Kieschnick, 1978, p. 6.

tween 1970 and 1976. As a fraction of total population, central-city residents have declined steadily since 1950. Moreover, Daniels and Kieschnick, in their summary of Birch's (1977) analysis of net migration flows, point out that large metropolitan areas (SMSA population greater than one million) lost population between 1970 and 1974, while small metropolitan areas and nonmetropolitan areas were net gainers. Daniels and Kieschnick conclude:

> If market growth or labor supply are important determinants of employment growth, these population figures present a picture of major redistribution of employment opportunities. (p. 8)

In their review of recent studies of employment shifts, Daniels and Kieschnick note that "employment has shifted from industrial regions to less industrial regions, from metropolitan to rural areas, and from central cities to suburbs." In short, employment shifts have been closely related to population shifts. The South Atlantic, East South Central, and Pacific census regions increased their share of employment relative to population, whereas the East North Central and Middle Atlantic regions lost employment relative to population. The extensive analysis of the components of recent employment changes by Allaman and Birch (1975) and Birch (1977, 1978) are reviewed by Daniels and Kieschnick. The series of earlier papers by Allaman and Birch are important because they demonstrate the relative unimportance of interregional migration in accounting for regional migration. Allaman and Birch classified net employment by firm status—births, deaths, expansions, contractions, immigrations, and out-migrations. When classified in this manner it becomes apparent

> that the actual migration of establishments from one state to another accounts for a very small fraction of employment change. The death, expansion, and contraction of existing establishments and the birth of new establishments is overwhelmingly more important than migration. The Birch data reveals little variation from state to state in the rate at which jobs are lost through the sum of the contraction and death of existing establishments. The main cause of differential employment growth rates is the difference in the birth and expansion of establishments. (Daniels and Kieschnick 1978, pp. 13–15)

The more recent work by Birch (1977, 1978) further highlights the role of the independent entrepreneur in the creation of new jobs, both in the birth of new firms and the expansion of existing firms. Daniels and Kieschnick, summarizing Birch's findings note that:

> when combined, births and expansions of independent firms create almost 75 percent of job gains. These figures hold across regions with only small variation, the most notable deviation being the relatively greater importance of branch plant expansions of out-of-state firms in the South. (p. 16)

When Birch (1978) also incorporated age of firm into the analysis, it was found that approximately 50 percent of all new jobs were created by young firms less than five years old. Old firms, both large and small, were responsible for very small fractions of all new jobs. These results did not vary significantly by region.

EMPIRICAL STUDIES OF INTRAMETROPOLITAN MANUFACTURING LOCATION PATTERNS

Of all industrial movement, that which occurs within single regions—usually within a single metropolitan area—has received the most careful analysis. This concentration is certainly appropriate because it is well known that the overwhelming majority of all industrial moves are over short distance (Schmenner 1977). These studies are also primarily focused on moves of manufacturing firms or subregional changes in manufacturing employment. Again this narrow focus is apparently justified because manufacturing employment has long been regarded as deserving special attention because it is thought to determine levels of employment in supporting industries, such as finance, wholesaling and distributing, and business services.

The most thorough of the recent empirical analysis of the intrametropolitan location decision is that of Struyk and James (1975). They point out that previous studies of intrametropolitan employment changes have been limited to single regions, and thus it has been extremely difficult to generalize the results. The purpose of their study was to apply the same methodology and data in several different urban areas in an attempt to discover common features in the spatial distribution of employment changes.

Struyk and James utilized Dun and Bradstreet Corporation information on all manufacturing establishments in the Cleveland, Minneapolis–St. Paul, Boston, and Phoenix metropolitan areas in 1965 and 1968.[8] The principal findings are summarized as follows:

> 1. A high rate of manufacturing employment mobility was found in all four metropolitan areas. Employment changes from new, moving, and failing establishments equaled 17 percent of total employment in 1965. Mobility rates were higher among smaller firms.
> 2. The general pattern of job movement was that of decentralization and for central cities to lose manufacturing employment, although some specific areas within the city gained employment.
> 3. The composition of net employment changes varied sharply between the SMSAs included, although there were some regularities:
>   a. The largest single component of net employment change was that of stationary firms, although again the direction varied and was not always the same as the total net change for the whole area.
>   b. The net impact of firm births versus deaths favored zones outside the central city and was responsible for a greater proportion of the total net increase in jobs outside the central city than was net migration. There was no evidence that central-city firms have a greater propensity to die than their suburban counterparts.
> 4. The hypothesis that central cities provide an "incubation" function in spawning new firms was not supported. Apparently some suburban sites provide an adequate level of external economies to facilitate new-firm birth.
> 5. Zones within three of the four SMSAs included had been classified by the Bureau of Census as poverty areas. All of these zones except one lost manufacturing employment during the study period. There was, however, an identifiable concentration of industries within these areas and some were growing. Growing industries within these areas tended to be those paying below-average wages and "nuisance" industries, such as chemicals, petroleum, and primary metals. No analysis was made to determine whether area residents were being employed by these firms.
> 6. Strong indirect evidence was found in support of the presence of external economies by the high concentrations of major industries within analysis zones across all included SMSAs.
> 7. When industries were divided on the basis of geographic concentration, the results indicated that concentrated industries grew more slowly and changed locations less frequently.

In a subsequent article Struyk (1976) summarizes the results of three other zonal studies of net employment change (Leone 1971, Schmenner

1972, Kemper 1973). All of these studies utilized the Dun and Bradstreet data base at the establishment level. Generally, Struyk is able to show that the empirical results of these three other studies are fully consistent with those reported in the Struyk-James (1975) effort. A fourth study by Williamson (1969) is also summarized by Struyk (1976). Williamson studied origins and destinations of manufacturing firms relocating in the Chicago area over a nine-year period. Zonal detail was especially rich because he utilized 576 separate transportation zones. In Williamson's statistical analysis, employment growth was found to be positively and significantly related to (1) the fraction of land in the zone devoted to manufacturing activity, (2) access to freeways, and (3) the availability of blue-collar workers; whereas employment declines were associated with high population densities and nearness to black residential areas.

Although the results of the previously described zonal studies of net employment change provide an invaluable description of patterns of intraurban industrial location, they lack an explicit theoretical foundation, and thus empirical models attempting to "explain" the observed locational patterns have been designed on an ad hoc basis. The usual approach has been to attempt to explain differences in the density of located industry across the included zones in terms of specific characteristics of each zone—for example, access to transportation, land availability and cost, local tax rates, and so on.

Although this ad hoc empirical strategy is quite respectable and, at least in some cases, yields results that have intuitive appeal—recall Williamson's results reported above—one important researcher in this area suggests that reliable empirical investigations of firm behavior can only be carried out using data disaggregated to the individual firm. Schmenner (1977) makes this claim in a recent provocative article where he proposes that an "evolutionary" theory of the firm be used to explore urban industrial location-decision behavior. In this article Schmenner outlines his theory and presents simulation results illustrating how firms will respond when confronted with a set of circumstances where their present location ceases to be profitable. The simulation exercise generates a pattern of firm moves that Schmenner argues are remarkably similar to the real-world observations of three previously cited studies (Leone 1971, Schmenner 1972, Struyk and James 1975). Schmenner concludes that studies aggregating data to the zone level are seriously flawed because the results are clearly dependent on the degree and manner (weighting) of aggregation. It should be pointed out that Schmenner's own earlier work (1972) is included in his criticism of empirical analysis of zonal data.

Because Schmenner's "evolutionary" model of firm location underpins his most recent work, which is discussed at length in the next section, it may be helpful to provide a description of this approach. According to the neoclassical theory of the firm, all management decisions are geared to the maximization of profits. Moreover, it is assumed that management is eager to exploit any opportunity to expand its profits. Of course, this willingness to alter firm operations to increase profits includes altering the firm's location if necessary. In the evolutionary theory of the firm, rigid pursuit of maximum profits is not assumed. Rather, decision rules dictate its response to a change in circumstances. To be more specific, Schmenner's evolutionary location model utilizes the following decision rules:

1. firms attempt to achieve an acceptable level of profits,
2. firms become mover candidates only when profits fall below the acceptable level,
3. the search for a new site is myopic in that they begin the search near the present location and expand the search only when an acceptable alternate site cannot be found.

Schmenner's principal argument in favor of an evolutionary theory of firm location is that the assumptions appear to coincide closely with what we know of firm behavior in selecting new locations.

> 1. A firm generally changes location only infrequently and can usefully be viewed as following an implicit decision rule of staying put unless there are radical disturbances to its selection environment.
> 2. The bulk of industrial relocations are made over short distances. (See Leone 1971, Schmenner 1973, and Struyk and James 1975.) Such local search may result from such factors as a firm's desire to keep its labor force intact and/or the only limited information a firm can gather about more distant locations. Firms clearly do not act as if they scan the urban horizon for least-cost or more-profitable sites; firms settle in acceptable sites.
> 3. The need for additional space has clearly prompted many growing firms to seek new locations and represents a clear disturbance to the firm's selection environment. (See Leone 1971, Schmenner 1973, Struck and James 1975.)
> 4. Even casual observation points up the tendency and desire of firms to deal with the same group of suppliers or customers over long stretches of time. Such behavior suggests that firms follow an explicit decision rule of trying to maintain existing distribution channels even at the expense of somewhat increased transportation costs. (Schmenner 1977, p. 180)

In a more recent study of manufacturing location decisions in Cincinnati and New England, Schmenner (1978) adopts an even broader theoretical perspective on locational decisions and suggests that plant location decision is part of a larger set of decisions concerning production capacity. Thus when a firm's "capacity planning proceeds past modest alterations to production control, subcontracting or existing process technology to consider additions to plant space, the company confronts on-site expansion, new branch establishment, and plant relocations.'' (Schmenner 1978, pp. 5–1) Here again Schmenner suggests a sequential decision-making process as follows:

1. The firm must first decide whether to pursue a multiplant strategy.
2. If a multiplant strategy is adopted, the contribution of specific plants to overall firm capacity must be evaluated.
3. Finally, the firm must decide on the specific characteristics of sites for branch plant expansions or relocations.

Schmenner's survey results suggest that the choice a firm makes among the alternatives to securing additional space—on-site expansion, branching, or relocation—will depend largely on the nature of the problems faced by the firm. For example, new branch plants are probably better able to deal with base plant problems of product proliferation, work-force size, and inadequate growth capacity, whereas base plant relocation is likely to be more responsive to problems of plant layout, materials handling, new process technology, production and inventory control, and lack of management depth.

Although it is true that Schmenner makes no attempt at direct evaluation of firm's responses to public policy initiatives directed at economic development, nevertheless his analysis of manufacturing activity in Cincinnati has important implications for public policy directed at retaining manufacturing employment in central cities. Schmenner's conclusions follow:

1. Public efforts at retaining the manufacturing employment base in the central cities should not be focused on the city's largest employers. For the most part these firms are likely to be multiplant concerns and good management practice is likely to dictate that they neither close their base plant nor open new branches within the city.
2. To be effective, public policy should focus on the small mover plants and those plants in marginal circumstances, that is, those about to go out of business or just beginning. Two-thirds of the net employment change in Cincinnati from 1971-75 was the result of plant "deaths" (branch plant closings, business failures, and relocations outside the metropolitan area) exceeding plant "births" (branch plant openings, new incorporations, and moves from outside the metropolitan area), and only 28.5 percent of net employment change resulted from moves from the central city to the suburb.
    a. Business failures and branch closings usually have little to do with existing public policies and are more often related to inadequate product demand or financing problems.
    b. Cities may be able to stimulate new company start-ups or increase the chances of survival for new firms by acting as an information clearing-house for local business services, space, and finance needs.

c. Cities may also be able to significantly increase their chances of retaining small mover firms if they become more aggressive in providing assistance in securing additional space. This follows because the overwhelming reason why firms move is to secure additional space and most move small distances. Firms moving longer distances tend to be larger firms with more complex needs. In some cases careful use of the power of eminent domain to permit on-site expansion may be sound public policy.

d. To be effective in retaining employment, cities must be able to react quickly to help meet the additional space needs of resident plants. Schmenner found that once a firm's need for additional space is triggered, it will move quickly to secure the additional space. The median time spent searching for a relocation site in the Cincinnati and New England firms surveyed was only six months. The establishment of a city ombudsman to help guide local businesses through local bureaucracy in an expeditious fashion may also increase the likelihood of a firm's remaining in the city even if it relocates.

3. State and local tax and financial incentive packages are not likely to have a significant influence on the firm-location decision. Schmenner found that only a quarter to a third of firms surveyed in the Cincinnati metropolitan area and in the New England region actually moved to districts with lower property-tax rates, and about a quarter of the moves were to jurisdictions with higher tax rates. Likewise, the survey results in both areas indicated that very small percentages of mover firms actually utilized financial inducements, such as industrial revenue bonds. In part, many financial incentive programs may suffer from inadequate marketing by public officials and therefore are largely unknown or poorly understood by potential clients.

4. The fact that the overwhelming fraction of all moves (perhaps 80 to 90 percent) are local and the general ineffectiveness of policies designed to lure out-of-area companies leads inevitably to the conclusion that localities should focus their economic development activities in "tending their own garden." This means that public efforts should be concentrated on:

a. assisting on-site expansion of resident firms,

b. helping small growing firms find additional space within the city limits, and

c. promoting the city's advantages as an initial location for new firms and new branch plants.

SURVEYS OF CENTRAL-CITY BUSINESS CONDITIONS

Several other parties interested in revitalizing the nation's central cities have attempted to learn more about the flight of business from the central city by direct survey of business. The results of these surveys are summarized next.

The First National Bank of Boston (Howell 1978) has recently completed a study of 226 manufacturing firms in six New England states, in which a series of questions were addressed to attempt "to identify the factors that are pushing business out of the city and to determine what it would take to bring business back into the city." Specific findings of the study are as follows:

1. Forty-seven percent of all firms and 61 percent of large firms surveyed indicated their principal reason for being in the central city is that they have always been there.

2. Forty-five percent of all firms were satisfied with their current central-city sites. Another 18 percent expressed dissatisfaction but indicated that they would probably stay in the city. Thirty-seven percent indicated that they would ultimately move to the suburbs.

3. Among firms contemplating relocation outside the central city, high property taxes were cited as the most important factor, followed closely by nonavailability of skilled labor and central-city crime.

4. Negative attitudes toward the nearest central city as a business location outweighed positive attitudes by four to one among non–central-city firms.

5. When non–central-city firms were asked to rank factors that would be influential in encouraging relocation in the central city, significant reduction in property taxes, adoption of a pro-business attitude by city officials, and significant reductions in crime were ranked one, two, and three. A significant improvement in availability of skilled labor was ranked as least important. Investment tax credits, accelerated depreciation, and new investment in public infrastructure also ranked relatively low.

In another recent survey directed at the problem of unemployment in central cities, the Subcommittee on the City of the House Committee on Banking, Finance and Urban Affairs (1978) addressed the following four questions to the 800 largest industrial and nonindustrial firms in the country:

1. Which of your corporation's operations are at present located in central cities, and how many persons do they employ out of your total work force?

2. What plans do you have to expand or contract these operations in the next five years? What major factors have influenced these plans?

3. What recruitment of job-training activities does your corporation sponsor that are specifically aimed at the unemployed in central cities?

4. Which existing Federal, State, or local policies, if any, discourage you from maintaining or locating operations in central cities? What new government policies would encourage you to maintain or locate operations in these areas?

Only 44 percent responded to the survey, and apparently no detailed analysis was made of the replies by the committee staff. The generality of the questions and the resultant variance in responses doubtlessly made careful analysis impossible. Nevertheless, the Committee staff did attempt to characterize the responses to two questions. First, firms with intentions of remaining in or expanding their central-city sites often mentioned the following reasons:

1. a desire to retain their present labor force,
2. the availability of a large labor pool,
3. easy access to other business services and necessary contacts,

4. the fact that it was not economic to scrap existing production facilities for new plant, and
5. an obligation to address the problems of the communities that fostered their original growth.

Second, the following factors were frequently mentioned as having a negative impact on decisions to remain or expand at central-city locations:

1. the high cost, limited availability, and difficulty in assemblage of urban land,
2. the low quality of public services, especially public education and public safety, which in turn increase production costs,
3. onerous and uncoordinated government regulation, especially environmental regulations,
4. the anti-business attitude of many local officials and needless red tape in local bureaucracies,
5. that given the level of services central-city property taxes are too high as compared to the suburbs, and
6. that the work force in central cities is often inadequately educated, is inexperienced, and lacks adequate motivation to successfully compete for entry-level jobs.

The Joint Economic Committee (Subcommittee of Fiscal and Intergovernmental Policy) has just released a very interesting and informative study entitled Central City Businesses—Plans and Problems (1979). The study was motivated by the Committee's desire to learn more about the factors that are most likely to be successful in encouraging business to remain in the central city and, in some instances, to be attracted back to the city.

From the outset it was realized that circumstances confronting central cities vary dramatically across the country, and thus an attempt was made to have a wide variety of cities included in the analysis. The Committee utilized data from Massachusetts Institute of Technology's Program on Neighborhood and Regional Change. From this data file of Dun and Bradstreet records on business establishments, a probability sample was drawn of 2,611 firms in ten central cities—Atlanta, Dallas, Detroit, Los Angeles, Minneapolis, New York, Phoenix, Pittsburgh, Seattle, and St. Louis. A total of 1,290 usable responses to the survey were received. Larger firms were overrepresented in the sample because of the selection methodology, but the various size classes of firms are probably adequately represented. In the final sample, 31 percent had fewer than 25 employees, 26 percent had 25 to 99, 27 percent had 100 to 499, and 16 percent had 500 or more employees. The distribution of sample firms by industrial classification was as follows:

7% construction
22% manufacturing

6% transportation/public utility
12% wholesale
12% retail
10% finance
31% service

It is estimated that the Dun and Bradstreet file contains 80 to 82 percent of all business establishments. Services, especially professional services, such as physicians and attorneys, are believed to be the major gap. For the remainder of business activity, the sample is thought to be representative. The major conclusions of the study are summarized next.

1. It is expected that disparities between growing and declining cities will continue. A major assumption underpinning the design of the study is that a business manager's perceptions of the overall business climate of a city is likely to be highly correlated with decisions to expand, reduce, or relocate business activity. The survey results confirmed this hypothesis. For example, firms in cities thought to have a highly favorable business climate (Dallas, Seattle, Phoenix, and Atlanta) were more likely to expand operations in the next five years than were firms in cities with less favorable—somewhat favorable (Pittsburgh, St. Louis, Minneapolis, and Los Angeles) and least favorable (Detroit, New York City)—business climates. In cities with the most favorable business climates, positive responses (expansions) outweighed negative responses (relocating, selling, going out of business) by two to one. Whereas in cities with the least favorable business climate, negative responses outweighed the positive by two to one. The conclusion that disparities in economic performance will continue between growing and declining cities is inescapable.

2. Mid-sized firms (25 to 499 employees) are the most likely to increase employment and expand operations in the next five years. Recent evidence (Birch 1977, 1978) suggests that small firms (50 or fewer employees) are responsible for the largest percentage of new jobs created between 1974 and 1976. According to Birch, firms having 50 or fewer employees created 69 percent of all new jobs during these two years. This finding points out a serious problem because the results of this survey also suggest that small businesses do not perform as well in central cities as they do in other locations. Thus the report concludes: "It is apparent that policies intended to assist local economies should focus on assisting small businesses to perform in cities as they do elsewhere, since small businesses generate most of the net new jobs."

3. The likelihood of changes in future levels of activity at central-city sites varied across industries. Financial-sector firms were the most likely to expand operations and employment, whereas manufacturing firms were most likely to reduce employment.

4. Factors affecting the overall quality of life were generally regarded as being more important than business-related factors (tax rates, business costs, and labor factors), although perceptions of business climate and quality of life were highly correlated. A major conclusion of the study is "that improving the quality of life in cities where it is poor, and maintaining it where it is good, can have an important impact on decisions of firms to relocate, alter the size of their work force and reduce or expand their operations."

5. When asked to make open-ended comments on public policy that would have a favorable impact on business, the need to reduce federal regulation and paperwork was the overwhelming response.

EMPIRICAL STUDIES OF FISCAL INCENTIVES TO ECONOMIC DEVELOPMENT

A wide variety of fiscal incentives to spur economic development are made available by state and local governments. Practically all states have some fiscal measures designed to attract business activity or to keep resident firms. These incentive programs take many forms: preferential property taxes for business property, low-interest loans, and public guarantees of loans or mortgages are common examples. Studies evaluating these policies are numerous and date back to 1950. Fortunately, this extensive literature has been reviewed recently in two excellent studies by Harrison and Kanter (1978) and Cornia, Testa, and Stocker (1978). Harrison and Kanter point out that the overall value of this literature is not very good because of poor statistical control, but that this does not really present a problem because the overwhelming conclusion of these studies is that there is little or no significant relationship between the presence of these fiscal incentives and plant relocations or expansions.[9] In the review conducted by Cornia, Testa, and Stocker, they conclude:

> Although existing research is far from conclusive, and a definitive test may never be carried out, the overwhelming consensus is that tax and fiscal concessions rarely have much effect on interstate or interregional choices of industrial location. Where adjacent states place sharply different tax burdens on industry, there may indeed be some noticeable location effect. These effects are evident also in metropolitan areas that contain jurisdictions with widely divergent tax rates.

Although their conclusion appears to suggest the possibility that fiscal incentives are important at the intrametropolitan level, the responses to questionnaire studies they cite suggest that other factors, such as crime and labor supply problems, are often more important than differentials in tax rates (Quante 1976, Mandell 1975, Hunker and Wright 1963). Indeed, Cornia, Testa, and Stocker found evidence of a significant relationship between taxes and economic activity in only two (Fox 1975 and Grieson et al 1977) of the eight intrametropolitan studies they reviewed. Harrison and Kanter (1976), in an earlier article on this subject, point out the paradox between findings of the research on fiscal incentives and their ubiquity. That is, why do these subsidy schemes remain so popular with most state and local officials in the face of a large literature that concludes overwhelmingly that they do not work? Harrison and Kanter resolve the paradox by suggesting that most state-local public officials may believe the primary contribution of these measures is in the promotion of a "pro-business" image for the state or locality. This is certainly plausible. Indeed, from another perspective it could be argued that state-local officials may feel that they have no choice in the matter; if other neighboring jurisdictions offer fiscal inducements, they will be forced to offer the same benefits in order to remain competitive. Of course, this interjurisdictional competition for industry places business in a strategic position of being able to induce competitive bidding between communities. Examples of this behavior are found in Apilado (1971). The end result, Harrison and Kanter (1976, 1978) conclude, is a redistribution of the cost of state-local government away from business—a form of "welfare grant" to the business sector. Likewise, Cornia, Testa, and Stocker (1978) express doubts about the desirability of these incentive schemes:

> . . . a careful consideration of the issues, together with the evidence available from empirical studies, suggests that benefits from these measures [tax and fiscal concessions] are typically modest while their costs may be substantial.

Schmenner (1978) suggests that state-local development policies have taken this path because fiscal incentives are so easy to offer. They are simple to administer and usually they appear to be inexpensive because they do not require front-end expenditures. On the other hand, taking other steps to enhance a community's image may require more effort and imagination. In 1967 a special committee of the National Tax Association charged with investigating the relationship between property taxes and interstate competition for industry concluded:

> . . . there are several local government factors other than taxation that contribute to a favorable climate for industry. These are the attitudes of government administrators (involving the quality of administration—is it fair, honest, reasonable, and so forth?); the control and effectiveness of expenditure policies; and policies directed toward developing, improving, and protecting natural resources, including human resources (e.g., highway development, air and water pollution control, water and sewage facilities, police and fire protection, as well as adequate educational facilities—technical, vocational, elementary-secondary, and college). These factors, combined with a "balanced" tax structure, will do more to improve a state's competitive position for industry than will tax exemptions or much advertising of tax comparisons. (Committee on Intergovernmental Fiscal Relations, 1967, cited in Cornia, Testa, and Stocker 1978)

CONCLUSION

For most firms the availability of subsidized capital or the existence of state and local fiscal incentives is not a major determinant of location choice. This suggests that the NDB could increase its contribution to economic development by targeting its efforts to the specific types of firms and types of distressed areas that do face a capital shortage.

The 1970s have witnessed a nationwide shift in the distribution of population and employment away from central cities, metropolitan areas, and the Northeastern and Midwestern regions of the country. Manufacturing activities in particular have been the most likely to make the move to the suburbs, rural areas, and the Southern and Western regions of the United States. These trends suggest that in order to contribute to economic development in distressed rural areas, NDB assistance to manufacturing activities may be most appropriate. For distressed central cities, however, concentrating efforts on nonmanufacturing activities may hold greater promise.

The studies reviewed here have identified several characteristics of firms that are likely to contribute the most employment growth to an area. By targeting funds to firms of these types, which lack access to private capital market, an NDB might increase the payoff to its economic-development efforts.

Firms already located in an area offer greater economic development promise than those which must be lured in from outside. Research indicates that the birth of new firms and the expansion of existing firms contribute more to employment growth than does the in-migration of firms. In addition, of firms that move, most move a relatively short distance. Firms that already are located within a central city are more likely to choose a city location than are firms currently located in the suburbs. Firms in industries that are heavily concentrated in one region, however, are not as likely to experience high employment growth. Thus, NDB efforts on behalf of a given distressed area are likely to be more effective if they focus primarily on local firms in nationally dispersed industries.

New firms, small firms, and independent firms offer greater promise to economic development efforts than established, large, or multiplant firms. Small firms tend to be the most mobile and the most likely to expand their employment. Thus, the NDB would be more likely to be assisting firms with long-run potential for growth if it concentrated its funds on new, small, and independent firms. Furthermore, public capital assistance may make the greatest difference to firms at the margin of life—those about to be born or to die.

Studies of firm-location decisions have uncovered a number of factors other than capital availability that are important to firms. High on the list of attractive characteristics are the availability of land and building space for expansion, a probusiness attitude of the local government, and good public services—represented primarily by protection against crime and high-quality public-education training of the local labor force. NDB-related assistance to local governments to provide this supporting framework for economic development may prove more important in encouraging employment growth in distressed areas than would the immediate NDB plan to subsidize capital availability.

CAPITAL MARKET IMPERFECTIONS AND THE NDB

THE ADMINISTRATION'S CASE FOR NDB

The Administration's support of the National Development Bank proposal (described earlier in this chapter) is perhaps best reflected in the testimony of Roger Altman (1978), Assistant Secretary of the Treasury for Domestic Finance, before the House Banking, Finance, and Urban Affairs Committee on August 1, 1978: "The Administration believes the National Development Bank will fill a significant void in the existing array of federal economic development tools and that it will do so efficiently."(p. 93)

The logic used by the Administration to justify the program is that many urban and rural areas are suffering from economic distress, and that these problems can be overcome through the creation of the NDB, which will bring jobs and income into these areas. Though the nature of the distress—the loss of jobs, regional population shifts, and the decline of central cities—is well documented, the same cannot be said for how the NDB will overcome this distress. It is simply assumed, with little supporting evidence, that firms will respond to the financial incentives of the National Development Bank in sufficient numbers to materially affect the economic base of distressed areas.

In its presentation the Administration did not draw on the long and ambiguous experiences of urban renewal, the Area Redevelopment Administration, the Economic Development Administration, the Appalachian Regional Commission, the Small Business Administration, and the Farmers Home Administration in their efforts to promote economic growth in distressed areas. These experiences demonstrate that financial incentives do not always work,[10] and that firms are not always eagerly awaiting the chance to locate in distressed areas. It needs to be remembered that areas are distressed because firms often do not want to locate there. They may have any number of other options. They can often obtain a wide range of subsidies and other inducements from state and local development authorities when locating in nondistressed areas.

It could, however, be argued that the political and social motivations for the NDB program outweigh the economic. There are important political constituencies in urban and rural areas that need to be satisfied. There are high social costs associated with distressed areas. The political method of dealing with distressed areas has always been to assuage local demands by enacting programs that will try to overcome the comparative disadvantages of an area through increased local infrastructure (industrial parks, sewer and water mains, or roads) or through federal credit to finance firms that locate in the area. The alternative approach of encouraging out-migration of labor to high growth areas has never been explicitly tried by the federal government. This would be socially and politically controversial because it would dilute local political power and would require a rethinking of the local booster approach to economic development.

CAPITAL MARKET IMPERFECTIONS AND DISTRESSED AREAS

Central to the arguments for a National Development Bank is the assumption that capital market imperfections exist for firms wishing to expand or locate in distressed areas. Thought on the issue can be divided into three schools. There is the argument that capital market imperfections do not exist, and that this very perfection is the reason why firms cannot obtain funds to locate in distressed areas. Another school is that imperfections do exist, which limit the ability of firms to obtain capital. A third view is that the question of capital market imperfections is irrelevant when one considers other more important factors that influence the location of firms.

The position that there are no imperfections focuses on the argument that capital is a scarce good, and that there will never be enough funds in the financial system to satisfy all the economic, political, and social demands placed on it (Smith 1977). The unique economic history of the United States and the sophisticated capital market structure that has developed are offered as proof that capital markets are working well. Sufficient capital has been available to foster economic growth, provide high per capita incomes, and a high standard of living.

Price, in the form of interest, has been the method of allocating funds. Price in turn has been based on risk assessment. The result is that funds go to larger, more successful firms. It goes to firms that can supply the highest, risk-adjusted returns. The result is that investors are unwilling to provide capital to firms in distressed areas (Daniels 1978). The perceived risks weighed against the expected returns on such investments are too great compared to opportunities available elsewhere.

The capital market imperfections school (reviewed above) argues that finance is not allocated in the most efficient manner because of transaction and information cost differentials that discriminate against small firms; regional concentration in the commercial banking industry that places small and especially rural borrowers at a disadvantage; imperfections in the venture capital market, making it difficult for many small to medium-sized firms to expand new product lines; and racial and geographic discrimination in lending, posing especially difficult problems in access to finance for minority borrowers in central cities.

Other imperfections may occur as a result of undue federal involvement in capital markets through tax policy and government regulations.[12] They also may exist because in the past small and medium-sized firms were squeezed out of the market during a credit crunch as financial institutions favored larger, low-risk firms. The result is that, over time, small and medium-sized firms become a smaller and smaller component of a financial institution's portfolio. The result is that many small, credit-worthy firms are unable to obtain financing. (Parshall 1978)

The argument in many cases goes on to state that because of higher labor, land, and other costs associated with distressed areas, access to capital at the market rate of interest is not a sufficient inducement. In order to help firms overcome higher costs it is necessary for the federal government to provide funds at a subsidized, below-market rate of interest (Parshall 1978).

The third school of thought holds that the question of capital market imperfections is irrelevant to the issue of economic development in distressed areas because capital is not a large factor in the costs of production, tending to vary between 5 and 7 percent of total costs (Daniels 1978). Capital availability is far less important than such things as attitudes, property taxes, crime, urban congestion, entrepreneurship, and expertise to put together viable projects (Howell 1978, Bearse 1978). According to this view, reductions in the cost of capital or its increased availability will not increase the number of viable projects that will expand or locate in a distressed area (Kelly 1978).

In both the perfect capital market and the market imperfection schools of thought there would be projects that could not obtain capital in distressed areas. Under the perfect capital market school these would be projects that did not meet market criteria, whereas under the imperfections school it would be due to considerations other than financial viability.

Under the perfect market argument the creation of a National Development Bank would cause market distortions and could lead to the inefficient use of a scarce good. It could result in macroeconomic costs by reducing national income and employment below levels that might otherwise have been achieved. Under the market imperfections argument, the creation of an NDB would help to perfect capital markets and could be justified on both equity and efficiency grounds because it would redistribute income and promote the efficient use of capital.

If capital is not an important determinant of location, or if the kinds of capital subsidies provided by the NDB are not large enough to induce investors to place funds in distressed areas, as is asserted in the third school of thought, then the question of perfect or imperfect markets becomes irrelevant from a policy point of view.

In summary, little evidence can be found in support of the first position that there are no capital market imperfections. Even those investigators who deny private market imperfections generally acknowledge that the inclusion of social benefits and costs may frequently dictate a different allocation than the private market outcome. Clearly, the second position, emphasizing capital market imperfections, is that taken by the Administration and most other proponents of an NDB. There is, however, widespread disagreement about the specific form that intervention in the capital market should take.

The third view, that the question of capital market imperfections is irrelevant to the issue of economic development in distressed areas, is the least orthodox, but in many ways the most compelling. Daniels (1978) and Daniels and Kieschnick (1978) argue forcefully that capital costs are almost never a principal reason why firms select a particular location. Capital costs are usually a small fraction of total costs, and, as a result, financial incentives can be expected to produce only a negligible effect on firm profits.

ABILITY OF THE NDB PROGRAMS TO ATTRACT FIRMS, CAPITAL, AND EMPLOYMENT

The objective of the NDB is to provide funding to established corporations that would employ a large number of people in distressed areas. The problem with this objective is that the bank would probably be directing its efforts toward firms that already have the ability to obtain funding in the nation's capital markets because the private-market test used by the bank would probably screen out many marginal firms. For enterprises that qualified for assistance, concern over the costs of funds or the ability to raise funds is probably not a pressing concern. Their decisions to locate are determined more by nearness to markets, labor supply, access to transportation, or other nonfinancial concerns. Firms of this type that locate in distressed areas would probably have located there without the capital subsidy. The result is that the NDB would be directing its efforts toward those firms where its incentives would have the least effect. It could be argued that this is an acceptable approach from a public policy point of view if it means that the subsidy would attract investors who otherwise would not have invested in a distressed area, leading to a net increase in investment in distressed areas. This will not be the case, however, if the firm would have located without the guarantee because the NDB program is oriented toward low-risk investors who would not normally invest in high-risk distressed areas.[13] Moreover, if the targeted "low-risk" firms also tend to be larger, older establishments, the research reviewed above suggests that the net employment gains are likely to be much smaller than those which might have otherwise accompanied the growth of younger, more dynamic firms.

NEGATIVE EFFECTS

Even if it is assumed that capital market imperfections exist, and that the NDB incentives are sufficient to overcome these imperfections, there are still a number of possible costs that must be weighed against the benefits. One cost already discussed is subsidies to firms that did not need them.[14] Another cost is the displacement of private by public capital. This would occur if the funds that went into the project came from investors who would otherwise have invested in small businesses or housing in the distressed area. In this situation, federal intervention would cause a shift in private capital from one use to another, rather than a net increase in investment.[15] Another displacement effect is channeling funds away from more productive investments elsewhere in the economy. Subsidies for firms that locate or expand in distressed areas give them a competitive advantage over those enterprises which locate and expand in these areas without this subsidy (Hubbell 1978). If NDB assistance becomes a common method of financing capital investment in designated areas, NDB assistance becomes a sine qua non in any financing arrangements in these areas. The result could be the widespread substitution of federally assisted credit for private credit in designated distressed areas.

A final possible negative effect is that a program that subsidizes capital may bias firms toward capital-intensive production processes. Without close control and monitoring of the projects that are assisted, a possible long-run result could be the substitution of capital for labor. This would run counter to the political and social intent of the NDB legislative proposal (Hubbell 1978).

OTHER MEANS OF ACHIEVING NDB OBJECTIVES

There are any number of ways that the NDB proposal can be changed. The means explored in this section can be characterized as either using existing or prior federal efforts as the basis for program design or by expanding the scope of bank activities. These changes could broaden the locational inducements offered firms to include assistance not now included in the Administration's program. This could increase the probable success of the program and could blunt some of the economic and political criticisms that have been directed toward the program.

EXISTING OR PRIOR FEDERAL EFFORTS

Building on existing or prior federal efforts can occur in at least three different ways. One is to incorporate existing federal economic development programs into the bank. The second is to expand existing programs and drop the NDB idea. A third is to enact legislation on a case-by-case basis to help a particular firm interested in locating in a distressed area.

A proposal to expand the NDB to include a number of already existing programs is included in the 1980 Budget. The bank would incorporate the direct and guaranteed loan programs of the Economic Development Administration and the Department of Housing and Urban Development.

Many of these programs have tools and goals similar to those found in the proposed NDB. The Economic Development Administration's business-development loan program finances firms willing to expand or establish operations in distressed areas. Assistance includes long-term low-interest loans for fixed assets, as well as the authority to provide working capital loans and guarantees, interest-subsidy guarantees of fixed asset loans made by private institutions, and lease guarantees for buildings and equipment. Obligations for this EDA program in the 1980 Budget are estimated at $176 million in fiscal 1980, up from $95 million in fiscal 1979.

The Farmers Home Administration (FmHA) in the Department of Agriculture has a number of economic-development grant, loan, and guarantee programs, which are available to rural areas and cities of less than 50,000. These programs include rural-development grants, which public bodies can use to assist in the acquisition or development of land or the construction of buildings, plants, or equipment. Grant obligations are estimated at $10 million in fiscal year 1980. Other FmHA programs include industrial-development loans and guarantees, which can be used to finance industrial acquisitions, land, equipment, working capital, and start-up costs. Industrial-development loans and guarantees in fiscal 1980 are estimated at $1 billion.

The Urban Development Action Grants of the Department of Housing and Urban Development are another development tool used to promote economic development and neighborhood revitalization in distressed cities and urban counties. It is estimated that $400 million will be obligated under the program in fiscal year 1980.

The Small Business Administration has a variety of programs available to small business in both distressed and nondistressed areas. Eligible enterprises must have less than $5 million in sales and employ fewer than 250 workers. SBA programs include loans for working capital, the purchase of inventories, equipment and facilities, and assistance to local development companies. The SBA under its regular loan program can guarantee up to 90 percent of any business loan originated by a private lender. The agency may also loan up to $150,000 to a firm when a private lender agrees to a minimum 25 percent participation on the project. When no private lender is available, the agency may make a loan for up to 100 percent of the project cost. It is estimated that in 1980 the agency will have outlays of $694 million, down from $1.5 billion in fiscal year 1979 and $2.8 billion in fiscal year 1978. This large change in SBA outlays is due to a proposed shift in SBA activities to guaranteed rather than direct loans. Guaranteed loans, as opposed to direct loans, only require an outlay when the guaranteed loan goes into default. They are a method of allocating private capital for a public purpose with minimum budgetary impact.

From an efficiency point of view, combining these various agencies under the National Development Bank could reduce program overlap and probably reduce costs. Carrying out such a program, though, would require dealing with interested parties in the public sector, Capitol Hill, and the executive branch who may be unwilling to agree to such a reorganization. Without a well-thought-out idea of how an expanded NDB would work and a carefully planned strategy for carrying out the consolidation, the effort might fail. The result could be the reduced effectiveness of federal economic-development activities.

The expansion of present federal economic-development assistance programs is another way of reaching the Administration's economic-development goals. This is particularly true because many currently operating programs either carry out many of the functions found in the NDB proposal or have the unused authority to implement such programs. Many existing programs have been used to assist large corporations of the type favored by the NDB proposal. The Economic Development Administration has received applications from at least six steel producers for loan guarantees of more than $50 million each, and $100 million in guarantees has been reserved by EDA for the reopening of the Campbell Works in Youngstown, Ohio.

In the past, the program has provided at least twenty guarantees of more than $1 million and four over $10 million. A large proportion of EDA's loan-guarantee assistance was used to help two shipbuilding companies. These firms have received a total of $113 million in guarantees. This is an amount equal to sixty percent of the amount of all guarantees authorized from fiscal year 1966 through June 30, 1977. One of the firms received a total of $83 million in guaranteed loans (U.S. General Accounting Office 1979).

The demand for additional large-scale assistance exists. The Chrysler Corporation recently asked for, and was denied, a $250 million loan guarantee from the Farmers Home Administration. This followed the exploration by the American Motors Corporation in the summer of 1978 of the possibility of a $109 million loan guarantee from the Economic Development Administration (Miller 1979). These examples indicate the possible demand for such expanded programs and the potential for existing agencies to make and monitor such loans. The problem is that these loans are often requested by firms in serious financial trouble. The subsidy provided is desired more for its ability to keep a firm afloat than its ability to promote the location or expansion of firms in distressed areas.

Another option is the enactment of special legislation. In the past such assistance has been geared toward particular firms or industries. The possible local economic impact of plant closings at times has been an argument used to justify such aid. The Emergency Loan Guarantee Act, P.L. 92-70, which authorized $250 million in loan guarantees to the Lockheed Corporation, stipulated that a guaranteed loan provided under the legislation had to be justified on the grounds that without it the borrower would be unable to continue in business and that this "would adversely and seriously affect the economy of or employment in the Nation or any region thereof." The use of federal credit assistance to help a particular firm or sector of the economy has a long history. Some precedents include the War Finance Corporation begun during World War I, the Reconstruction Finance Corporation, loan guarantees authorized under Title V of the Interstate Commerce Act to assist railroads, the unused interim emergency financial assistance available to railroads under the Railroad Passenger Service Act of 1970, and the financial assistance provided under the Rail Reorganization Act of 1972 (Mitrisin 1974).

The call for legislation of this type occurs periodically when a particular sector of the economy experiences difficulties and one or two firms need assistance. In 1975 it was help for the electric utility industry, in 1978 it was a guarantee to finance the Alaska pipeline, and recently there have been suggestions that special credit assistance may be provided for the Chrysler Corporation (Miller 1979).

The use of special-purpose legislation to assist large firms locating in distressed areas is a possible alternative approach to the NDB. The programs run by HUD, EDA, FmHA, and SBA could finance smaller projects and the particular constituencies they were designed for. Projects costing tens or hundreds of millions of dollars would require special legislation. A possible advantage of this approach is that it would require very special circumstances to justify the effort needed to pass such legislation. This would force firms to use all other options before taking this approach. In all probability, only those projects which had sufficient economic and noneconomic justifications would receive assistance. More marginal requests would not survive the congressional process. Such a process, because of the political trade-offs that would occur, would probably not be the most economically efficient way of promoting growth in economically distressed areas. At times it could assist poorly run firms selling products or services for which there was no demand.

OTHER OPTIONS

A number of proposals have been made on how a development bank might work. A brief discussion of three proposals follows in order to provide an idea of ways, other than the Administration proposal, a bank might work. Daniels and Kieschnick (1978), in a draft study done for EDA in July 1978, propose a development bank that would:

1. Have the authority to make direct loans,
2. Target guaranteed loans to new, small, or otherwise risk ventures,
3. Not have the authority to provide interest subsidies,
4. Provide technical assistance,
5. Encourage the use of industrial-development bonds by small corporations, and
6. Provide venture capital through existing Small Business Administration programs.

Smith (1977), in his study also done for the Economic Development Administration, calls for an institution that would finance:

1. Small and medium-sized firms,
2. State and local development corporations,
3. Public works,
4. Environmental control projects, and
5. Large-scale projects that could not be done by authorities.

The assistance to firms would include subsidized loans to small businesses for plant and equipment regardless of location, loans to minority firms, and working capital loans to firms in distressed areas. Assistance to publicly owned, nonprofit development groups could include direct loans, loan guarantees, loan insurance, or the purchase of loans made by such groups. The bank would have the authority to purchase the indebtedness of industrial revenue authorities, states, and municipalities when it was used to promote economic development, municipal infrastructure, pollution control, and urban revitalization

Parshall (1978), in his discussion of a National Development Bank, proposes an institution that would not be part of a federal line agency and would not be included under civil service. The bank would make loans, loan guarantees, and grants but would not participate directly in equity investments. The bank would be financed by the purchase of one billion dollars of stock by the U.S. Treasury and the transfer of Department of Housing and Urban Development (UDAG) grants to the bank. Assistance would be directed toward urban areas and would be used to underwrite land assembly costs to finance plant expansion, and for working capital costs. Venture capital would be provided to innovate firms, as well as assistance to small business.

A discussion of some of the various changes mentioned follows.

EQUITY FINANCING

Equity financing by the National Development Bank is not an option included in the current Administration proposal, although it was favored by the Department of Housing and Urban Development in the initial development bank discussions in 1977.[16] Proponents of equity financing argue that the riskier a venture, the higher the proportion of funding that should consist of equity. Because distressed areas, by their very nature are high risk, ventures in these areas should be heavily financed by equity.[17] There is a lack of clarity, however, on the types of firms that would be eligible for and would use equity financing (Parshall 1978).

This not-so-minor problem aside, the advantages of this financing method are that it would permit the NDB to fund potentially high-risk ventures. These can be characterized as smaller, high-risk firms that are not now the focus of the Administration proposal. For these firms, the advantages of equity financing, unlike debt financing, is that it does not require a steady commitment of funds in the form of interest payments. This permits more latitude in the use of whatever cash flow is generated. This is particularly important in the first years of operation.

For assisted firms, equity financing has the potential disadvantage of extensive NDB involvement in daily operations because this is the only way the bank could protect its investment. From the federal perspective, equity participation, as a general rule, is not the accepted form of financing used to promote economic development.[18] The increased involvement by the NDB in the daily operations of particular firms would require additional staff. These additional costs might not be worth the benefits. In addition, and perhaps more important, equity financing would expose the bank to a greater risk of loss. In the event of a failure, the NDB would have no recourse to pledged collateral or other assets of the firm or its owners, as could be the case with a direct or guaranteed loan.

VENTURE CAPITAL

The literature search described above indicates the possibility that capital market imperfections exist in the availability of venture capital for high-risk, high-technology firms. Enterprises of this type have the potential of creating a large number of long-term jobs, as well as the high possibility of failure. An NDB engaged in such financing would have to be willing to sustain a high loss rate. In many instances, equity participation might be the most appropriate form of assistance because high-technology enterprises do not usually generate profits in the first few years. The Administration objective of locating projects in distressed areas might have to be altered, because some high-technology entrepreneurs might need proximity to a university or other specialized facility to bring projects to fruition. Even if venture-capital projects were not all located in distressed areas, their activities, if successful, could help distressed areas. This could happen in two ways. Direct employment could be provided distressed-area residents to the extent that semiskilled manufacturing or service jobs resulted from the venture. Additional, less-direct employment effects would occur as a result of the increased economic activity within the metropolitan or nonmetropolitan area. Some of this increased activity would produce additional jobs and income for distressed-area residents.

Participation in high-technology, high-risk projects, although more reasonable in terms of Administration objectives of overcoming capital market imperfections, might be hard to justify. High-technology projects take time to mature and are subject to a high failure rate. Until projects matured, it would be hard for the NDB to justify its expenditures. Even when a project succeeded, it might be difficult to show how distressed areas were helped, particularly if the venture was not located in such an area.

TARGETING

The present proposal has very liberal eligibility criteria. As written they would permit approximately 12,000 localities to apply for NDB assistance.[19] If all applied, and the funds were divided equally, each locality would receive about $83,000 for each billion dollars of assistance provided by the bank. More selective targeting of bank assistance would increase the potential effectiveness of the programs offered by the bank, depending of course on the effectiveness of the particular programs. The criteria used to limit assistance would depend on the goals of the development bank. They could either further restrict the number of eligible places or the number of eligible firms. The number of eligible places could be reduced by altering the required unemployment, population growth, employment growth, and per capita income figures found in the Administration proposal. The number of eligible firms could be reduced with the goal of either increased efficiency or equity.

Efficiency criteria could eliminate proposals that had little prospect of generating new long-term jobs or increased income in distressed areas.[20] Equity could be promoted by limiting assistance to small firms, firms employing low-income persons, the unemployed and minorities, or enterprises run by community development corporations (Daniels and Kieschnick 1978). These two approaches in general represent the opposing positions taken by the Treasury Department and the Department of Housing and Urban Development on how to provide assistance. Each has its strong and weak points.

The Treasury position favored limiting assistance to larger, more established, manufacturing firms. Although participation by nonmanufacturing firms was not ruled out, it was proposed that firms primarily serving local markets and nonprofit enterprises not be aided. The HUD position favored broad-based stimulus of the overall economy of the targeted distressed area in contrast to the focus on manufacturing and export-base activity featured in the Treasury position.[21] HUD argued that the bank should not be unduly restricted as to the type of activity that it can support, but rather it should be allowed to judge projects on their individual merits. The Treasury position would limit assistance to firms that may not be influenced by the capital subsidies now proposed. The HUD position is likely to have a higher default rate, and in some cases the emphasis may be on maintaining jobs rather than creating new ones.

ASSISTANCE TO SMALL AND MEDIUM-SIZED FIRMS

The thrust of the Administration's NDB proposal is assistance to large firms employing several hundred or more workers in distressed areas. An alternative, and perhaps more promising, approach is federal assistance to small and medium-sized firms that would expand or locate in distressed areas. The literature search described above supports this conclusion on two grounds. First, the literature clearly indicates that capital is less available and is more expensive to smaller firms and in some cases is unavailable at any price and, second, that small to medium-sized firms are responsible for the largest net employment gains.

It is indeed a paradox that those enterprises which have the greatest potential for reducing our unemployment problems are often the same firms which encounter the greatest difficulty in securing the needed finance to expand. Moreover, another problem exists in formulating effective public policies to assist these firms. It is clear that there is no known road to success, but at least one important conclusion emerges from the literature, namely, that priority should be given to the assistance of firms already located in distressed areas rather than emphasizing policies designed to encourage new firms to locate there.

MUNICIPAL BOND BACKSTOP

Another option for the NDB is an alternative borrowing source for cities and localities unable to sell their bonds on the private market (Parshall 1978). Such an option would be attractive to localities facing short-term cash-flow problems, which restrict or eliminate their ability to borrow. An NDB backstop facility would permit these localities to obtain financing without going through the drawn-out and complicated procedure faced by New York City. Such a facility would probably only be justified when the locality's inability to borrow was short-term in nature and not due to long-term structural changes in the area's economy. If the locality's problems were the result of long-term changes, more fundamental problems would have to be dealt with. Backstop financing would be a handy way of permitting local officials to avoid coming to grips with these problems, although it would run counter to the present NDB objectrives of promoting long-term growth.

No backstop facility now exists. Localities with financing difficulties either have to sharply reduce expenditures, raise taxes, or obtain special legislation. Special legislation is time consuming and difficult. It would probably be unacceptable to most localities and would also not be subject to the kind of abuses that could occur with a backstop facility. Such a facility would be subject to a variety of pressures to provide assistance to unqualified applications, pressures that might be difficult to resist.

NDB AS A COORDINATOR AND PACKAGER

The NDB as now formulated is a passive institution responding to requests for assistance. As contemplated it would not take an active role in formulating or packaging projects. Using the alternative approach, an NDB would find projects, locate financing, and utilize the knowledge and expertise of existing state and local development institutions (Daniels and Kieschnick 1978 and Parshall 1978). This concept of what an NDB should do is closely akin to the view expressed by Chinitz and Fairchild (1977):

> Our tentative preference is for an NDB which specializes in assisting the financing of large scale complex projects which are developmental in nature, i.e., projects which shape development patterns rather than respond to development patterns. . . . the financial needs of small scale developmental projects can be met by existing techniques and institutions such as the EDA and SBA programs. . . . To reverse the momentum [of urban decline] it is necessary to

> operate on a large scale, both spatial and temporal. The effort must be substantial and sustained. Our experience suggests that neither private conventional lending mechanisms nor government agencies are capable of meeting these requirements. (pp. 357-58).

This approach would provide a service that is now lacking at the federal level. The NDB in this role could not assist many localities at the same time because extensive time and manpower would be required to find and effectively promote a project. An institution strong enough to reject a proposal, even after it has devoted considerable time and money in investigating its possibilities, would be required.

CONCLUSION

Proposals for the National Development Bank should be evaluated in the context of the wide variety of federal economic-development assistance programs already in operation. Identifying what is expected to be different about the NDB should help reduce duplication of federal program efforts, help avoid the pitfalls of previous experiences, and help design a program that fills a void in the existing set of federal economic-development tools.

For some types of economic-development efforts, the goals motivating the NDB proposal might be better accomplished by the expanded application of existing programs or by the enactment of special economic-relief legislation. A new NDB-type program may be appropriate if this flexibility in program administration or legislative relief is not forthcoming. In addition, a new program may be called for if promising economic-development proposals do not fit into any category of existing federal programs.

This analysis suggests that the effectiveness of a National Development Bank could be enhanced by a redefinition of the current proposal targeting NDB efforts 1) to projects least likely to be covered by other private or federal programs, 2) to types of firms and areas for which capital shortages can be identified, and 3) to projects contributing to economic growth that would not have taken place without federal aid.

ISSUES TO CONSIDER WHEN DECIDING ON THE APPROPRIATENESS OF A NATIONAL DEVELOPMENT BANK

This chapter does not provide a definitive answer on whether a national development bank is a good or bad idea, and neither does it advocate one approach over another in promoting economic development. It indicates that the issues involved are complex, and that there is no universally agreed on approach to promoting development. It shows that a considerable body of literature exists that deals directly with the development bank and closely related issues and indicates that some approaches, from an economic point of view, appear to show more promise than others as a means of promoting development.

The presence of literature on the subject indicates that information exists that can be used by policymakers to make more reasoned decisions on the most appropriate approach to solving the problems of distressed areas. The literature can be used to help decide if a bank is a good idea and, if it is, what tools might be used. Perhaps most important, the literature suggests a variety of analytic methods that can be used to evaluate the effectiveness of various bank ideas and development tools.

For any detailed evaluation of the NDB to be of assistance to policymakers some basic policy decisions must be made about the purposes of any proposed development bank. Without such basic policy determinations, it is unlikely that any analysis useful to policymakers will be done because it would not be able to address the essential issues in the most fruitful way.

One issue that needs to be addressed is whether the assistance is aimed at overcoming long-term structural changes or short-term cyclical problems. Each may require a different approach. Another issue is the role of the federal government versus the private sector. For example, guarantees and insurance are a means of allocating private credit for a public purpose. These tools, if selected, would be used to encourage loans by institutions that currently, for any number of reasons, are unwilling to provide financial support. The use of direct loans would place the burden of selecting and monitoring projects with the federal agency. This could require budget outlays that may be unacceptable in times of concern over the increasing size of federal expenditures.

A central policy decision regards targeting. Shall the assistance be for a large number of areas, or just a few? Should the orientation be urban, rural, metropolitan or nonmetropolitan? How shall eligible areas be determined? What types of firms should be eligible for assistance within the targeted areas—large or small firms, capital-intensive or labor-intensive enterprises?

The issue of targeting the bank's activities is closely related to the question of how much political and financial risk the bank is willing to assume. Political risk is minimized by spreading the available funding as widely as possible. Financial risk is minimized by lending to well-established, mature firms. The literature reviewed in this chapter suggests that the decision to minimize one or both or these risks may substantially reduce the potential effectiveness of the National Development Bank. The choices here are not easy.

NOTES

1. See Altman, 1978, p. 57. Although a number of legislative proposals to create development banks have been advanced over the past decade, the focus of this chapter is the Carter Administration's program detailed in HR13230 nd S3233 (June 21, 1978).
2. The Budget of the United States, Fiscal Year 1980 (Washington, D.C. 1979), p. 21.
3. Ibid., p. 199.
4. Ibid., pp. 200-201.
5. "To Establish a National Development Bank," Hearings before the Subcommittee on Economic Stabilization of the House Committee on Banking, Finance and Urban Affairs, Aug. 1 and 2, 1978, Appendix II, "Questions Submitted to Administration Witnesses and Replies," pp. 557-60.
6. Statement before the Subcommittee on Economic Stabilization of the Committee on Banking, Finance and Urban Affairs, Aug. 1, 1978, Treasury Department news release, p. 2.
7. Ibid., p. 8.
8. The Dun and Bradstreet firm level data included primary and secondary SIC codes, total employment at the site as well as that of the parent organization (if any), firm net worth and annual sales, the address and postal zip code, and the year the firm began operations. Each of the metropolitan areas included was divided into small geographic areas (analysis zones). These analysis zones were then used to examine the pattern of net changes in employment during the 1965-68 period. Net employment changes were examined by components (moving, new and dying, and stationary firms) and by industry mix. Results are presented for each city and in aggregate.
9. This conclusion offered by Harrison and Kanter is, of course, easily criticized because they cannot prove that a properly designed statistical analysis would not uncover a significant relationship between fiscal incentives and plant mobility.
10. Two critical studies of the National Development Bank idea were done on contract for the Economic Development Administration in the Department of Commerce. A study by Belden Daniels and Michael Kieschnick (1978, draft of July 10, 1978) found that the guarantee provisions in the NDB proposal would increase a firm's profits by only one-tenth of a percent, whereas the grant proposals would increase the rate of profit by 2.4 percent. A study by Kenneth Hubbell (1978), also done for the EDA, concluded that there was little reason to believe that the availability of grants or interest subsidies would induce firms to locate in core cities.
11. For a discussion of state assistance see *Industrial Development Magazine,* Jan./Feb. 1979. Most of the issue is devoted to assistance available from each of the fifty states.
12. The most thorough review of the impact of government regulation and taxation on the functioning of private capital markets is contained in Daniels and Kieschnick. They examine: (1) the chartering of commercial banks, (2) the implications of the new "prudent man" rule of the Employee Retirement Income Security Act (ERISA) of 1974, (3) Federal Reserve interest rate controls—a form of price controls on finance, (4) information and transactions cost implications of Securities and Exchange Commission (SEC) rules, and (5) the implications of federal tax policies with respect to capital gains, the investment tax credit, and contributions to social security.
13. On this point, see Daniels and Kieschnick (1978, draft of July 10, 1978), pp. 256-57, and Hubbell (1978), p. 30.
14. See Daniels and Kieschnick (1978), p. 222, and Parshall (1978), p. 333.
15. Daniels and Kieschnick (1978), p. 256.
16. See U.S. Department of Housing and Urban Development, "The Urban Development Bank: Options for Discussion," Sept. 18, 1977, p. 6.
17. See Daniels and Kieschnick (1978, draft of July 10, 1978), p. 249, on this point.

18. One example of public-sector equity financing at the level of state government is the recently formed Connecticut Produce Development Corporation. A discussion of this interesting innovation is found in Fournier (1978).
19. A full listing of eligible communities under the Administration's NDB proposal is contained in the Aug. 1 and 2, 1978, hearings on HR13230 before the Subcommiteee on Economic Stabilization of the House Committee on Banking, Finance and Urban Affairs, pp. 213-486.
20. See U.S. Department of the Treasury, 1977, p. 17.
21. See U.S. Department of Housing and Urban Development, 1977, pp. 7-8.

BIBLIOGRAPHY

Allaman, Peter, and Birch, David. "Components of Employment Change for Metropolitan and Rural Areas in the United States by Industry Groups, 1970-1972." Working paper #8, Inter-Area Migration Project, Joint Center for Urban Studies of M.I.T. and Harvard University, 1975.

Altman, Roger C. Statement before Subcommittee on Economic Stabilization of the House Committee on Banking, Finance and Urban Affairs. "To Establish a National Development Bank." Aug. 1 and 2, 1978. Pp. 57-102.

Apilado, Vincent P. "Corporate-Government Interplay: The Era of Industrial Aid Finance." *Urban Affairs Quarterly* 7 (Dec. 1971): 219-41.

Archer, S. H., and Faerden, L. G. "Firm Size and the Cost of Externally Secured Equity Capital." *Journal of Finance* 21 (Mar. 1966): 69-83.

Baty, G. "Initial Financing of New Research-Based Enterprise in New England." Research report for the Federal Reserve Bank of Boston, from Master's thesis, Massachusetts Institute of Technology, 1964.

Bearse, Peter J. "Influencing Capital Flows for Urban Economic Development: Incentives or Institution Building?" *Journal of Regional Science* 19 (Feb. 1979).

———. ed. *Mobilizing Capital for Economic Development: Institutional Innovation and the New Urban Policy.* Papers and proceedings from a conference held at Princeton University, Apr. 27, 1978. Center for New Jersey Affairs, Woodrow Wilson School of Public and International Affairs, Aug. 1978.

———. "Concluding Observations." In *Mobilizing Capital for Economic Development*, edited by Peter J. Bearse, Princeton, N.J.: Center for New Jersey Affairs, Woodrow Wilson School for Public and International Affairs, Aug. 1978. Pp. 356-72.

Birch, David. "Regional Differences in Factor Costs: Labor, Land, Capital, and Transportation." Paper presented at the symposium Alternatives to Confrontation: A National Policy toward Regional Change, Austin, Tex., Sept. 24, 1977.

———. "The Processes Causing Economic Change in Cities." Prepared for a Department of Commerce Roundtable on Business Retention and Expansion in Cities held Feb. 22, 1978.

Bosworth, B.; Duessenberry, J.; and Carron, A. *Capital Needs in the Seventies.* Washington, D.C.; Brookings Institution, 1975.

Brookings Institution. "Roundtable Discussion on Urban Development Banking." Washington, D.C.; Brookings Institution, 1977. Mimeographed.

Cannon, Donald S.; Lachman, M. Leanne, and Bernhard, Arlyne S. "Identifying Neighborhoods for Preservation and Renewal." *Growth and Change* 8 Jan. 1977): 35-38.

Chandross, R. "The Impact of New Bank Entry on Unit Banks in One Bank Towns." *Journal of Bank Reserve,* Autumn 1973.

Charles River Associates, Inc. "An Analysis of Venture Capital Market Imperfections." Prepared for National Bureau of Standards, Experimental Technology Incentives Program, 1976. NBS-GCR-ETIP76-12.

Chinitz, Ben, and Fairchild, Chuck. "Establishing a National Development Bank." Prepared for ABT Associates in a report to EDA. Reprinted in Hearings before the Subcomittee on Economic Stabilization of the House Committee on Banking, Finance and Urban Affairs, Oct. 4, 5; Nov. 1, 1977. Pp. 323-80.

Cornia, Gary C.; Testa. William A.; and Stocker, Frederick D. "State Local Fiscal Incentives and Economic Development." Urban and Regional Development Series no. 4. Columbus, Ohio: Academy for Contemporary Problems, 1978.

Daniels, Belden. "Capital is Only Part of the Problem." In *Mobilizing Capital for Economic Development,* edited by Peter J. Bearse. Princeton, N.J.: Center for New Jersey Affairs, Woodrow Wilson School of Public and International Affairs, Aug. 1978. Pp. 2–19.

———. and Kieschnick, M. "Theory and Practice in the Design of Development Finance Innovations." Prepared for U.S. Economic Development Administration, July and Nov. 1978.

Dennis, R. *Investment in the Eighties.* Washington, D.C., National Planning Association, 1975.

Federal Reserve System. "Financing Small Business." Report to the Committee on Banking and Currency and the Select Committe on Small Business, United States Congress. Washington, D.C.: Government Printing Office., 1958.

Fox, William. "Intrametropolitan Tax Differentials and Industrial Location." Ph.D. dissertation, Ohio State University, 1975.

Fournier, Arthur. "Capital for New Technology." In *Mobilizing Capital for Economic Development,* edited by Peter J. Bearse. Princeton, N.J.: Center for New Jersey Affairs, Woodrow Wilson School of Public and International Affairs, Aug. 1978. Pp. 47-60.

Fraser, D., and Rose, P. "Bank Entry and Bank Performance." *Journal of Finance* 27, no. 1 (Mar. 1972): 65-78.

Gardner, C. "Banking Regulation and Urban Growth." The Rand Corporation, P-5057, July 1973.

Garvin, W. "The Small Business Capital Gap: The Special Case of Minority Enterprise." *Journal of Finance* 26(2)(May 1971): 445-57.

Grieson, Ronald E., et al. "The Effect of Business Taxation on the Location of Industry." *Journal of Urban Economics* 4 (Apr. 1977).

Harrison, Bennett, and Kanter, Sandra. "The Political Economy of States' Job-Creation Business Incentives." *Journal of the American Institute of Planners* 44, no. 4 (Oct. 1978): 424-35.

Heggestad, A. "Market Structure, Risk, and Profitability in Commercial Banking." *Journal of Finance* 32, no. 4 (Sept. 1977): 1207-16.

Howell, James H. Comments before the Subcommittee on Fiscal and Intergovernmental Policy of the Joint Economic Committee, Hearings on Keeping Business in the City, Mar. 6-7, 1978.

———. "The Northeast's Regional Economic Dilemma." In *Mobilizing Capital for Economic Development,* edited by Peter J. Bearse. Princeton. N.J.: Center for New Jersey Affairs, Woodrow Wilson School for Public and International Affairs, Aug. 1978. Pp. 20-25.

Hubbell, Kenneth. "Development Banking and Financial Incentives for the Private Sector." Prepared for a conference sponsored by the University of Missouri-Kansas City on the Federal Response to the Fiscal Crisis in American Cities, June 15 and 16, 1978.

Hunker, Henry L., and Wright, Alfred J. *Factors of Industrial Location in Ohio.* Columbus, Ohio: Bureau of Business Research, Ohio State University, 1963.

Jacobs, D. *Business Loan Costs and Bank Market Structures.* National Bureau of Economic Research, 1971.

Jusenius, Carol L., and Ledebur, Larry. "The Migration of Firms and Workers in Ohio, 1970-75." A Great Lakes Regional Research Report. Columbus, Ohio: Academy for Contemporary Problems, 1978.

Katzman, M., and Daniels, B. "Development Incentives to Induce Efficiencies in Capital Markets." Prepared for the New England Regional Commission and the International Center of New England, Inc. (Revised) ed. June 1976.

Kelly, Eamar. "Development Banking." In *Mobilizing Capital for Economic Development,* edited by Peter J. Bearse. Princeton, N.J.: Center for New Jersey Affairs, Woodrow Wilson School for Public and International Affairs. Aug. 1978. Pp. 248-50.

Kemper, Peter. "The Location Decision of Manufacturing Firms within the New York Metropolitan Area." Ph.D. dissertation, Yale University, 1973.

Kieschnick, M., and Daniels, B. "Preliminary Research on Capital Markets and Economic Development." National Rural Center, May 1978.

Knight, Kenneth E., and Dorsey, Terry. "Capital Problems in Minority Business Development: A Critical Analysis." *American Economic Review* 66, no. 2 (May 1976): 328–31.

Kraft, G., Williams, A., Kaler, J., and Meyer, J. "On the Definition of a Depressed Area." In: *Essays in Regional Economics*, edited by J. Kain and J. Meyer. Cambridge, Mass.: Harvard University Press, 1971. Pp. 58–104.

Leone, Robert. "The Location of Manufacturing Activity in the New York Metropolitan Area." Ph.D. dissertation, Yale University, 1971.

Levenson, Albert M. "Interest Rate and Cost Differentials in Bank Lending to Small and Large Business." *Review of Economics and Statistics* 44, (May 1962): 190-97.

Mandell, Lewis. *Industrial Location Decisions: Detroit Compared with Atlanta And Chicago.* New York: Praeger Publishers, 1975.

Marcus, Bruce. "Economic Development and the Development Bank—A Different View." *Mobilizing Capital for Economic Development,* edited by Peter J. Bearse. Princeton, N.J.: Center for New Jersey Affairs, Woodrow Wilson School for Public and International Affairs, Aug. 1978. Pp. 269-91.

McCall, A., and Peterson, M. "The Impact of DeNovo Commercial Bank Entry." *Journal of Finance,* 32, no. 5 (Dec. 1977): 1587-1604.

Meadows, George Richard, and Call, Steven T. "Combining Housing Market and Resident Attitudes in Planning Urban Revitalization." *Journal of American Institute of Planners* 44, no. 3 (July 1978): 297-305.

Michelson, Stephan. "Community Based Development in Urban Areas." In *Central City Economic Development.* Papers and speeches from a conference held at State University of New York at Binghamton, Oct. 17-18, 1977. Center for Social Analysis, State University of New York at Binghamton, June 1978.

Miller, Judith. "U.S. Move Blocks Aid to Chrysler." *New York Times,* Feb. 3, 1979. Pp. 25 and 29.

Mitrisin, John. "Emergency Federal Financial Assistance to Private Enterprise: A Selective Examination of Past Loan and Loan Guarantee Programs of the Federal Government." Congressional Research Service, Nov. 29, 1974.

Nathan, Richard P., and Adams, Charles. "Understanding Central City Hardship." *Political Science Quarterly* 91, no 1 (Spring 1976): 47-62.

———. and Dommel, Paul R. "The Cities." In *Setting National Priorities: The 1978 Budget,* edited by Joseph A. Pechma. Washington, D.C.: Brookings Institution, 1977. Pp. 293-316.

National Tax Association Committee on International Fiscal Relations. "Property Taxation and Interstate Competition for Industry." 1967.

New York Stock Exchange. *The Capital Needs and Savings Potential of the U.S. Economy: Projections through 1985.* New York Stock Exchange, 1974.

Parshall, William. "Institutional Innovations for Mobilizing Capital: The National Development Bank." In: *Mobilizing Capital for Economic Development,* edited by Peter J. Bearse. Princeton, N.J.: Center for New Jersey Affairs,

Woodrow Wilson School for Public and International Affairs, Aug. 1978. Pp. 292-354.

President's Urban and Regional Policy Group. "Cities and People in Distress: National Urban Policy Discussion Draft." Washington, D.C., Nov. 1977.

Quante, Wolfgang. *The Exodus of Corporate Headquarters from New York City.* New York: Praeger Publishers, 1976.

Schmenner, Roger W. "City Taxes and Industrial Location." Ph.D. dissertation. Yale University, 1972.

———. "The Manufacturing Location Decision: Evidence from Cincinnati and New England." Research report prepared for Economic Development Administration, Mar. 1978.

———. "Urban Industrial Location: An Evolutionary Model." *Journal of Regional Science* 17, no. 2 (Aug. 1977): 179-94.

Shaul, Marnie. *Capital Shortages the Next Decade: An Assessment.* Public Finance Series no. 2. Columbus, Ohio: Academy for Contemporary Problems, 1977.

———. "Availability of Capital for Investment in the Great Lakes." (Working Draft). Academy for Contemporary Problems, Mar. 24, 1978.

Sinai, A., and Brinner, R. *The Capital Shortage: Near-term Outlook and Long-term Prospects.* Lexington, Mass.: Data Resources, 1975. (Economic Studies No. 18).

Smith, Edward K. "A Proposal for a Development Bank for the United States." Discussion paper for ad hoc advisory group meeting, U.S. Department of Commerce, Economic Development Administration, Mar. 3, 1977. OER 7-22518.

Straszheim, Mahlon R. "An Introduction and Overview of Regional Money Capital Markets." In: *Essays in Regional Economics,* edited by John F. Kain and John R. Meyer. Cambridge, Mass.: Harvard University Press, 1971. Pp. 218-39.

Struyk, Raymond J. "Empirical Foundations for Modeling Urban Industrial Location." *Journal of the American Institute of Planners* 42, (Apr. 1976): 165-73.

———. and James, Franklin J. *Intrametropolitan Industrial Location.* Lexington, Mass.: Lexington Books, 1975.

Sullivan, Timothy G. "The Cost of Capital and the Market Power of Firms." *Review of Economics and Statistics* 60. no. 2 (May 1978): 209-17.

Tassey, Gregory. "The Effectiveness of Venture Capital Markets in the U.S. Economy." *Public Policy* 25, no. 4 (Fall 1977): 479-97.

U.S. Congress. House Committee on Banking, Finance and Urban Affairs. Subcommittee on Economic Stabilization. "To Establish a National Development Bank." Aug. 1 and 2, 1978.

———. Subcommittee on the City. "City Need and the Responsiveness of Federal Grants Programs." Washington, D.C.: Government Printing Office 1978.

———. Subcommittee on the City. "Large Corporations and Urban Employment." Washington, D.C.: Government Printing Office, Feb. 1978.

U.S. Congress. Joint Economic Committee. Subcommittee on Fiscal and Governmental Policy. "Keeping Business in the City." Hearings, Mar. 6 and 7, 1978.

———. Subcommittee on Fiscal and Intergovernmental Policy. "Central City Business—Plans and Problems." Washington, D.C.: Government Printing Office., Jan. 1979.

U.S. Department of Housing and Urban Development. "The Urban Development Bank: Options for Discussion." Sept. 18, 1977.

U.S. Department of the Treasury. "The Proposed Urban Development Bank." Memorandum, Sept. 8, 1977.

U.S. General Accounting Office. "Legislation Needed to Establish Specific Loan Guarantee Limits for the Economic Development Administration." FGMSD-78-62, Washington, D.C., Jan. 5, 1979.

Williamson, Harold F., Jr. "An Empirical Analysis of the Movement of Manufacturing Firms in the Chicago Metropolitan Area." Ph.D. dissertation, Yale University, 1969.

AN EVALUATION OF THE RECONSTRUCTION FINANCE CORPORATION WITH IMPLICATIONS FOR CURRENT CAPITAL NEEDS OF THE STEEL INDUSTRY

James M. Bickley

INTRODUCTION

Secular shifts in the relative importance of different sectors of the economy have occurred in the past and will continue to take place. Initially, our economy was primarily agrarian, but then manufacturing grew and supplanted farming as the major source of employment. Presently, the service sector is expanding at the expense of both agriculture and manufacturing. Numerous mature industries, such as railroads, automobile production, shipbuilding, and steel manufacturing, are on the relative decline because of foreign competition, shifting consumer preferences, varying resource prices, and changing technology. For example, the American steel industry is losing its market share to foreign competitors who are undercutting U.S. prices. In addition, the relative importance of steel is diminishing as other materials, such as aluminum and plastics, are substituted for steel.

These long-term changes have been accentuated by current economic conditions. The sustained increase in consumer prices over the past ten years has created inflationary expectations. The general public has responded by decreasing its saving rate, which has contributed to a lower rate of capital accumulation. The high cost and limited availability of funds have encouraged some declining industries to seek federal assistance. It has been suggested that the U.S. government start a federal financial intermediary modeled after the old Reconstruction Finance Corporation (RFC). The financial intermediary would be designed to forestall the continuing decline of mature American industries by providing loan guarantees.

The next section establishes a framework to determine the relevance of the old RFC to current capital needs in the steel industry. First, the rationale for starting the RFC is explained by placing the corporation in historical context and describing prior major federal credit programs. Second, the RFC's function in macroeconomic stabilization and resource allocation is considered. Third, these two functions of the corporation are indicated by examining the major sectors of the economy that received RFC credit. Fourth, RFC's accomplishments, including its default level, are evaluated. Fifth, the economic and political reasons for the termination of the RFC are presented, including the primary justification that changed economic conditions no longer warranted the continued operation of the corporation. The third section critically evaluates the applicability of the old RFC to present capital requirements of the steel industry by using the analytical framework earlier developed. Appendix A describes the economic conditions in the 1920s and 1930s and federal credit corporations preceding the RFC. Appendix B presents details of RFC's program, which includes financing, organization, administrative problems, and management.

This brief study demonstrates that the RFC was established to help revive the U.S. economy. During World War II the corporation served an important role in reallocating resources into defense production. Both major functions are inconsistent with providing support to a mature industry. However, the concept of an "emergency finance corporation" that would grant aid to firms or industries on a case-by-case basis may be relevant. Before aid is provided, the total costs of assistance should be critically compared with the aggregate benefits.

EVALUATION OF THE RECONSTRUCTION FINANCE CORPORATION

ECONOMIC RATIONALE FOR RFC

In order to understand the reasons for the establishment of the RFC, a brief description of the economic conditions and prior federal credit corporations is essential.[1] During the 1920s the economy was prosperous, with low unemployment, stable prices, and sustained economic growth. The total or aggregate demand for output suddenly slumped in the late 1920s, however, and this slump resulted in the Great Depression. The early 1930s were a period of falling prices, rising unemployment, declining international trade, and diminishing gross national product (GNP). The widespread collapse of banks caused a sharp contraction of the money supply and reduced credit availability, exacerbating deflationary conditions.

The depressed economy caused some private and public interest in reestablishing the War Finance Corporation (WFC). The WFC had been founded in 1918 to strengthen private capital markets and grant credit for defense industries. During the 1920–22 recession the WFC was changed into an emergency loan operation with authority to provide loans to exporters, farmers, and financial institutions giving agricultural loans. Rather than revive the WFC, however, the federal government first attempted to revive the economy by creating a private $500 million credit pool to assist commercial banks that had liquidity problems. Because the private loan plan failed to provide sufficient credit support, the federal government finally established the Reconstruction Finance Corporation (RFC), which was modeled after the WFC.

FUNCTIONS OF RFC

The objectives of a government program are classified in three distinct categories:

1. *Allocation* concerns the process by which total resource use is divided among different goods and services, that is, the composition of total output.
2. *Distribution* refers to adjusting the distribution of income and wealth to assure conformity with what society considers to be a "fair" state.
3. *Stabilization* is the use of a policy tool to promote full employment, price stability, economic growth, and balance-of-payment equilibrium.

At first the RFC was only concerned with stabilization—more specifically, returning the economy to full employment. In signing the Reconstruction Finance Corporation Act, President Herbert Hoover stated, "Its purpose is to stop deflation in agriculture and industry and thus to increase employment by the restoration of men to their normal jobs."[2] Since the downturn was believed temporary, the RFC was able to make loans only during the first two years, and all funds had to be repaid within ten years.

During 1932 most RFC loans were given to financial institutions, agricultural credit intermediaries, and railroads. The financial institutions were considered vital in providing a credit flow to private businesses. The railroad industry was also crucial because it was the primary form of intercity freight transportation. The decline in aggregate demand was so huge, however, that RFC operations were too limited to generate an economic recovery. Nevertheless, the corporation's lending activities served an important cushioning role and thus helped prevent a further decline in real GNP.

During 1933 and 1934, the new Roosevelt Administration raised RFC funding. Financial institutions, agricultural financing institutions, and railroads received most of the support. The corporation's lending was drastically curtailed from 1935 to 1939, even though the Great Depression continued. The reduced funding resulted from the development of Federal Deposit Insurance Corporation insurance, the establishment of such federal programs as unemployment compensation and work relief, and a limited economic upturn. Exhibit 9 also shows the relative increase in loans to business enterprises and public agencies. The Roosevelt Administration pursued limited distributional goals by attempting to provide relatively more credit for smaller firms and the poor, while it imposed a ceiling on the earnings of top executives of corporations receiving loans.

The New Deal economic policies failed to provide sufficient stimulus for the system to rebound. U.S. unemployment was extremely high throughout the 1930s and only reached politically acceptable levels after World War II had commenced. The deficiency in aggregate demand was so enormous during the Great Depression that the correct federal fiscal policy was to raise government spending drastically and to lower tax rates sharply. In addition, an expansion by the Federal Reserve of the money supply was needed to prevent the collapse of much of the U.S. banking system and the subsequent reduction in both credit availability and buying power.

The lack of understanding of the national economic system, that is, of macroeconomics, impeded government actions necessary to effect an economic recovery. For example, Roosevelt felt in the summer of 1937 that it would be politically popular to balance the federal budget even though unemployment averaged 14.3 percent for that year. Hence, he proceeded to reduce spending on public works and raised tax rates. In October 1937 Roosevelt ordered Jesse Jones, director of RFC, to stop all lending, even though RFC loans did not appear in the budget. The result of these policies was an economic contraction and a subsequent rise in the unemployment rate to 19 percent in 1938.[3]

Although the RFC is known primarily for its operations during the Great Depression, it played its major funding role during World War II. From 1940 through 1945, 80 percent of RFC loans were for defense-related activities, and most of the remaining 20 percent were for business enterprises, as shown in Exhibit 9. Over one-half of all RFC financing took place during World War II. Defense subsidiaries helped construct and equip war plants, purchase and stockpile strategic materials, manufacture arms, and even insure property against damage from military conflict. As shown in Exhibit 9, RFC's total employment rose substantially during World War II and reached a peak in 1945. Workers assigned duties with the corporation's defense subsidiaries were considered to be RFC employees.

EXHIBIT 9
GRAPHIC SUMMARY OF RFC ACTIVITY

GRAPH 1
LOANS AND INVESTMENTS AUTHORIZED, 1932-1939

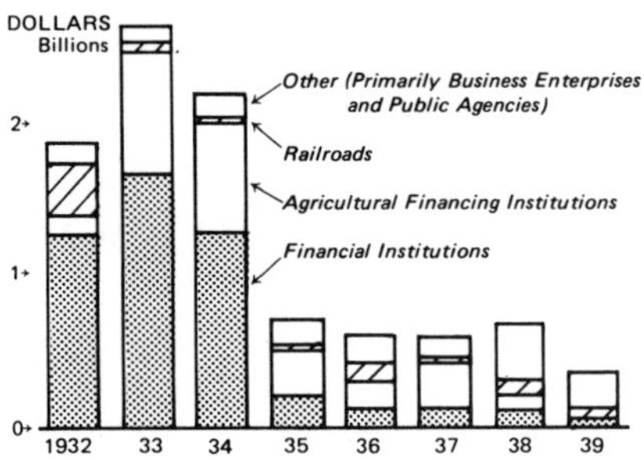

GRAPH 2
LOANS AND INVESTMENTS AUTHORIZED, 1940-1945

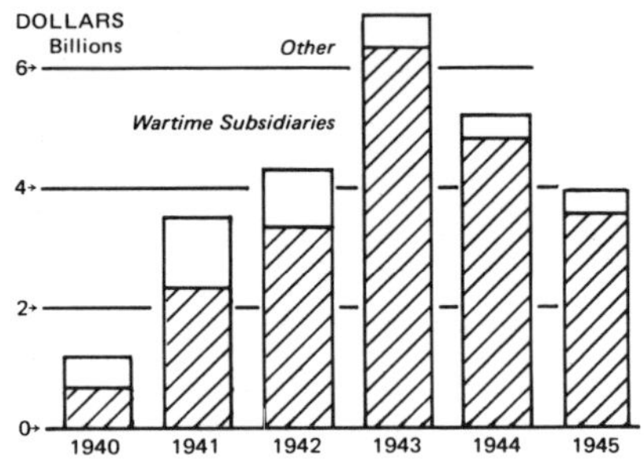

GRAPH 3
RFC EMPLOYMENT (As of June 30, 1935-1956)

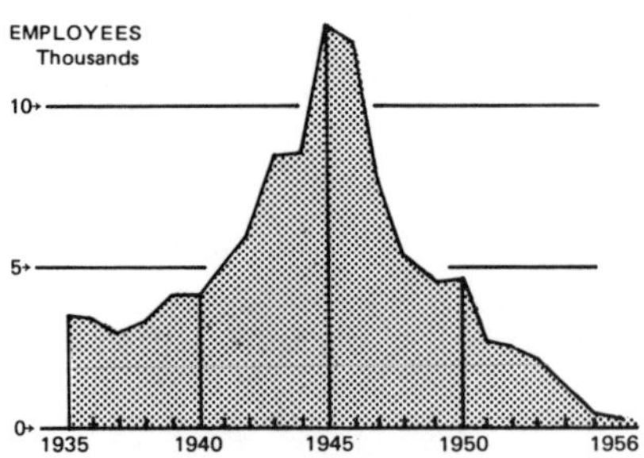

GRAPH 4
LOANS AND INVESTMENTS AUTHORIZED, 1946-1953

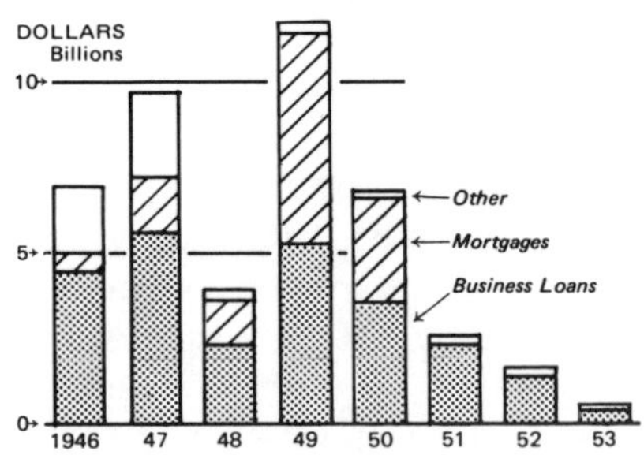

Source: Secretary of the Treasury, *Final Report of the Reconstruction Finance Corporation* (Washington, D.C.: Govt. Print. Off, 1959).

After World War II, RFC's lending was sharply curtailed and its wartime subsidiaries sold. Most of the corporation's postwar credit was for mortgages or business loans, as shown in Exhibit 9. The Federal National Mortgage Association, the Export-Import Bank, and the Small Business Administration evolved from the RFC. The corporation discontinued making new loans in June 1954 and liquidated outstanding loans by 1957.

MAJOR ECONOMIC SECTORS RECEIVING RFC LOANS

In evaluating the RFC it is important to understand the scope of its operations, which eventually became more varied and broad. Some sectors first received limited credit, whereas the total level of RFC operations was curtailed during the second half of the Great Depression, while other industries were allocated loans during World War II. Hence, the corporation did not play a significant peacetime resource-allocation role. Both the stabilizing and wartime allocative functions of the RFC are evidenced by the types of industries selected for assistance. The eight major economic sectors receiving RFC loans were banks and other financial intermediaries, railroads, agricuture, commercial and industrial businesses, mortgages, public agencies, national-defense industries, and miscellaneous loans consisting of several small categories.

The original RFC Act allowed insolvent banks and trust companies to borrow funds to assist them in reorganization. Later the corporation was able to provide credit to any bank on the recommendation of the U.S. Treasury. Eventually, the RFC was able to loan money to most kinds of financial intermediaries including insurance companies, building and loan associations, mortgage companies, and agricultural lending institutions. Many financial institutions were saved from bankruptcy by RFC assistance.

The railroad industry was particularly damaged by the Great Depression because vigorous competition with the trucking industry had developed. Furthermore, a high percentage of total railroad costs are fixed, that is, they cannot be reduced if demand for railroad service declines. Yet, because railroads played a crucial transportation role in the economy, the federal government had to ensure that the railroad system operated efficiently. Consequently, railroad credit assistance was specifically mentioned in the original RFC legislation.[4]

Regional agricultural credit corporations were established by the initial RFC law to provide loans to farmers. In 1933 the RFC was authorized to make funds available to joint-stock land banks, and in 1936 the corporation was directed to funnel monies into the Commodity Credit Corporation, which made agricultural loans. Also in 1936 the RFC was authorized to lend funds to the Rural Electrification Administration to make loans available for rural electrical-power projects. In 1941 the RFC was empowered to advance credit to tenant farmers so that they could acquire land.

In 1934 the RFC was authorized to make business loans provided that the firms could not obtain bank loans at the prevailing rate and that the loans were "adequately secured." The maximum term was five years and the ceiling amount to any borrower was $500,000. In 1935 the term "adequately secured" was changed to the less restrictive phrase, "so secured as reasonably to assure repayment." The five-year maturity limit was replaced with a deadline of January 31, 1945, and the ceiling on the amount obtainable by any single borrower was eliminated. In 1938 the risk clause was further loosened by restating it, "of such sound value, or so secured, as reasonably to assure retirement or repayment." In 1940 the maturity deadline was extended until January 31, 1955.[5]

From 1932 to 1934 several RFC Act amendments authorized the lending of funds for home mortgages. In 1935 the RFC was given the power to subscribe to the capital stock of mortgage loan companies in order to help in the reestablishment of a normal mortgage market. The corporation later set up two mortgage subsidiaries: the RFC Mortgage Company and the Federal National Mortgage Association (FNMA). From 1935 to 1947 the RFC Mortgage Corporation provided funds for 103,525 loans worth $660,901,581, and from 1938 to 1950 the FNMA authorized the purchase of 414,449 mortgages valued at $3,084,211,324.[6]

The original legislation empowered the RFC to make loans or purchase securities for self-liquidating public projects. The act specifically mentioned public housing corporations, bridge construction, tunnel construction, and natural-resource development projects. Later, the corporation was authorized to finance federal, state, and municipal projects and irrigation districts. From 1934 to 1941 the corporation made loans to the Public Works Administration to reduce the unemployment rate. Finally, between 1935 and 1947 the RFC was authorized to advance monies to public school districts to enable them to refinance debt.[7]

During World War II the RFC played an important role in shifting resources from civilian output to military production. Subsidiary corporations were formed to funnel credit into various war-related needs. The Defense Plant Corporation, an RFC subsidiary, constructed and equipped more than 2,300 defense plants. After their completion these facilities were leased to private firms for a fixed charge or for a fee based on production volume, dollar sales, or profits. By the end of World War II the federal government obtained a dominant position in numerous major industries, such as shipping, nonferrous metals, machine tools, synthetic rubber, and aircraft production. Another RFC wartime subsidiary was the Defense Supplies Corporation, which purchased and stockpiled commodities essential to the war effort and dispensed subsidies to stabilize consumer prices. Other defense subsidiaries stockpiled strategic metals, insured property against damage from military conflict, purchased war materials overseas to deny them to the enemy, acquired natural rubber abroad, and purchased oil products overseas.

Finally, the RFC loaned funds for several less costly purposes. In 1932 the corporation was authorized to provide some monies to states to assist the unemployed. In 1940 the RFC was empowered to provide credit to the Export-Import Bank to assist in the economic development of countries in the Western Hemisphere. In 1941 the corporation was authorized to make loans to foreign countries, and it eventually provided credit to such countries as Great Britain, Greece, Turkey, the Philippines, and Nationalist China.[8]

RFC'S ACCOMPLISHMENTS AND DEFAULT LEVEL

The RFC played an important stabilization role in the early part of the Great Depression, from 1932 to 1934. Numerous financial institutions and railroads continued to operate because of RFC assistance. Hence, many borrowers had access to credit, and the national transportation system was not disrupted. Agricultural loans allowed many farmers to avoid foreclosure and lessened the reduction in farm income. Most observers believe that the decline in real gross national product and the rise in unemployment would have been significantly worse without the RFC, but the corporation served a cushioning rather than a corrective role.

RFC's effectiveness from 1935 to 1939 was reduced because the corporation's funding was limited compared to the deficiency in aggregate demand. During World War II the RFC was useful as a powerful allocative tool in shifting resources from civilian production to the defense sector. In the postwar period the corporation was unimportant as a mechanism for macroeconomic stabilization because the level of aggregate demand was usually excessive.

The RFC contributed to a revolution in U.S. housing finance by providing long-term mortgages through the Federal National Mortgage Association. Prior to the Great Depression, home mortgages were usually intermediate-term loans with large required down payments. Consequently, only one third of U.S. families owned their living quarters in 1929, although now two-thirds of all families are homeowners.

Both the Small Business Administration (SBA) and the Export-Import Bank evolved from the RFC. The SBA provides direct loans and loan guarantees to small businesses to assist them in competing with larger firms. the justification is that smaller concerns do not have "fair" access to financial capital and, furthermore, the U.S. government should provide "seed" money to start new enterprises that will expand employment. The Export-Import Bank provides loan guarantees to exporters of U.S. products, which results in lower prices for foreign buyers of American products. The role and value of the SBA and the Export-Import Bank are both controversial.

Considering the unstable economic conditions under which the RFC operated, its loan default rate was very low. All of the $3.1 billion borrowed from the public was repaid, but of the $51.3 billion borrowed from the U.S. Treasury, $12.85 billion was canceled. More than $9.3 billion of canceled loans, however, were unrecovered costs of national defense, war, and reconversion. These defense-related losses were anticipated and were primarily incurred by defense subsidiary corporations.

REASONS FOR RFC TERMINATION

The Small Business Act of 1953 (P.L. 83-163, approved July 30, 1953) provided for the end of the Reconstruction Finance Corporation and the establishment of the Small Business Administration. Earlier, the Export-Import Bank and the Federal National Mortgage Association had evolved out of the RFC. The operations of the corporation actually ceased on June 30, 1954, and by 1957 almost all remaining RFC loans had been liquidated.

Of the many arguments for terminating the RFC, the most important concerned changed economic conditions. The corporation had been established in 1932 to help the nation recover from the Great Depression, but in 1953 the economy was prosperous. There was public apprehension about inflation, and most economists felt that the lending operations of the RFC would aggravate inflation by raising aggregate demand. In addition, free-market advocates asserted that the private financial markets allocated capital more efficiently than a governmental agency. Furthermore, critics charged that the RFC was involved in numerous cases of political favoritism and even some instances of corruption.[9] Finally, discontinuing the corporation was supported by many leading fiscal experts, including Jesse Jones, former administrator of the RFC; Herbert Hoover, former U.S. president and chairman of the Hoover Commission on Organization of the Executive Branch of the government; Senator Harry F. Byrd; and Marriner S. Eccles, former chairman of the Federal Reserve Board.

IMPLICATIONS OF THE RFC TO CURRENT CAPITAL NEEDS OF THE STEEL INDUSTRY

In recent years the U.S. steel industry has faced vigorous foreign competition, which has contributed to a lower rate of return on some facilities. Furthermore, many steel users are shifting to substitute materials, such as aluminum and plastics, reducing the growth in steel demand. The seventeen largest domestic steel firms averaged only 7.05 percent after-tax return on invested capital during the first nine months of 1979.[10] The companies' low earnings are insufficient to modernize or replace existing plant and equipment. The U.S. steel industry is a classic example of a mature or declining industry; consequently, it must contend with a low profit margin unless federal assistance is forthcoming. Steel executives and labor leaders are seeking federal assistance, which could consist of tariff protection, import quotas, tax law preferences, an easing of pollution-control standards, and loan guarantees. The industry has already received some tariff protection under a complicated "trigger price" system, and the U.S. government has relaxed some of the more rigorous air-quality control standards.

At present five U.S. steel companies are receiving approximately $365 million in 90 percent federal loan guarantees from the Economic Development Administration. Ironically, Lukens Steel filed suit to prevent Phoenix Steel from obtaining a federal loan guarantee, claiming that Phoenix Steel would receive an "unlawful" competitive advantage. On January 10, 1980, a federal judge ruled that the loan guarantee was legal, although Lukens Steel is considering appealing the decision.[11] Currently, steel-industry supporters are actively seeking an expansion of federal loan guarantees and even an examination of the feasibility of reestablishing the old Reconstruction Finance Corporation.

The justification for creating the RFC was macroeconomic stabilization; more specifically, the federal government wanted to reduce unemployment, stabilize prices, and encourage economic growth. The corporation was not created to assist any particular industry but rather to aid the entire economy. Initially, most RFC loans went into financial intermediaries and railroads because their economic revitalization would bolster the whole economic system. In the second half of the Great Depression, more general business loans were made, but all major economic sectors were eligible for this assistance. Furthermore, these funds were advanced in an attempt to return the economy to a full-employment state. Today, our economy has only 6.2 percent unemployment but double-digit inflation.

During World War II, the RFC served an important allocative function by providing funds to the defense sector. War-related industries, including steel, obtained extensive RFC credit; however, the corporation's objective was not to subsidize a monetarily weak industry but rather to assist the nation in winning an armed struggle. Today, this country is not actively engaged in a military conflict, and our steel industry already has much idle capacity.

After World War II, RFC's lending operations were reduced and eventually terminated in 1954. Critics argued that the RFC was less efficient in allocating credit than the private market, and economic stimulus was no longer necessary because prosperity had resumed. The primary accomplishments of the RFC were cushioning the economic downturn in the early 1930s and efficiently shifting resources to defense needs during World War II.

In summary, the reason for the establishment, purpose, accomplishments, and termination of the old RFC are inconsistent with future steel-industry loan guarantees. In other words, assisting the U.S. steel industry by establishing a government credit corporation modeled after the old RFC may not be appropriate. An entirely new public finance organization, such as an Emergency Finance Bank, would be necessary in order to assist large firms or industries on a case-by-case basis.

A federal loan guarantee provides a recipient with the lowest cost funds but requires other borrowers to pay higher interest rates. In addition, some marginal borrowers may be "crowded out," that is, unable to obtain credit. Hence, there are substantial social and economic costs resulting from the granting of a loan guarantee. The U.S. steel industry has three potentially valid claims for federal loan guarantees.

First, domestic producers claim that they are facing unfair competition from foreign firms. This unfair competition could involve dumping, that is, a foreign firm's charging a lower price in the United States than in its home market. Another form of unfair competition concerns a foreign company's receiving a government subsidy that reduces its production costs. Thus, the subsidized foreign firm can charge lower prices on its output, which will allow it to increase its exports. If a subsidized foreign commodity is permitted to be freely sold in the United States, then our domestic industry may suffer lower profits, lost sales, and a reduction in employment.

Currently, a producer that believes it is facing such unfair competition may take legal action. Any firm or industry that claims that it is being damaged may file a petition with the Department of Commerce. Then the Department of Commerce conducts an investigation to determine the existence and amount of the unfairly competitive practice. The U.S. International Trade Commission undertakes a parallel investigation to decide whether domestic producers are being injured by unfair competition.

If both investigations are affirmative, then the Department of Commerce levies compensatory (antidumping or countervailing) duties to eliminate the unfair price differential of the imported product. Hence, any domestic firm or industry presently has legal recourse if it is being injured by either dumping or subsidized foreign exports.

An additional policy consideration is important regarding unfair import competition. Though such practices may impose costs on the steel producers, they also yield benefits in the form of lower prices provided to American purchasers of the product.

Second, foreign steel sources may not be dependable during periods of worldwide prosperity or war. If there is a strong international economic expansion and a steel shortage occurs, foreign producers may give priority to domestic needs over export demand. Conceivably, an international steel cartel could organize and collectively reduce output to force up prices. In this case U.S. steel users could find their access to foreign steel curtailed, reducing their ability to produce goods and services. Furthermore, overseas sources may be unavailable for U.S. defense needs. A supplying nation may want to avoid being drawn into a conflict, sympathize with the enemy, possess steel facilities destroyed by combat, or have its steel shipments blocked by naval action. The probability and costs of a supply disruption must be compared with the expense of government assistance.

Third, the social costs of closing down steel facilities will fall disproportionately on certain states, regions, and groups. These social costs, such as unemployment, crime, community disruption, and emotional stress, may be so high that it might be appropriate to provide some public support to the steel industry. Other public policies to soften the dislocations of a declining industry could be used in conjunction with or possibly in place of direct government assistance to the industry. Examples of these other government policies are retraining the unemployed, relocating workers, and providing information about available job openings.

The benefits of any program should be carefully weighed against the costs. Different methods of achieving a given policy objective should be critically compared and long-term implications considered. It is beyond the scope of this chapter to evaluate the validity of arguments for public support for the U.S. steel industry.

APPENDIX A

ECONOMIC CONDITIONS IN THE 1920s AND 1930s AND FEDERAL CREDIT CORPORATIONS PRECEDING THE RFC

ECONOMIC CONDITIONS OF THE 1920s

After a sharp but brief recession in 1920-21, the U.S. economy expanded at a rapid pace during the 1920s with real gross national product rising an average annual rate of 4 percent. Also during this decade there was a large increase of 28 percent in real gross national product per man-hour because of improved equipment, capital accumulation, mass-production techniques, and scientific methods.[12]

Three primary sectors of the U.S. economy had dramatic growth, which sustained the 1920s' expansion. First, the automobile industry achieved an exceptional increase in production and accounted directly or indirectly for nearly 4 million jobs in a labor force of 45 million people in 1925. Such industries as concrete, oil, glass, and steel experienced strong demand as the result of the automotive revolution. Second, there was intense demand for electrical equipment and consumer durables because of the development of new products and the availability of electricity. Unit output of such appliances as electric irons, washing machines, refrigerators, and vacuum cleaners surged. Third, the capital-goods industry expanded because of demand for residential housing and high corporate outlays to augment productive capacity.[13]

THE GREAT DEPRESSION

Despite the prosperity of the 1920s, the U.S. economy possessed five major weaknesses, which eventually resulted in a collapse in output, employment, prices, and world trade. First, the residential construction industry slumped, owing to previous overbuilding and a decline in the birthrate. Second, corporate and household debt had reached unusually high levels in 1929, which meant that a large percentage of corporate and household income was needed merely to pay interest. These interest payments in turn sharply reduced demand for current output of both capital goods and consumer products. Third, exceptional increases in agricultural productivity because of improved scientific methods and better equipment raised output and lowered agricultural prices and incomes. Fourth, greater income inequality developed in the 1920s, reducing the momentum of consumer spending. Finally, European economic weakness and high tariffs worldwide disrupted international trade patterns and credit flows.[14]

Consequently, there was an unexpected and large reduction in the nation's total or aggregate demand for output by consumers and investors. From 1929 to 1933 real GNP fell by more than 30 percent, the unemployment rate rose from 3.2 percent to 24.9 percent, and industrial production declined by over 36 percent. The magnitude and duration of the slump were underestimated by both public officials and business leaders; hence, the initial phase of the Great Depression was met with by little federal action. The concept of fiscal policy, that is, changing tax rates and the level of government spending in order to stabilize the economy, had not been formulated.

The Federal Reserve System (Fed) had been established in 1913 to support the nation's banking system during periods of financial duress. The Fed was to provide elasticity to the money supply by rediscounting commercial paper during periods of monetary stringency. Once the Great Depression started, however, the Fed did little to prevent thousands of commercial banks from closing, which caused a dramatic reduction in the nation's money supply. Because there was no federal insurance on bank deposits, many customers withdrew their funds to avoid possible losses, which further reduced credit to businesses. The prevailing view of most economic historians is that the Federal Reserve System's inaction greatly contributed to the failure of the economy to rebound.

WAR FINANCE CORPORATION

As the Great Depression deepened, President Hoover was urged to reestablish the War Finance Corporation (WFC). When Hoover eventually set up the Reconstruction Finance Corporation, he modeled it after the WFC and specifically cited the operation of the WFC.

The WFC was started by Congress in 1918 to strengthen private capital markets and provide funds to war-related industries. Sectors receiving WFC loans included chemical production, railroads, public utilities, mining, and banking. Most WFC monies were loaned to commercial banks, which in turn provided credit to the war sector, but in certain situations funds were loaned directly to defense industries. The corporation's capital of $500 million was completely subscribed by the federal government, but during World War I only $67 million was actually loaned. During the 1920-22 recession Congress overrode a presidential veto and turned the WFC into an emergency loan corporation with power to grant loans to exporters, farmers, and financial intermediaries providing farm credit. In 1924 the corporation stopped making new loans and began liquidating, and by 1929 the initial $500 million was repaid as well as $64 million in net profits.[15]

NATIONAL CREDIT CORPORATION

In 1931 the federal government attempted to revive the economy by establishing a private $500 million credit pool to assist commercial banks with liquidity problems. The nation's lending bankers reluctantly agreed to support the private credit plan, but only under the condition that if the system failed the WFC would be revived. The private National Credit Corporation (NCC) was organized with the authority to issue $1 billion in debentures, with private banks purchasing $500 million of that total. The NCC officers were so skeptical of their organization's success, however, that they imposed stringent loan requirements to protect themselves. The NCC advanced loans on only 40 percent of the market value of collateral and accepted U.S. government securities only at 75 percent of market value. The U.S. economy was so depressed and the NCC operated on such a limited scale that a large number of additional banks failed, and gross national product continued to decline. Finally, the Reconstruction Finance Corporation was established with power to provide large direct loans to major corporations.[16]

APPENDIX B

RFC'S PROGRAM DETAIL

FINANCING THE RFC

Funding for the corporation was obtained from the sale of capital stock borrowing, net profits, and the sale of assets of terminated programs. The original RFC Act stated that $500 million in capital stock were to be purchased by the U.S. government. The RFC retired stock worth $175 million, $225 million, and $65 million in the years 1941, 1948, and 1957, respectively. The dominant method of financing was borrowing, with $51.3 billion borrowed from the public. Prior to June 30, 1948, all earnings from RFC operations were available for its own needs. After June 30, 1948, the corporation was required to make dividend payments on its accumulated net earnings to the U.S. Treasury.[17]

RFC'S ORGANIZATION

The RFC headquarters was located in Washington, D.C., and 31 loan agency offices were scattered across the country in order to be accessible to potential borrowers. Lending policies were developed in Washington and then implemented by the loan agency offices. The manager of each loan office was selected by the RFC Board of Directors or, after May 4, 1951, the RFC administration. In Washington responsibilities for lending operations were divided among subordinate units according to the types of loans.

Initially, the headquarters had to approve every loan, but later only large loans needed Washington's approval. As a general rule, if a direct business loan was under $100,000 or if the RFC participated with banks on a loan of less than $350,000, then Washington's acceptance was not required. Any loan rejected by a loan agency office was automatically sent to RFC headquarters with the denial justifications, but Washington could overturn the loan agency's negative decision.[18]

The corporation's administrative responsibilities relating to the national defense effort were handled primarily through wartime subsidiary corporations. Nevertheless, the supervisory role of the loan agencies substantially increased because war contracts had to be managed, war-plant rentals collected, and subsidy claims audited.

ADMINISTRATIVE PROBLEMS

The role of the RFC relative to other federal programs was never clearly delineated; consequently, overlapping duties with other federal agencies occurred. This overlapping resulted in some waste, confusion, and internal administrative conflict. Another administrative weakness was that the requirements for obtaining an RFC loan gradually became so loose and vague that subjective case-by-case decisions were often made. The probability of obtaining a loan often depended on political contacts, and unfortunately some credit may have been granted as compensation for political support.[19]

RFC'S MANAGEMENT

From February 1932 until May 1951, RFC was managed by a board of directors. At its inception the board consisted of seven members, including the chairman of the Federal Reserve Board of Governors, the secretary of the treasury, and the farm loan commissioner, as ex officio members. The other four members were appointed by the president with the advice and consent of the Senate. On August 1, 1932, by law the chairman of the Fed and the farm loan commissioner were replaced by two additional presidential appointees.[20]

On February 24, 1938, the board was reduced to five members, all appointed by the president with the advice and consent of the Senate. Not more than a simple majority could belong to any one political party, and at most one member could be appointed from any one Federal Reserve district. Terms of office and procedures for filling vacancies were changed occasionally over the life of the corporation. Initially, terms were for two years, but in May 1938 three-year staggered terms were implemented. If a vacancy occurred before a completed term, then the appointed replacement would complete only the remainder of that term. Before May 25, 1948, the board selected its own chairman, but after that date the president designated a member to serve as chairman for a period coextensive with his term.

In 1951 a reorganization of the RFC replaced the board of directors with an administrator and deputy administrator, and both were appointed by the president with the advice and consent of the Senate. The reorganization plan also established the RFC Loan Policy Board, which was empowered to determine general policies to evaluate financial-assistance applications. This board was composed of the administrator, deputy administrator, secretary of commerce, secretary of the treasury, and one presidential appointee selected with the advice and consent of the Senate. Finally, on June 30, 1954, the secretary of the treasury was assigned the responsibility for the liquidation of the remnants of the RFC.[21]

NOTES

1. More detailed descriptions are presented in Appendix A.
2. Secretary of the Treasury, *Final Report of the Reconstruction Finance Corporation* (Washington, Government Printing Office 1959), p. 1.

3. Jesse H. Jones and Edward Angly, *Fifty Billion Dollars, My Thirteen Years with the RFC (1932-1945)* (New York: Macmillan, 1951), pp. 266-67.

4. Herbert Spero, *Reconstruction Finance Corporation Loans to Railroads, 1932-37* (Boston: Bankers Publishing Co., 1939). pp. 12–15.

5. Secretary of the Treasury, p. 10.

6. Ibid.

7. Ibid., pp. 7-9.

8. Ibid., pp. 16-18.

9. U.S. Congress, Senate, Committee on Banking and Currency, Subcommittee on Reconstruction Finance Corporation, *Study of Reconstruction Finance Corporation and Proposed Amendment of RFC Act*. Senate Report no. 649. 82nd Congress, 1st session, (Washington, D.C. Government Printing Office, 1951), pp. 40-95.

10. "Steel: High Hopes for More U.S. Aid," *Business Week*, no. 2619, Jan. 14, 1980, pp. 96–97.

11. "Lukens Loses Its Suit to Deny Phoenix Steel Federal Loan Backing," *Wall Street Journal*, January 10, 1980, p. 35.

12. Harry N. Scheiber, Harold G. Vatter, and Harold Underwood Faulkner, *American Economic History*, 9th ed. (New York: Harper & Row, 1976), pp. 334–35.

13. Ibid, pp. 335–36.

14. Joseph S. Davis, *The World between the Wars, 1919–*39: *Economist's View*, (Baltimore, Md., The Johns Hopkins University Press, 1975), p. 112.

15. Paul Studenski and Herman E. Krooss, *Financial History of the United States*, (New York: McGraw-Hill, 1952), p. 32.

16. James Stuart Olson, *Herbert Hoover and the Reconstruction Finance Corporation, 1931–33*, pp. 27–32.

17. Secretary of the Treasury, pp. 33–43.

18. Ibid, pp. 28–29.

19. U.S. Congress. Senate. Committee on Money and Currency, p. 409.

20. Secretary of the Treasury, p. 25.

21. Ibid., p. 28.

BIBLIOGRAPHY

Culbertson, John M. *Money and Banking*. 2d ed. New York: McGraw-Hill, 1979.

Davis, Joseph S. *The World Between the Wars: 1919–39: Economist's View*. Baltimore, Md.: The Johns Hopkins University Press, 1975.

Doan, Michael. "An Aging Giant Tries to Regain Youthful Vigor." *U.S. News and World Report*, 38, no. 5, (Feb. 11, 1980): 68–70.

Heilbroner, Robert L., and Singer, Aaron. *The Economic Transformation of America*. New York: Harcourt, Brace, Jovanovich, 1977.

Herber, Bernard P. *Modern Public Finance*. 4th ed. Homewood, Ill.: Richard D. Irwin, 1979.

Jones, Jesse H., and Angly, Edward. *Fifty Billion Dollars, My Thirteen Years with the RFC (1932–45)*. New York: Macmillian, 1951.

"Lukens Loses Its Suit to Deny Phoenix Steel Federal Loan Backing." *Wall Street Journal*, Jan. 10, 1980, p. 35.

McConnell, Campbell R. *Economics*. 7th ed. New York: McGraw-Hill, 1978.

Musgrave, Richard A., and Musgrave, Peggy B. *Public Finance in Theory and Practice*. 2d ed. New York: McGraw-Hill, 1976.

Olson, James Stuart. *Herbert Hoover and the Reconstruction Finance Corporation, 1931–1933*. Ames, Iowa: Iowa State University Press, 1977.

Robertson, Ross M., and Walton, Gary M. *History of the American Economy*. 4th ed. New York: Harcourt, Brace, Jovanovich, 1979.

Sauliner, R. J.; Halcrow, Harold G.; and Jacoby, Neil H. *Federal Lending and Loan Insurance*. Princeton, N.J.: Princeton University Press, 1958.

Scheiber, Harry N.; Vatter, Harold G.; and Faulkner, Harold Underwood. *American Economic History*. 9th ed. New York: Harper and Row, 1976.

Shultz, William J., and Harriss, C. Lowell. *American Public Finance*. 6th ed. New York: Prentice-Hall, 1954.

Spencer, Milton H. *Contemporary Economics*. 2d ed. New York: Worth Publishers, 1974.

Spero, Herbert. *Reconstruction Finance Corporation Loans to the Railroads, 1932–1937*. Boston: Bankers Publishing Co., 1939.

"Steel: High Hopes for More U.S. Aid." *Business Week*, no. 2619, Jan. 14, 1980, pp. 93–100.

Studenski, Paul, and Krooss, Herman E. *Financial History of the United States*. New York: McGraw-Hill, 1952.

"Treasury Issues." *Wall Street Journal*, January 28, 1979, p. 30.

U.S. Congress. House. Committee on Banking, Finance and Urban Affairs. Subcommittee on Economic Stabilization. *Catalog of Federal Loan Guarantee Programs*. 95th Congress, 1st session. Washington, D.C.: Government Printing Office, 1977.

U.S. Congress. House. *Reconstruction Finance Corporation Act with Amendments*. Washington, D.C.: Government Printing Office, 1947.

U.S. Congress. Senate. Committee on Banking and Currency. Subcommittee on Reconstruction Finance Corporation. *Study of Reconstruction Finance Corporation and Proposed Amendment of RFC Act*. Senate Report no. 649. 82d Congress, 1st session. Washington, D.C.: Government Printing Office, 1951.

U.S. Congress. Senate. Committee on Money and Currency. *Hearings, Government Lending Agencies*. Washington, D.C.: Government Printing Office, 1953.

U.S. Congressional Budget Office. *Economic Conversion: What Should Be the Government's Role?* Washington, D.C.: Government Printing Office, 1980.

———. *Loan Guarantees: Current Concerns and Alternatives for Control*. Washington, D.C.: Government Printing Office, 1979.

U.S. Executive Office of the President. Office of Management and Budget. *The Budget of the United States Government*, 1981. Appendix. Washington, D.C.: Government Printing Office, 1980.

U.S. General Accounting Office. "A Methodology for Estimating Costs and Subsidies from Federal Credit Assistance Programs." Washington, D.C., exposure draft, July 17, 1979.

U.S. Library of Congress. Congressional Research Service. "A National Development Bank: Survey and Discussion of the Literature on Capital Shortages and Employment Changes in Distressed Areas." (Report no. 79-89 E) George R. Meadows and John Mitrisin.

———. "Large Loan Guarantee Programs Which Assist Government Entities and Private Corporations," John Mitrisin, Washington, Feb. 24, 1978 (CRS typed report) Updated, Charlotte Breckenridge, Oct. 22, 1979.

U.S. Secretary of the Treasury. *Final Report of the Reconstruction Finance Corporation*. Washington, D.C.: Government Printing Office, 1959.

U.S. Treasury Department. *Liquidation of Reconstruction Finance Corporation*. Washington, D.C.: Government Printing Office, 1958.

THE FISCAL IMPACT OF ECONOMIC-DEVELOPMENT PROGRAMS: CASE STUDIES OF THE LOCAL COST-REVENUE IMPLICATIONS OF HUD, EDA, AND FmHA PROJECTS

Robert W. Burchell
David Listokin

SUMMARY

1. Investments by the federal government in economic-development programs are intended to accomplish a number of objectives, of which the most important is the creation of jobs for structurally unemployed persons and the disadvantaged. However, one of the main thrusts of economic-development programs is to strengthen the revenue base of distressed communities.
2. This study presents a methodology for computing the fiscal impacts on local governments of projects assisted under federal economic-development programs. This methodology is applied on an exploratory basis in eleven case studies of assisted projects in New Jersey communities. Projects examined were aided under HUD's UDAG program; EDA's public-works, business-development, and Title IX programs; and FmHA's business and industrial loan program.
3. Due to the small sample of projects, and their concentration in a single state, they are not necessarily representative of the full range of federal economic-development efforts, nor are the results useful for comparing

the fiscal impacts of projects assisted under the various federal economic-development programs. Considerably more research would be needed to obtain definitive results.

4. In most cases, HUD, EDA, and FmHA-sponsored economic-development projects appear to have a significantly *positive* effect on the local fisc of the host community. Of eleven case studies of selected HUD, EDA, and FmHA nonresidential developments in seven very different New Jersey communities (growing/declining, metropolitan/nonmetropolitan, large/small, expansive/basic public service systems, etc.), ten demonstrated *primary* public-service revenue-to-cost ratios of at least 1.5 to 1. (The large majority of cases were found at ratios of 1.5 to 3.0 to 1.)
5. In examining *secondary* (growth-induced residential/nonresidential development) public-service demand/supply, revenue-cost relationships through altered fiscal flows from local, state, and federal revenue sources, they were found to be positive in eight of eleven cases.
6. Given definite thresholds of maximum direct servicing costs (costs do not vary directly with scale of facility), larger economic-development projects seemed more fiscally beneficial than did smaller ones.
7. From the results of a limited number of case analyses, economic-development programs appear most fiscally effective in larger, declining communities (excess capacity in an established service system), which are relatively poor (receive compounding benefits from additional school aid per newly attracted pupil), and whose local housing costs allow a share of the moderate-income labor force to reside within the community (dampening effect of school-aid loss due to tempered wealth increase of the community as a result of economic development).
8. Taking the possible secondary impacts of the projects into account, local revenue returns from economic-development activities compared to federal dollar outlays were positive in nine of eleven cases, typically at ratios of 1.0 to 3.0 to 1. This suggests that federal economic-development assistance may be a highly efficient form of fiscal assistance: that is, one dollar of federal economic-development assistance may generate more than one dollar of additional net revenues to recipient local governments.
9. The fiscal effects of economic development are an area of public policy that needs much more intense and long-term research. The case studies included here barely scratch the surface of the types of communities/projects that require detailed analyses before definitive statements can be made on the relationship between economic development and local fiscal stability.

INTRODUCTION

The purpose of the following analysis is to investigate the local fiscal implications of federal economic-development programs: to compare the costs incurred by the municipality in providing public services and other development accommodations to the revenues garnered as a result of development through the property tax, local income/sales taxes, and such other local revenues as user charges and miscellaneous revenues, as well as intergovernmental transfers from both the state and federal governments. Statements will then be made concerning (1) the federal and local costs versus benefits of urban and rural economic-development efforts, (2) the types of projects and the fiscal environments that tend to yield either the greatest or the least fiscal benefits, (3) the appropriateness of the structure and form of federal allocation programs, and (4) the capacity of current evaluation methods to accurately chart cost and revenue flows for a number of projects in a variety of settings.

This is an exploratory effort, and the focus will be on developing methods that could be used in the future by the federal government to assess the fiscal impacts of its economic development programs and by localities to estimate the fiscal advantages of particular projects. In order to test the methodology and to demonstrate its applications, eleven case studies were made of particular projects assisted under federal economic-development programs in a number of New Jersey communities. The results of the study of these eleven projects provide suggestive insight into the general nature of the fiscal impacts of economic-development projects and how these impacts compare with the costs to the federal government of the assistance provided to the projects. However, much more research is needed for definitive results to be obtained.

The projects to be studied have been drawn from selected economic-development efforts of the Department of Housing and Urban Development (HUD), the Economic Development Administration (EDA), and the Farmers Home Administration (FmHA). They represent a small, convenient sample of characteristic programs of these agencies. Municipalities of selected projects were visited for interviews with local city managers, economic-development directors, and municipal department heads to determine public-service extensions to as well as revenues generated by specific economic-development activities. In addition, project files were analyzed, and the projects themselves were visited to uncover any local revenue concessions made during development that allowed the projects to be more economically feasible, as well as to obtain information on the current status of the project and specific characteristics of its labor force. The results in no way permit a comparison of the effectiveness of the programs of the various agencies in providing fiscal assistance. Projects may not be representative of the projects that are assisted by the various agencies, and sample sizes are far too small to be meaningful.

The report that follows is organized into four sections:

I. Economic-Development Activities of Major Federal Agencies—Program Thrusts of HUD, EDA, and FmHA
II. Example Economic-Development Activities and Selection of Cases to be Studied.
III. Methods of Approach to Fiscal and Economic Impact Analysis—Conceptual and Technical Issues
IV. The Fiscal and Economic Impacts of Economic-Development Activities—Results of the Analyses/Implications for Policy

I. ECONOMIC-DEVELOPMENT ACTIVITIES OF MAJOR FEDERAL AGENCIES—PROGRAM THRUSTS OF HUD, EDA, AND FmHA

INTRODUCTION

The purpose of the following section is to discuss featured economic-development programs of the Department of Housing and Urban Development (HUD), the Economic Development Administration (EDA), and the Farmers Home Administration (FmHA) as a prelude to selecting representative projects for case analysis. For each of these agencies discussion will encompass: (1) authorization for and scope of the agency's activities, (2) locations and types of projects for which its resources are allocated, and (3) eligible applicants and procedures for application to the agency.

Generally speaking, the federal government is involved in economic development because private-sector investment is not occurring in targeted areas.[1]. Private sector-investment is not occurring because:

1. firms are unable to obtain credit from private lenders.
2. firms are deterred from locating in certain areas because of characteristics of these areas that reduce their competitiveness or profitability.[2]

Sustained and diversified private-sector investment is in the public interest because it:

1. strengthens the local tax base and promotes balanced community growth.
2. creates jobs and entrepreneurial opportunities for the resident labor force.
3. diversifies the local economy and thus dampens the potential for sole-source economic disaster (technological obsolescence, natural disaster, federal installation closings, etc.)
4. increases national productivity.

Because the federal government cannot directly remove many of the obstacles to private-sector investment, especially those resulting from the characteristics of the areas targeted for economic development, its economic-development incentives are limited. Most federal economic-development programs rely on capital and infrastructure incentives, consist of grants and direct and guaranteed loans to private firms or local governments to assist firms or to construct or rehabilitate infrastructure.[3]

The following section discusses the various incentives employed by those agencies charged with economic-development stimulation, as well as resource-allocation profiles of these agencies.

U.S. DEPARTMENT OF HOUSING AND URBAN DEVELOPMENT—URBAN DEVELOPMENT ACTION GRANT (UDAG) PROGRAM

AUTHORIZATION AND SCOPE

The purpose of the UDAG program is to revitalize distressed cities by providing public seed money to stimulate private redevelopment. Grants are available to distressed cities and urban counties for neighborhood, industrial, and commercial revitalization projects. The seed money from the public sector allows distressed cities to achieve a more competitive economic position to attract nonresidental development vis-à-vis growing, economically healthy localities.[4]

Authorized under the 1977 Housing and Community Development Act, during the first two years of the program (through FY 1979) UDAG presented to 382 cities 521 Action Grant project awards in the amount of $967 million. Under the UDAG program, cities or urban counties can use UDAG funds for a wide variety of purposes, including (1) the acquisition and development of land; (2) the acquisition, construction, and rehabilitation of public works or facilities, residential property, and commercial and industrial buildings; and (3) the provision of direct financial assistance to firms and nonprofit entities.[5]

LOCATION OF ACTION GRANTS AND APPLICABLE ACTIVITIES

Exhibit 10 provides an analysis of Action Grant activities since its inception in 1977. For the first two years of the program authorized budget levels were at the $400 million level; for FY 1980 the budget was increased to $675 million. The average grant per project for the first two years was approximately $1.7 million to $2 million.[6]

EXHIBIT 10

U.S. DEPARTMENT OF HOUSING AND URBAN DEVELOPMENT
URBAN DEVELOPMENT ACTION GRANT (UDAG) PROJECTS AND DOLLARS
BY CITY* TYPE AND FISCAL YEAR

Fiscal Year	Number of Projects	Percent of Projects	Action Grant Dollars ($000)	Percent of Action Grant Dollars	Action Grant Dollars per Project ($000)
All Cities					
Total	521	100.0%	$967,496	100.0%	$1,857
FY 1978	236	45.3	489,326	50.6	2,073
FY 1979	285	54.7	478,170	49.4	1,678
Metropolitan Cities					
Total	277	53.2%	$763,401	78.9%	$2,756
FY 1978	131	55.5	393,419	80.4	3,003
FY 1979	146	51.2	369,982	77.4	2,534
Small Cities					
Total	244	46.8%	$204,094	21.1%	$ 837
FY 1978	105	44.5	95,907	19.6	913
FY 1979	139	48.8	108,187	22.6	778

*Metropolitan City category includes urban counties.

Source: Data Systems and Statistics Division, Office of Management, Community Planning and Development (CPD), U.S. Department of Housing and Urban Development, Summer 1980.

Exhibit 10 also presents Urban Development Action grant activity (number of projects and total dollars) by type of city recipient. As is indicated, although the number of projects was distributed relatively evenly between small and metropolitan cities, nearly 75 percent of the Action Grant dollars went to the latter category of cities. Exhibit 11 indicates Action Grant activity by type of project, that is, industrial, commercial, and neighborhood. Whereas the number of projects is equally represented in the above three categories, the dollar amount invested favors commercial redevelopment by almost two to one over both industrial and neighborhood projects. When location of Action Grant projects (small city–metro city) is cross-tabulated with type of project, metro-city locations favor commercial and neighborhood projects, whereas small cities are the sites of extensive industrial redevelopment.[7]

EXHIBIT 11

U.S. DEPARTMENT OF HOUSING AND URBAN DEVELOPMENT
URBAN DEVELOPMENT ACTION GRANT (UDAG) PROJECTS AND DOLLARS—
ALL CITIES BY PROJECT TYPE AND FISCAL YEAR

Project Type/ Fiscal Year	Number of Projects	Percent of Projects	Action Grant Dollars ($000)	Percent of Action Grant Dollars	Action Grant Dollars Per Project ($000)
Industrial					
Total	185	35.5%	$235,887	24.4%	$1,275
FY 1978	85	36.0	115,573	23.6	1,360
FY 1979	100	35.1	120,314	25.2	1,203
Commercial					
Total	176	33.8%	$476,693	49.3%	$2,709
FY 1978	84	35.6	243,551	49.8	2,899
FY 1979	92	32.3	233,143	48.8	2,534
Neighborhood					
Total	160	30.7%	$254,915	26.3%	$1,593
FY 1978	67	28.4	130,202	26.6	1,943
FY 1979	93	32.6	124,713	26.0	1,341
All Projects					
Total	521	100.0%	$967,495	100.0%	$1,857
FY 1978	236	100.0	489,326	100.0	2,073
FY 1979	285	100.0	478,170	100.0	1,678

Source: Data Systems and Statistics Division, Office of Management, Community Planning and Development (CPD), U.S. Department of Housing and Urban Development, Summer 1980.

Approximately 65 percent of the UDAG projects and grant dollars are equally distributed between the Northeastern and North Central regions of the United States. The South follows at about two-thirds of the penetration rate of those regions, and the West trails at one-third the rate (see Exhibit 12). Finally, one-half of the UDAG projects are found in central cities, one-third in nonmetropolitan areas, and one-sixth in suburban areas.

PROCESS FOR APPLICATION

Urban Development Action Grant funds are targeted to cities or urban counties that meet minimum standards of distress as defined by several

EXHIBIT 12

U.S. DEPARTMENT OF HOUSING AND URBAN DEVELOPMENT
URBAN DEVELOPMENT ACTION GRANTS
BY REGION AND POPULATION SIZE

REGION

Region	Eligible Popu- lation	Percent Total Eligible Popu- lation	Number of Projects	Percent of Total Projects	Action Grant Dollars ($100)	Percent of Action Grant Dollars
Northeast	22,792,874	28.1%	179	34.4%	$305,405	31.6%
North Central	22,394,127	27.6	171	32.8	314,575	32.5
South	24,557,155	30.2	125	24.0	235,740	24.4
West	11,450,145	14.1	46	8.8	111,775	11.5
Total	81,194,301	100.0%	521	100.0%	$967,495	100.0%

POPULATION SIZE

Population Size	Number of Projects			Percent of Projects		
	Total	FY 1978	FY 1979	Total	FY 1978	FY 1979
Over 500,000	60	25	35	11.5%	10.5%	12.3%
250,000–500,000	63	26	37	12.1	11.0	13.0
100,000–249,999	64	30	34	12.3	12.7	11.9
50,000–99,999	67	34	33	12.9	14.4	11.6
25,000–49,999	61	33	28	11.7	14.0	9.8
10,000–24,999	70	32	38	13.4	13.6	13.3
Under 10,000	136	56	80	26.1	23.7	28.1
Total	521	236	285	100.0%	100.0%	100.0%

Source: Data Systems and Statistics Division, Office of Administration, Community Planning and Development (CPD), U.S. Department of Housing and Urban Development, Summer 1980.

variables: age of housing, per-capita income change, population/job decline, unemployment, poverty, and so on.

The major prerequisites to preliminary Urban Development Action Grant approval are:[8]

1. clear demonstration that the Action Grant is stimulating private development
2. a firm private commitment to develop the site subject only to the award of a UDAG
3. a firm financing commitment
4. a commitment for equity money, as appropriate
5. a commitment for any other public money required to complete the project
6. explanation of how the land is to be controlled
7. generally, that the grant must not cause relocation of jobs from one distressed metropolitan area to another.

The Action Grant process consists of six steps:[9]

1. City is designated as "distressed" based on Census and Labor statistics (334 metro cities or urban counties and 10,000 small cities are categorized as distressed),
2. City is determined eligible to apply by demonstrating results in providing equal opportunities in housing development and city employment to low/moderate-income persons,
3. An application containing the following information is received at the HUD area office containing:
    a. project description
    b. commitment to project
    c. identification of money sources—private and public
    d. description of prerequisite public expenditures
    e. estimate of new permanent jobs (as well as interim construction jobs)
    f. project schedule
    g. description of how land is to be controlled
    h. acknowledgment that, on award, the private firm will execute legally binding commitment
    i. written acknowledgment that "but for award" the firm would not proceed with the planned action.
4. Preliminary grant approval
5. Grant agreements between city/HUD and private business/HUD, which set forth conditions precedent to the release of grant funds
6. Funding—grant funds are released—no funds are released until private sector is legally bound to complete a development project.

UDAG grants contain no mandatory local public-sector matching requirements but definitely require firm and significant financial participation from the private sector. By regulation, UDAG requires private-to-public leveraging ratios of 2.5 to 1.0 and averages ratios of 5.8 to 1.0.[10] Federal funds cannot be drawn until the local recipient has secured legally binding commitments from private participants. Grants may be made to an initial grantee and then granted or loaned to others. Repayment can subsequently be used by initial grantee for other economic-development purposes.

U.S. DEPARTMENT OF COMMERCE—ECONOMIC DEVELOPMENT ADMINISTRATION (GRANTS/LOANS/ GUARANTEES)—AUTHORIZATION AND SCOPE

The Economic Development Administration has multiple programs with which to carry out its mission of stimulating lagging local economies in both urban and rural areas.[11] The main programs are grouped under the following three categories: *Business Development (loans and guarantees), Public Works (grants), and Economic Adjustment Assistance (grants).*Authorization for these activities originates in the Public Works and Economic Development Act of 1965, as amended. Cumulatively and currently, the largest program (dollars allocated) is Public Works, followed by the Business Development and the Economic Adjustment Assistance programs (see Exhibit 13).[12]

BUSINESS DEVELOPMENT LOANS AND GUARANTEES

The purpose of the Business Development Program is to support private investment in economically distressed places through the provision of direct loans and loan guarantees to private firms unable to obtain funds due to credit unavailability in specific locations.[13] Loans or guarantees may be made for fixed assets (land acquisition/improvement, machinery and equipment, construction and rehabilitation) or for working capital (including start-up and operating costs). Direct loans are at the federal borrowing rate; guarantees are linked to the market rate for a financial institution's preferred customers. Typical equity participation for both fixed assets and working capital is 15 percent; the term of the loan is twenty-five years or useful life for fixed assets; up to five years for working-capital loans. EDA requires that the requested financial assistance not be available from other sources on terms and conditions that would permit the accomplishment of the project.[14]

In FY 1979, EDA approved 160 direct Business Development loans for

EXHIBIT 13

ECONOMIC DEVELOPMENT ADMINISTRATION (EDA)—
SUMMARY OF EDA OBLIGATED PROJECTS BY PROGRAM

FY 1979 AND CUMULATIVE TO DATE*

	Public Works		Business Development			Technical Assistance	
	No. of Projects	Amount ($000)	No. of Projects	Loans ($000)	Guarantees ($000)	No. of Projects	Amount ($000)
FY 1979	350	239,488	222	132,002	417,079	362	32,943
Cumulative to Date	5,396	2,640,580	1,002	655,393	737,937	4,422	214,871

	Planning Grants		Economic Adjustment		State Totals	
	No. of Projects	Amount ($000)	No. of Projects	Amount ($000)	No. of Projects	Amount ($000)
FY 1979	467	38,182	117	85,754	1,518	945,443
Cumulative to Date	2,840	177,880	340	396,737	14,000	4,823,395

*Excluding Drought Assistance and Local Public Works

Source: Economic Development Administration. *Annual Report 1979* (Washington, D.C.: U.S. Department of Commerce, 1980), pp. 53–54.

$132 million, or an average loan of $825,000 (see Exhibit 14). Over the program's fourteen-year history, there has been a 50-loan-per-year average, with an average face value of $875,000. Loan concentrations by type of industry include the industrial categories of food and kindred projects, leather and leather products, and textile-mill products.[15]

Sixty-two Business Development loan guarantees were approved by EDA during FY 1979. The average guarantee was $700,000 (see Exhibit 14). Current and historical substantive areas of lending concentration include two of the above categories—food and kindred products and textile-mill projects. As of September 1979, the bulk of the Business Development Loans and Guarantees were found in cities of various sizes in New York, California, New Jersey, Texas, and Pennsylvania.[16]

EXHIBIT 14

ECONOMIC DEVELOPMENT ADMINISTRATION
BUSINESS DEVELOPMENT LOAN/GUARANTEE
PROJECTS BY MAJOR PROJECT TYPES

BUSINESS DEVELOPMENT LOANS

	Fiscal Year 1979		Cumulative FY 1966–79	
	No. of Projects$^{\Psi}$	EDA Investment ($000)	No. of Projects	EDA Investment ($000)
Electrical and Electronic Equipment	9	7,450	28	19,583
Food and Kindred Products	11	8,805	82	88,509
Leather and Leather Products	35	20,560	92	51,600
Machinery (except electrical)	9	8,630	32	28,238
Miscellaneous Manufacturing	9	3,965	32	24,120
Rubber and Miscellaneous Plastic Products	9	5,310	43	29,949
Textile Mill Products	30	21,660	99	75,389
Total	160[1]	132,002*	756	655,395

Ψ only categories of 8 or more projects included here
* includes collateral protection
[1] figures do not add to total due to excluded categories

BUSINESS DEVELOPMENT GUARANTEES

	Fiscal Year 1979		Cumulative FY 1966–79	
	No. of$^{\Psi}$ Projects	EDA Investment ($000)	No. of Projects	EDA Investment ($000)
Food and Kindred Projects	11	16,515	39	59,415
Primary Metal Industries	8	317,137	16	357,836
Textile Mill Products	10	14,625	31	30,938
Total	62[1]	417,080	246	737,937

Ψ only categories of 8 or more projects includced here
[1] figures do not add to total due to excluded categories

Source: EDA, *Annual Report*, 1979, pp. 47–48.

PUBLIC WORKS GRANTS

In FY 1979, the Economic Development Administration approved grants of close to $240 million for more than 350 public-works projects (see Exhibit 15). Two-thirds of these (265) fell within the aegis of a development program or strategic plan of a local government or economic-development district; the others were part of a public-works "impact" program to create jobs in sudden, severely economically depressed areas.[17]

Grants to states, counties, and localities may be used for rehabilitation, repair, or construction of public-works facilities primarily for industrial, commercial, or tourism development. To be eligible for a grant an area must (1) demonstrate economic distress as reflected in abnormally high unemployment or low median incomes, and/or significant declines in per-capita income; and (2) have in force or be in part of an Overall Economic Development Program (OEDP).[18]

The federal share varies from 50 to 80 percent; local share must be in place before federal funds are dispersed. Grants cannot be passed through or reused by organizations other than the initial grantee. EDA's 1979 Public Sector Investment Program included 144 grants for industrial development and 49 for commercial development. In addition, 42 infrastructure development grants were approved to improve the economic climate for nonresidential development. The purpose of these grants was to retain or create private-sector jobs through nonresidential growth in urban and rural areas, which would not have been possible without the grant. In FY 1979, the average public-works grant was $700,000; over the period 1966–79, the public-works grant average was approximately $500,000. As of September 1979, the bulk of the projects were concentrated in Arkansas, California, Kentucky, Mississippi, Oklahoma, and Texas.[19]

TITLE IX—ADJUSTMENT ASSISTANCE

Areas that experience sudden and severe economic dislocation or face long-term deterioration in their economies are eligible for special economic-development and adjustment assistance under Title IX of EDA's basic authorizing act. The purpose of EDA grants under this program is to attempt to arrest and reverse long-term economic decline and resulting reductions in jobs and income.[20]

Grants are made to states, counties, and localities for development of economic-development strategies, technical assistance, construction of public works, capitalization of revolving funds, land-banking activities, and the like. Eligible locations must (1) be part of a designated redevelopment area, (2) prepare an OEDP, and (3) be experiencing (compared to national averages) high unemployment, low per-capita income or chronic economic distress.[21]

EXHIBIT 15

ECONOMIC DEVELOPMENT ADMINISTRATION
PUBLIC WORKS AND ECONOMIC ADJUSTMENT
ASSISTANCE PROJECTS BY TYPE OF PROJECT

OBLIGATED PUBLIC WORKS PROJECTS

	Fiscal Year 1979		Cumulative FY 1966–79	
	No. of Projects	EDA Investment ($000)	No. of Projects	EDA Investment ($000)
Industrial park/site development facilities	86	53,903	1,133	535,279
General industrial/commercial development facilities	151	97,070	2,595	1,155,185
Recreation/tourism facilities	16	23,603	403	254,292
Educational facilities	6	6,704	204	142,457
Port/harbor facilities	9	11,241	147	159,210
Airport facilities	2	1,398	67	34,530
Health facilities	4	1,767	109	71,846
Other public facilities	76	43,803	738	287,777
Total	340	239,489	5,396	2,640,576

OBLIGATED ECONOMIC ADJUSTMENT ASSISTANCE PROJECTS

	Fiscal Year 1979		Cumulative FY 1966–79	
	Number of Projects	EDA Investment ($000)	Number of Projects	EDA Investment ($000)
Industrial park/site development facilities	5	8,407	8	11,396
General industrial/commercial development facilities	12	7,001	19	31,946
Recreation/tourism facilities	2	975	2	975
Port/harbor facilities	2	4,507	3	12,757
Other public facilities	83	60,941	266	319,367
Not elsewhere classified	13	3,921	42	20,298
Total	117	85,752	340	396,739

Source: EDA *Annual Report*, 1979, pp. 44, 50

During FY 1979, EDA approved 117 Title IX grants for a total of $85.7 million. This includes $44.9 million for long-term deterioration grants and $40.8 million for sudden dislocation grants. Obligated adjustment-assistance projects by type of project are shown in Exhibit 15. The largest of the classified group currently and cumulatively include (1) industrial park/site development facilities and (2) general industrial/commercial development facilities. In 1979 the former category of site infrastructure development averaged $1.8 million per grant; the latter category of general industrial/commercial development, $600,000 per grant.[22]

Economic Adjustment Assistance Projects are distributed at the level of one to three per state in 60 percent of the states, are not found at all in 20 percent of the states, and exist at double the one to three project level in the remaining 20 percent. California and Texas bulk large as current and historic project sites. Within-state locations depend on the nature of the economic adjustment: urban/rural, short/long-term economic dislocation, and so on.[23]

ECONOMIC DEVELOPMENT ADMINISTRATION—PROCESS FOR APPLICATION

PUBLIC WORKS GRANTS AND TITLE IX—ADJUSTMENT ASSISTANCE

For the Economic Development Administration Title IX and Public Works programs, an Overall Economic Development Plan (OEDP) must be developed by a committee representative of a cross-section of the community. Within the OEDP, projects are listed by type/area by priority. Prescreening occurs in conferences between the applicant and state representatives (EDRs). Profiles on projects having potential for funding are sent to regional directors for review by Project Review Committees (PRCs). Projects selected by PRCs are submitted to Washington for review and concurrence. The applicant is then authorized to prepare a full application, it is processed through the regional office, funds are reserved, and the applicant is notified and has three weeks to accept the offer.[24]

BUSINESS DEVELOPMENT LOANS AND GUARANTEES

Private Sector Investment (Business Development Loans and Guarantees) programs also must be consistent with the OEDP. As in the Title IX and Public Works programs, prescreening occurs in conferences between the private-sector applicant (for loan or guarantee) and the EDA state representative. Profiles on projects having potential for funding are sent to the national office for review and comments. Applicant meets with the regional professional staff, and a decision is made whether to invite a full application. A full application is submitted by the applicant to the regional office and, if it is accepted and approved, funds may flow in sixty to ninety days.[25]

FARMERS HOME ADMINISTRATION— BUSINESS AND INDUSTRIAL (B&I) LOAN PROGRAM

AUTHORIZATION AND SCOPE

The Business and Industrial Loan Program has been administered by FmHA primarily as a guaranteed loan program due to budget restrictions since its inception. The program was legislated in 1972 under Section 310B of the Consolidated Farm and Rural Development Act. The program is self-perpetuating unless repealed or not funded by Congress.[26]

The Rural Development Act does not specifically identify the size or types of loans or businesses to be considered for assistance. FmHA departmental policy has been to guarantee loans up to $10 million (usually $350,000 to $10 million), with priority given to the "retain" rather than "create" job category. Annual targeting goals direct a portion of the guarantees to those most in need according to the following criteria:[27]

$ 75 million to minority-owned businesses
$ 75 million to women-owned businesses
$100 million to revitalize small community downtowns
$100 million to depressed areas (with high unemployment)
$100 million to alternative energy projects

Applicants with successful track records, proven management skills, a product, and a market, are given priority in loan guarantees.

FmHA uses a rule of thumb of $20,000 loan-guarantee-to-job ratio and attempts to target the bulk of its lending toward rural development. It is believed by this agency that through the vehicle of the loan guarantee, private capital will be transferred from large capital-centered metropolitan areas to small rural communities in nonmetropolitan areas to help stem labor-force out-migration from these areas. Application awards thus favor projects in open-country, rural communities and towns of 25,000 and smaller.[28]

Exhibit 16 provides an analysis of Business and Industrial Loans both budgeted and obligated over the period 1974–79. Over the five-year period, annual obligated funds have increased by more than $1 billion—from approximately $200 million to $1.2 billion. As also indicated in the exhibit, the average loan guarantee has increased over this same period from $550,000 per loan to approximately $900,000. Historically, however, four-fifths of the loans processed are for less than $1 million.

EXHIBIT 16

FARMERS HOME ADMINISTRATION
BUSINESS AND INDUSTRIAL LOAN GUARANTEES
BUDGETED, OBLIGATED, AVERAGE LOAN SIZE

FYs 1974 - 1979

Fiscal Year	Budgeted ($000)	Obligated ($000)	Average Loan Size ($000)
1974	$200,000	$181,000	$555
1975	350,000	302,000	581
1976	437,000	398,000	681
1977	350,000	340,000	621
1978	1,000,000	988,000	902
1979	1,100,000	1,200,000	820

Source: U.S. Department of Agriculture, "FmHA Report on the Business and Industrial Loan Program," 1980, pp. 14, 16.

LOCATION OF LOAN GUARANTEES AND APPLICABLE ACTIVITIES

Characteristics of loan guarantees indicate that nearly 75 percent have been placed in communities of less than 10,000 population and more than 50 percent in communities of population size 5,000 or less (see Exhibit 17). Furthermore, over 50 percent of the dollar lending guarantees have been for manufacturing industries, 20 percent for service activities of one type or another, and nearly 14 percent for retail/wholesale trade (see Exhibit 18).

FmHA's principal economic-development vehicle is the loan guarantee. The guarantee fee is 1 percent of the principal loan amount multiplied by the percent of guarantee. It is a one-time fee paid by the lender, who usually passes it on to the borrower. FmHA contracts to reimburse the lender in case of a loan default for a maximum of 90 percent of principal and interest actually lost by the lender. Lenders are responsible for making and servicing loans. Applicants apply for loans through private money sources. In special cases where a guaranteed loan is not available, FmHA may directly make and service a loan.[31]

For guaranteed loans, the interest rate may be fixed, variable, or multiple and is determined between the lender and the borrower. The interest rate on direct loans—which FmHA has made only in limited cases—is computed on the cost of Treasury borrowing plus an increment to cover administrative

EXHIBIT 17

FARMERS HOME ADMINISTRATION
BUSINESS AND INDUSTRIAL LOAN GUARANTEES
BY POPULATION SIZE INCLUDING TOTAL JOBS

FYs 1974 - 1979

Population	Number of Borrowers	Percent of Borrowers	Dollar Amount Obligated	Percent of Dollar Amount Obligated	Total Jobs	Percent of Total Jobs
Under 5,000	2,209	53.5%	$1,476,978,365	46.4%	83,028	46.7%
5,000 - 9,999	856	20.7	622,587,224	19.6	30,036	16.0
10,000 - 24,999	634	15.3	612,439,383	19.2	35,061	19.7
25,000 and over	433	10.5	417,704,041	14.8	29,759	16.7
Total	4,132	100%	$3,184,009,013	100%	177,884	100%

Information was collected from the Rural Community Facilities Tracking System and represents 93 percent of total funds obligated.

Source: U.S. Department of Agriculture, "FmHA Report on the Business and Industrial Loan Program," 1980, p. 25.

EXHIBIT 18

FARMERS HOME ADMINISTRATION
BUSINESS AND INDUSTRIAL LOANS
BY STANDARD INDUSTRIAL CODE

FYs 1974 - 1979

Project Classification Created/Saved	Jobs Created/Saved	Number of Borrowers	Dollar Amount	Percent of $ Amount
Agriculture, Forestry and Fishing	3,554	141	$ 73,621,020	2.3%
Mining	2,258	69	79,518,850	2.5
Construction	8,339	168	83,579,300	2.6
Manufacturing	99,845	1,428	1,646,943,254	51.7
Transportation, Communications, Electric and Sanitary Services	9,353	275	154,864,678	4.9
Wholesale Trade	7,424	445	215,040,424	6.7
Retail Trade	11,711	720	217,289,974	6.9
Finance, Insurance and Real Estate	6,790	160	100,232,376	3.1
Services	28,585	725	611,519,107	19.2
Public Administration	25	1	1,400,000	0.1
Total	177,884	4,132	$3,184,009,013	100%

Information was collected from the Rural Community Facilities Tracking System and represents 88 percent of total funds.

Source: U.S. Department of Agriculture, "FmHA Report on the Business and Industrial Loan Program," 1980, p. 25.

costs; for public bodies borrowing to install community facilities necessary for community development, the rate is 5 percent.[32]

PROCESS FOR APPLICATION

Loan guarantees are potentially available to all types of businesses, including shoe companies, processing and textile plants, toy manufacturers and retailers, commuter airlines, restaurants, grain elevators, nursing homes, farm machinery companies, and retailers.

The basic requirements are that applicant projects are proposed for rural areas, they create or retain employment, and they meet private-sector tests for credit worthiness (FmHA does not apply an "availability of credit elsewhere" test). Screening procedures in this process include A-95 comments and the projects' eligibility and alignment with overall program objectives. Through subsequent conferences with the lender and applicant, a completed application is then developed and the various terms negotiated.[33]

Upon satisfactory completion of the above negotiations, the business and industry chief reviews the completed application and makes recommendations to the FmHA State Loan Review Board. The state director, through the county supervisor, will then notify the applicant of the FmHA decision. In the event that the decision is favorable, FmHA will issue the "Conditional Commitment of Guarantee," setting forth all conditions under which the Loan Note Guarantee will be issued.[34]

SUMMARY

This section has detailed the major economic-development programs of HUD, EDA, and FmHA. What is clear from the analysis is the differing geographic locational foci of these agencies, the form or way they choose to allocate their resources, and the types of projects they favor for resource distribution. These patterns of agency behavior are reflected in the form and composition of funded projects. In the next section this behavior is converted to examples of program activity, which then form the basis for the selection of cases.

II. EXAMPLE ECONOMIC-DEVELOPMENT ACTIVITIES AND SELECTION OF CASES TO BE STUDIED

INTRODUCTION

The previous section of this report detailed the program activities of the three principal federal agencies concerned with economic development. All of these programs share a common purpose: the promotion of private-sector investment in selected geographic areas. They also share sets of assumptions about why public interest is served by stimulating private-sector development in those areas and why private-sector investment is not occurring. Yet, the agencies give their programs different emphases in terms of locational allocation, types of activities funded, and amounts of funding—depending on the objectives or targets that, by virtue of their statutes and regulations, they are to address. Further, federal agencies have considerable discretion over the type and structure of resource allocation—grant, loan, loan guarantee—as well as procedures for the division of resources between state/local entities and private lenders.

This section reviews resource-allocation emphases of the major economic-development agencies en route to establishing example activities for each agency. From these examples, projects are subsequently drawn for fiscal and economic analysis. The purpose of this selection procedure is to ensure, within resource constraints, that a full range of projects is considered for potential analysis.

ALLOCATION EMPHASES

GEOGRAPHIC LOCATION OF RESOURCE ALLOCATION

Two of the three agencies listed above have distinctly different geographic loci of resource allocation. The HUD UDAG program concentrates its grant activities in large metro cities (75 percent) as well as smaller independent cities throughout the nation. FmHA Business and Industrial loan guarantees are specifically slotted for fledgling nonmetropolitan areas (towns, townships, and so on) of minimal population size. (In FY 1979 all of FmHA's direct and guaranteed loans were made in rural areas.) EDA's economic-development efforts, reflecting the agency's various programs, encompass rural areas, suburban municipalities, and urban locations as well. In FY 1978, 64 percent of EDA Title IX funds and 35 percent of its Public Works funds went to central cities. Of the three agencies, EDA is probably the largest current lender in suburban metropolitan jurisdictions (metropolitan areas—non-central city).[35]

Forty percent of EDA's Business Development Loan Guarantees (FY 1978) were made in central cities, compared to 24 percent in the suburbs and 35 percent in nonmetropolitan areas. Twenty-eight percent of EDA's direct Business Development Loans were made in central cities, 35 percent in suburbs, and 37 percent in nonmetropolitan areas.

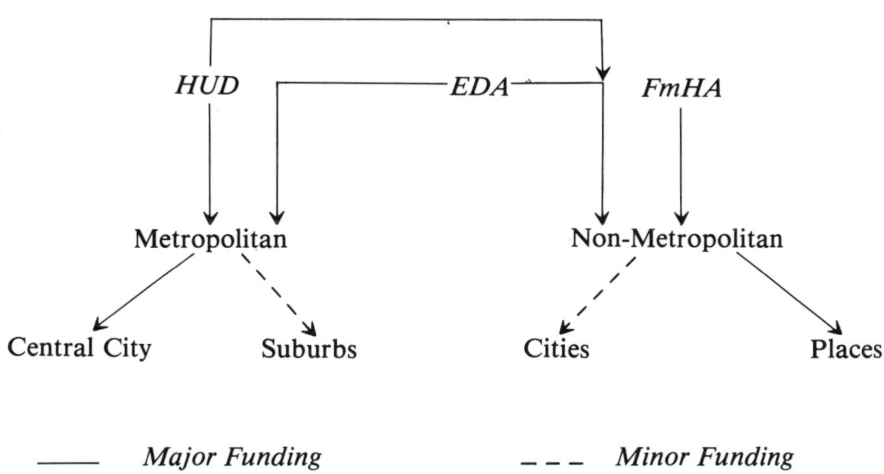

The HUD Urban Development Action Grants and EDA's Public Facilities and Title IX Adjustment Assistance Grants are targeted to distressed areas through hardship formulas. EDA's Private Sector Investment Program (Business Development Loans and Guarantees) is also targeted to areas on the basis of distress. FmHA's Business and Industrial loan guarantees are not specifically targeted except in a very broad-based way to rural, nonmetropolitan areas.[36]

FORM OF THE TENDERED RESOURCES

The three economic-development sponsoring agencies also vary significantly in the form of the resources tendered to local areas. HUD's UDAG program and EDA's Title IX and Public Works programs make grants to local governments or area organizations. EDA's Private Sector Investment Program and FmHA's Business and Industrial Loan Program offer loan guarantees and to a lesser extent direct loans to private sector firms.[37] The agency decision to grant, lend, or guarantee is based on two principal factors: (1) geographical area of the agency's coverage versus available program resources to meet coverage requirements; and (2) level of impaction of the believed problem and degree of assistance required by those at the site of the problem. FmHA's coverage requirements for business and industrial support are large (all nonmetropolitan areas). Its mission—to encourage nonresidential growth in rural areas—and finally, the level of economic impaction in these areas, are more modest. It thus chooses a widely distributive, shallow subsidy, the loan guarantee, to carry out its mission.[38]

HUD in its UDAG program deals in a more finite geographic arena—severely distressed metro and small cities. The mission is more encompassing, however: (1) encouraging economic growth in areas where other economic activities may have previously failed; and (2) reducing local unemployment through the inclusion of a portion of the presently unemployed in the labor force of the renewed facility. Further, the level of impaction in its locus of operation is usually severe. HUD employs a steep subsidy—the direct grant.[39]

EDA, when its mission directs its resource-allocation activities to severely or suddenly impacted areas, usually employs a grant (Title IX). When this agency operates in primitive public-service locations and its mission is to develop public facilities there, it continues to use the grant mechanism (Public Works Program). When, however, its coverage is extended, and its goal is to boost or support sagging private sector firms in less-impacted, "grey" areas, it frequently employs the direct loan or the loan guarantee.

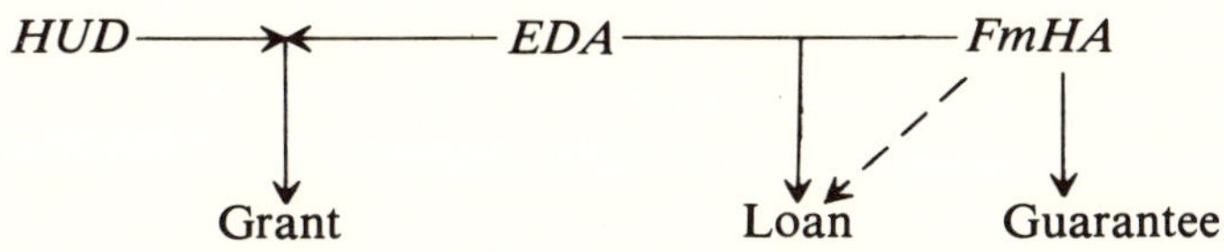

——— *Major Funding* — — — *Minor Funding*

In terms of scope, except for the cases of loans and guarantees to primary-metal producers, HUD Urban Development Action Grants and EDA Title IX and Public Facilities Grants tend to be of larger magnitude than FmHA Business and Industrial Guarantees or the EDA Private Sector Loans/Guarantees.

TYPE OF ACTIVITY FUNDED

The type of activity to which resources are directed also varies significantly by agency. Historically, HUD has been involved in housing redevelopment and commercial urban renewal. These activities, although by no means dominant, are nonetheless reflected in its economic-development activities. Similar statements may be made concerning EDA's continuous involvement with basic industry support (metals, leather products, textiles) and FmHA's primary concern with agriculture-related, rural industries.

HUD (FY 1978, 1979) in metro-cities committed almost equal resources to the three substantive grant categories: commercial, industrial, and neighborhood. In small cities, the category of industrial grant dominated. EDA, currently (FY 1979) and historically (FY 1966-79), has funded industrial over other forms of economic redevelopment. In FY 1979, 70 percent of the obligated Public Works Projects were industrial; 66 percent of Economic Adjustment Assistance Projects (not for public facilities) went to industrial-park site development or general industrial activities. Further, fewer than 10 percent of EDA's private-sector loans or guarantees went for anything other than industrial development (trade/general merchandise, eating/drinking places, amusement services, and so on). Sixty-five percent of FmHA's Business and Industrial dollar guarantees also were directed toward industrial facilities; the remaining amount flowed to commercial activities in the form of consumer/business services (19 percent); retail/-wholesale trade (13 percent); and finance, insurance, and real estate (3 percent). As city size increases toward 10,000 at the loan site, the guaranteeing activity of FmHA moves noticeably away from industrial development to the support of commercial and service activities.[40]

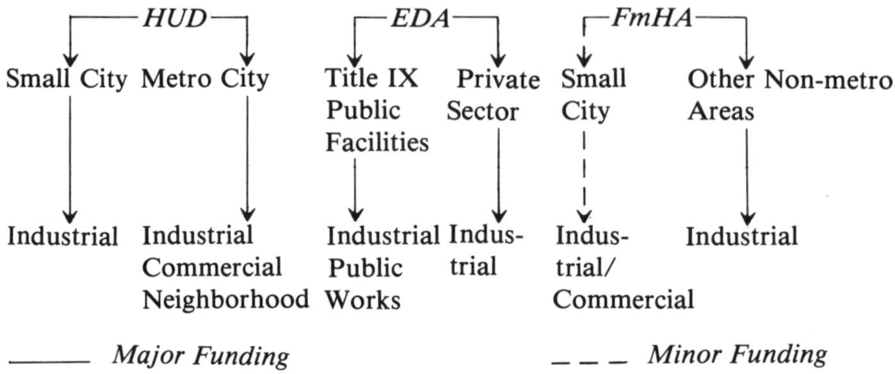

EXAMPLES OF FEDERAL ECONOMIC-DEVELOPMENT ACTIVITIES

Patterns of the substantive lending activities of the three sponsors of economic development begin to merge from the previous discussion. They are presented in the left-hand portion of Exhibit 19. HUD, through its UDAG program offers grants to severely distressed communities, which are used to support a wide range of industrial, commercial, and neighborhood projects in both larger and smaller communities. FmHA uses private-sector loan guarantees to stimulate primarily industrial development in less severely distressed, rural townships and small nonmetropolitan cities. EDA employs the techniques discussed above to support a variety of industrial-development and public-works infrastructure provisions in cities of varying degrees of hardship/stress.

CASE SELECTIONS—SPECIFIC FACILITIES

The right-hand portion of Exhibit 19 summarizes the case selections of economic-development activities of HUD, EDA, and FmHA. They are presented in parallel with the mode of activities undertaken by the respective agencies. The case selections are sited in New Jersey, a Middle-Atlantic state of the Northeast region. In each instance, the case selections follow the project type and locational emphases of the three agencies, and each economic-development programmatic thrust is represented at least once in the eleven cases.

HUD's UDAG program is illustrated by four metro-city examples and one small-city example. The substantive thrusts of industrial, commercial, and neighborhood redevelopment are also represented. Projects vary in scale from $170,000 to $4.2 million. Reflective of the UDAG program, all projects are of the grant type of resource disbursement.

FmHA's Business and Industrial (B&I) Loan Guarantees are represented by three examples in the typical size cohorts of the nonmetropolitan locations where FmHA is active. The program is further represented by both industrial and commercial loan guarantees and, within industrial guarantees, by FmHA's most frequent SIC lending categories. Loan guarantees range from $300,000 to $3.1 million, paralleling general trends in the scale of FmHA guarantees by community size of the applicant.

EDA's economic-development efforts are characterized through four examples, one in each of its major activities: Public Works Grants, Economic Adjustment Assistance, Business Development Loans, and Business Development Guarantees. Projects parallel EDA, SIC-lending emphases and include a primary-metals producer, a public-works industrial park, and a mixed-use (commercial/industrial) Adjustment Assistance development. Project scale runs from $2 million to $12 million and follows the trends in grant/loan size across EDA's categories of programs. It must be realized, however, that, whereas selected projects parallel general program emphases, there is no intent to suggest that a statistically representative sample has been derived.

CASE SELECTIONS—DETAILED SUMMARIES

The HUD-UDAG examples include (1) a $170,000 grant for the refitting of an abandoned factory in Salem, N.J., to accommodate an electronic-parts manufacturer; (2) a $296,000 grant for construction of a structure in Newark, N.J., to house a regional wholesaler of poultry and meat products; (3) a $1 million grant to convert an old brewery in Newark to a multi-tenant, industrial park; and (4) a $4.2 million grant to build a multi-use, industrial-residential facility to anchor a portion of the Paterson, N.J., central business district.

The electronic-parts manufacturer in Salem has added 15 new jobs to this declining rural city of approximately 7,000 population. The $296,000 grant to the wholesale poultry distributor added 70 jobs to the job base of the City of Newark and allowed another 67 jobs to be retained (population size 310,000). The UDAG grant to convert the Newark brewery supplied 480 jobs to the city and retained 1,000 others. The creation of the industrial-residential facility adjacent to Paterson's CBD will, upon completion, add 180 jobs and retain 120 more in this city of approximately 145,000 population.

FmHA Business and Industrial Loan program is represented by (1) a $300,000 loan guarantee for land acquisition and construction of a structure to house the operations of a paint-pigment manufacturer in rural West Amwell, N.J.; (2) a $625,000 loan guarantee to build a recreational tennis facility to answer the recreational demands of exurbanites drawn to

EXHIBIT 19

EXAMPLES AND CASE SELECTIONS OF FEDERAL (HUD, EDA, FmHA) ECONOMIC-DEVELOPMENT ACTIVITIES

EXAMPLES				CASE SELECTIONS			
Agency/Program	Program Partition	Type of Project	Average Grant/ Loan/Guarantee	Agency/ Program	City/ Size	Type of Project	Grant/Loan/ Guarantee
U.S. DEPARTMENT OF HOUSING AND URBAN DEVELOPMENT (HUD)				U.S. DEPARTMENT OF HOUSING AND URBAN DEVELOPMENT (HUD)			
URBAN DEVELOPMENT ACTION GRANTS				URBAN DE-VELOPMENT ACTION GRANTS			
	Small City	Industrial (Manufac-turing)	$ 818,000– 844,000	Small City	Salem, N.J. (7,000)	Wire-Pro Inc. (Industrial-Electronic Parts)	$ 170,000
	Metro City	Commercial, Neighborhood Industrial	$2,083,000–2,257,000	Metro City	Newark, N.J. (310,000)	Schnoll Poultry (Commercial-Wholesale)	$1,000,000
					Newark, N.J. (310,000)	Balco-RAR Properties (Industrial Park)	$1,000,000
					Paterson (145,000)	Marshall St. and Bale Avenue Industrial Park (Neighborhood-Industrial-Residential-Commercial	$4,200,000
ECONOMIC DEVELOPMENT ADMINISTRATION (EDA)				ECONOMIC DEVELOPMENT ADMINISTRATION (EDA)			
BUSINESS DEVELOPMENT LOANS AND GUARANTEES				BUSINESS DEVELOPMENT LOANS AND GUARANTEES			

EXHIBIT 19 (*Continued*)

EXAMPLES AND CASE SELECTIONS OF FEDERAL
(HUD, EDA, FmHA) ECONOMIC-DEVELOPMENT ACTIVITIES

	Guarantees	Primary Metals	$40,000,000	Guarantees	Perth Amboy (35,000)	Raritan River Steel Co. (Manufacturing—Primary Metal)	$12,000,000
	Loans	Textile Mill/ Products	$700,000	Loans	Paterson, N.J. (145,000)	ATP Processors, Inc. (Textile Printers)	$1,900,000 $1,900,000
PUBLIC WORKS GRANTS				PUBLIC WORKS GRANTS			
	Grant	Industrial Development—Industrial Parks	$700,000		Lakewood, N.J. (30,000)	Lakewood Township Industrial Campus	$2,176,000
TITLE IX—ADJUSTMENT ASSISTANCE				TITLE IX—ADJUSTMENT ASSISTANCE			
	Grant	Common Industrial/Communication	$ 580,000		Paterson, N.J. (145,000)	Great Falls Historic District	$11,112,200
FARMERS HOME ADMINISTRATION (FmHA)				FARMERS HOME ADMINISTRATION (FmHA)			
BUSINESS AND INDUSTRIAL LOAN PROGRAM (GUARANTEE)				BUSINESS AND INDUSTRIAL LOAN PROGRAM (GUARANTEE)			
	10,000–12,000 Population	Commercial (Service)	$ 800,000	10,000–12,000 Population	Hopewell Twp. (11,500)	Tencor, Inc. (Tennis Facility)	$ 625,000
	5,000–10,000 Population	Industrial (Manufacturing)	$1,000,000	5,000–10,000	Salem, N.J. (7,000)	Fosterglass (Industrial Glass Production)	$3,100,000
	Less than 5,000 Population	Industrial (Manufacturing)	$ 60,000	Less than 5,000	West Amwell, N.J. (2,500)	Breen Color, Inc. (Industrial Color Dyes)	$ 300,000

Hopewell, N.J.; and (3) a $3.1 million fixed-asset and working-capital loan guarantee to bolster a component of the glass industry of southwestern New Jersey.

The paint-pigment manufacturer has added 14 new jobs to West Amwell Township (population size 2,500); the tennis facility, 9 new jobs to Hopewell Township (population size 11,500); and the glass manufacturing firm, 25 jobs to the City of Salem.

EDA's several economic-development strategies are found in case examples of (1) a $12 million loan guarantee for the replacement, with a steel mill, of an abandoned copper mill in the industrial shore community of Perth Amboy, N.J.; (2) a $2.2 million public-works grant for the development of an industrial campus as a stabilizing factor for the tourist-oriented, shore economy of Lakewood, N.J.; (3) a $1.9 million working-capital and fixed asset loan for a bankrupt textile mill in Paterson; and (4) and $11.1 million economic-adjustment assistance grant for the refurbishing and conversion of industrial buildings in Paterson's Great Falls Historic Zone.

The steel mill has added 420 new jobs to Perth Amboy's employment base (population size 35,000); the Lakewood industrial park will house 6,000 new employees over a ten-year period in this township of 30,000. The stabilizing of the bankrupt textile mill and nonresidential development of Paterson's historic district, in the first case, has introduced 250 jobs locally and, in the second, will add 1,000 jobs and retain close to 400 others, over a four-to-five-year period.

NEW JERSEY AS THE SITE OF ANALYSIS

As is indicated in the foregoing analyses, selected projects have been chosen to parallel basic program allocation and scale emphases of HUD, EDA, and FmHA. That is, the types and scale of projects, in-state geographical location, and levels of community economic distress have been taken into account in the selection of cases.

New Jersey has been selected as the generic site of analysis due to resource constraint and for familiarity on the part of the authors with the fiscal structure of the communities in which economic development is taking place as well as with the financial system of the state as a whole.

New Jersey, as a component of the Northeast region, is a major recipient of all forms of the previously discussed economic-development assistance activities. It receives currently, and has received historically, a substantial share of UDAG grants, EDA grant/loans, and FmHA loan guarantees.

As one of the Middle Atlantic states, it demonstrates a fiscal profile that is close to the mode of local and state revenue-raising alternatives nationally. The state's localities employ a real-property tax of moderate proportion to fund a share of both municipal and school-district costs. They rely to lesser degrees on other taxes, user charges, and miscellaneous revenues to fund the range of public services. A state lottery and income tax are applied to school-district costs, and individual supplements are keyed to the hardship of the specific district.[41] The levels of other state and federal aid that contribute to the support of local public expenditures are considered average nationally.[42]

SUMMARY

The above-listed case selections serve as example public economic-development activities that will be analyzed for their current local fiscal and economic impacts. They have been selected from characteristic activities of three federal agencies that support economic development. It is quite obvious that the sample is limited and is one drawn partially for the sake of convenience and resource constraint. As such, only tentative inferences should be made from the results stated in the last section of this paper.

III. METHODS OF APPROACH TO FISCAL AND ECONOMIC IMPACT ANALYSIS— CONCEPTUAL AND TECHNICAL ISSUES

INTRODUCTION

The purpose of this section is to overview, and describe in detail where necessary, the procedures used to carry out both fiscal and economic impact analyses. It is the intent of the pages that follow to relate in narrative form a "walk through" example of a generalized impact-analysis case. As procedures are described, certain features of the selected projects and communities will be highlighted to illustrate specific points. Thus, the information presented here will vary in specificity and emphasis according to the degree to which a procedure affects or an issue surrounds the fiscal and economic impact analyses of the eleven case examples.

The section follows the general order of Exhibit 20 and covers fiscal impact projection techniques involved in estimating:

Primary Costs
Primary Revenues
Secondary Costs
Secondary Revenues

The final portion of this section considers the procedures and assumptions used to tally the local return to federal outlay ratios. This last measure is important because it provides a crude indication of the effectiveness of federal dollars in stimulating local revenue generation. As a prelude to the

EXHIBIT 20

EVALUATING THE IMPACT OF ECONOMIC DEVELOPMENT: ANALYTIC STRATEGY AND PROCEDURAL STEPS

I. LOCAL FISCAL IMPACT

A. *PRIMARY FISCAL-IMPACT CALCULATIONS*

1. Public-Service Costs of Economic Development
   a. Method I projection[1]
   b. Method II projection[1]
   c. Method III projection[1]
   d. Other method projections[1]
   e. Total primary service costs (synthesis[1] of a–d)

2. Public Revenues Generated by Economic Development
   a. Local revenues (i.e., property taxes)
   b. State intergovernmental (i.e., school aid)
   c. Federal intergovernmental (i.e., Revenue Sharing)
   d. Total primary revenues (summation of a–c)

3. Primary Local Fiscal Impact—Compare total primary service costs to total primary service revenues

B. *SECONDARY FISCAL-IMPACT CALCULATIONS*

1. Secondary Public-Service Costs Affected by Economic Development
   a. Residential sector costs
   b. Commercial sector costs
   c. Industrial service sector costs
   d. Total secondary service costs (summation of a–c)

2. Secondary Public Revenues Generated By Economic Development
   a. Residential sector revenues
   b. Commercial sector revenues
   c. Industrial/service sector revenues
   d. Total secondary revenues (summation of a–c)

3. Secondary Local Fiscal Impact—Compare total secondary public-service costs to total secondary public revenues

II. LOCAL RETURN TO FEDERAL OUTLAY ANALYSIS

A. *FEDERAL (and local) OUTLAYS OF ECONOMIC DEVELOPMENT*

1. Federal Outlays of Economic Development (i.e., annual loan repayments)
2. Other Local Outlays (i.e., street/road improvements)
3. Total Federal and Local Outlays (summation of 1 and 2)
4. Total Federal Outlays

EXHIBIT 20 (*Continued*)

EVALUATING THE IMPACT OF ECONOMIC DEVELOPMENT: ANALYTIC STRATEGY AND PROCEDURAL STEPS

B. *LOCAL RETURN OF ECONOMIC DEVELOPMENT*
   1. Total Local Fiscal Impact
   2. Other Local Revenues (i.e., business-loan repayments)
   3. Total Local Revenues (summation of 1 and 2)
   4. Net Local Return (total of local revenues minus other local outlays)

C. *NET LOCAL RETURN TO FEDERAL OUTLAY RATIO*—Compare net local return to federal outlays

---

[1] See text.

discussion procedures, certain aspects of definition and analytical focus will be briefly addressed.

BACKGROUND

Fiscal impact analysis is a technique that involves a comparison of the local public-service costs and revenues associated with residential or nonresidential growth.[43] It indicates whether growth will generate a net fiscal gain or loss with attendant consequences to local taxpayers.

Fiscal-impact analysis has been conducted over a forty year period, with its emphasis of attention changing over time. Although fiscal-impact analysis has been in use for this period, only during the past ten years have projection techniques been standardized and refined. Because this period coincided with the suburban emphasis of the discipline, it is not surprising that the fiscal-impact techniques that were devised were most applicable to suburban conditions—new construction in communities with under-developed service systems.

The 1980s are witnessing a new wave of residential and nonresidential development within cities. Fiscal-impact analysis is now being called on to answer the questions that surround the local fiscal effect of such development. This redirection of fiscal impact from suburbs to cities raises many conceptual and procedural issues. The following sections discuss these issues and outline applicable fiscal-impact techniques within the urban context.

LOCAL FISCAL IMPACT: CONCEPTUAL ISSUES AND FOCUS

AREAL FOCUS

The fiscal-impact analysis compares the annual local service expenditures engendered by the incoming nonresidential facility and the secondary growth it spurs to the changes in annual local revenues occasioned by both the primary and secondary growth. The focus of the analysis is a *local* comparison—that is, a pairing of the service costs of the municipality, school district, and other local units of government in which the new or redeveloped facility is located to the public revenues received by these same host jurisdictions attributable to the facility. The focus on local impact reflects a key objective of most economic-development programs—to improve the local financial health of impacted communities by encouraging development that will strengthen their revenue bases. The fiscal-impact analysis thus measures how successful individual projects are in achieving this community fiscal revitalization objective. Although it is true that redevelopment activity will also likely affect other, more-encompassing units of government, it is beyond the scope of this analysis to examine such effects.

COST/REVENUE COVERAGE AND TIME FRAME

The fiscal analysis is comprehensive; it considers the full range of local costs—operating, statutory*, and capital—forced by development, as well as the full set of local revenues—property and other local levies, along with net changes in state and federal intergovernmental assistance (see Exhibit 20). A full tally, especially of revenues, is essential when considering effects in distressed communities, as these jurisdictions increasingly rely on intergovernmental support to fund their basic services, often to a greater extent than traditional local revenues. In Newark, N.J., for example, the State of New Jersey finances 75 percent of local educational expenditures, while the federal government pays for about one-quarter of municipal outlays.[44] As state/federal aids are often granted inversely to local wealth, development that affects per-capita income, property-tax base, and other local wealth indices may markedly decrease intergovernmental assistance. The fiscal-impact analysis traces these net intergovernmental revenue additions/subtractions triggered largely by the value of the economic development facility.

Another characteristic of the fiscal-impact calculation is that

---

*Statutory costs—costs relating primarily to employee benefits (health, pension, etc.) that have been formulated into law via legislative action.

costs/revenues are both expressed on a *current annual* basis. This treatment reflects the need to address all components of the fiscal-impact equation in equivalent fashion. Thus, capital costs would be expressed in terms of the current annual payback of a bond issued to pay for infrastructure improvements. Treated in this fashion, the capital outlay, amortized into the future, is added to annual operating and statutory costs in order to determine total local current costs. In similar fashion, all revenues generated by economic development are summarized to a common annual denominator.

SCOPE OF ANALYSIS: INCLUDED PRIMARY AND SECONDARY EFFECTS

The fiscal analysis, as described here, traces two rounds of local service costs/revenues. The first is termed *primary impact* and includes the *direct* fiscal effects—both costs and revenues—of the specific project under review. This analysis is coupled with a much more tentative analysis of *secondary impact* encompassing the generated *second-tier* fiscal consequences—both costs and revenues—of primary-generated, secondary growth (residential, commercial, and/or industrial—see Exhibit 20).

The specific differentiation of primary versus secondary effects is a temporal factoring of anticipated events. The primary cost impact of a nonresidential project is typically the added police/fire/public-works expenditures associated with protecting and providing traffic control for direct employees and goods. The primary revenue impact is the property-tax dollar and other local-levy dollar increases triggered by the new or revamped nonresidential facility. The secondary effect goes beyond these immediacies and encompasses the financial consequences of the series of events set in motion by the incoming nonresidential complex. These include (1) a portion of the employees taking residence locally and generating municipal and school expenditures/revenues associated with residential development; (2) a share of the wages of the local employees being spent in the community of residence and thus supporting local commercial establishments, which in turn generate local costs/revenues; and (3) the nonresidential facility itself spending on local goods and services and likewise supporting other local businesses, with their attendant costs/revenues (see Exhibit 20).

Both rounds—primary and secondary—generate local public costs and revenues, and these are addressed, in turn. The fiscal-impact analysis, therefore, first compares *total primary costs* versus *total primary revenues* to derive a *primary local fiscal impact*. In a parallel fashion, *total secondary costs*, *total secondary revenues*, and *secondary local fiscal impact* are also approximated. The fiscal impact analysis is thus composed of two stages, individually analyzed with results *not* aggregated. Primary and secondary impacts are not aggregated to a single figure because of a substantive difference between direct and indirect impact and because of the difference in magnitude between the two numbers. Secondary effects are usually larger and would overly influence any combined tally of the two impacts.

SCOPE OF THE ANALYSIS: EXCLUDED EFFECTS

Before turning to discussion of the federal outlays to local return analysis, it is important to consider what is *not* considered in the specification of local costs and revenues and why these elements are not included.

One issue deals with the scope of fiscal impact analysis, that is, the point at which the relationship between value generated and its stimulating effect will be terminated. Although cognizant of a potentially continuing dynamic, that is, tertiary costs/revenues, and so on, the analysis practically limits itself to primary and secondary effects because this level of tracing covers the main types of actions and responses that can be legitimately anticipated. Even here, relationships between primary and secondary growth are speculative due largely to the availability of data on resident workers' spending patterns. The tertiary and subsequent rounds, while adding further layers of costs/revenues, are much too vague and undefined in their composition to even begin to specify impact.

Another issue is the psychological impact of a redevelopment project. Such activity may act as a psychological boost—an affirmation to owners of nearby residential and industrial buildings that there are not merely possibilities but realities of both outside aid and better times in the future. This affirmation may encourage further local reinvestment, which in turn will generate a local fiscal benefit. The fiscal-impact analysis does not count this consequent fiscal gain because in some cases it is only conjectural. Even where it is present, it is very hard to measure and is likely the result of multiple interventionary forces—not solely the consequence of the single economic-development project under study.

Another issue concerns the potentially harmful effect of competition. An assisted redevelopment project, for example, an in-town shopping center, can adversely compete with existing local businesses, in this case, CBD retailers. If the competition results in the downturn or demise of extant local firms, then the actual net fiscal benefit of the new redevelopment project is dramatically reduced. This fiscal-impact analysis does not factor in a loss due to displaced competition for the same reasons as the exclusion of the positive effects of the psychological boost—the effect of competition is undefined and even if present often cannot be ascribed solely to the individual redevelopment project being examined. A basic assumption of economic redevelopment is that a critical mass will be formed that will attract consumers to this geographical location in the region. If an individual entrepreneur has goods that are in direct competition with the goods of the proposed facility, that entrepreneur has the option of changing the goods line or being replaced by a facility whose merchandise or service is not in direct competition with the redeveloped facility. The individual or goods lines may go out of business, but the store and its tax dollars are assumed to remain.

LOCAL RETURN VERSUS FEDERAL OUTLAY ANALYSIS: CONCEPTUAL ISSUES AND FOCUS

In addition to local fiscal impact, the analysis of the economic impact of federally assisted economic development also compares the relationship of the full local revenue return to the extent of the federal dollar outlay.

The specific federal outlay depends on the depth and scope of the federal assistance. In the case of a federal economic-development grant, the federal cost is assumed to be the annual federal interest and amortization repayment of a Treasury bond issued to raise the grant funds.* In the case of a federal below-market-interest-rate development loan, the federal cost is assumed to be equal to the difference between the federal interest and amortization obligation and the amount it receives from the private loan repayment. In addition, an imputed loss factor, taking into account the projected program default rate in the below-market-interest-rate portfolio, is also added. Finally, when a federal loan guarantee is given, the federal expense is assumed to be the obligation to reimburse lenders on that share of the guaranteed loan portfolio that does not succeed.

The calculation of federal costs is restricted to actual federal outlays or surrogates of outlays based on default rates. Program administrative expenses are not considered, as they would cloud comparisons between the revenue result and the actual scope (dollars tendered) of the federal subsidy.

Local returns of economic development are compared to the program outlays of the various federal agencies. Aggregate local dollar benefits are termed the *total local return* and equal the total fiscal impact (surplus or deficit) plus additional local financial benefits accruing primarily from a redevelopment-loan repayment. UDAG projects, for example, incorporate such repayments when the redevelopment agency elects to use a portion of the UDAG grant to provide the long-term, low-interest loans to interested entrepreneurs. This provides an additional stimulus for private capital investment.

Federal benefits, such as added personal income or corporate taxes

*A conceptually similar procedure would be to calculate the discounted present value of the grant amount.

generated by redevelopment, are *not* included because the analysis here focuses on how successful the redevelopment programs are in achieving one of their primary objectives—the strengthening of the local fiscal status of targeted, distressed communities. In addition, there is a very real question whether such federal benefits should be counted as a consequence of the redevelopment assistance because, even in the absence of such aid, the redevelopment projects would likely have been built in the nation or region (reflecting the results of required market analyses), albeit probably not in the distressed communities. If the projects would have come to fruition without redevelopment assistance, it is unfair to count additional federal (tax and other) revenues as a consequential benefit of the redevelopment programs.

After the derivation of the federal cost and the local return, the final step is to compare these features. This comparison indicates the scale of "local economic bang" afforded by the federal economic development "buck."

FISCAL-IMPACT ANALYSES: SPECIFIC CALCULATION PROCEDURES

The previous discussion outlined the overall strategies of the analyses and the issues involved in their practical implementation. This and the following section consider the component aspects of impact projection as well as necessary assumptions to proceed from step to step. The reviews in these two sections highlight the key considerations and variables. A more thorough guide to generalized procedures and assumptions of fiscal-impact analysis is found in *The Fiscal Impact Handbook*[45], published by Rutgers University and HUD.

PROJECTING PRIMARY COSTS AND REVENUES

Local service costs of nonresidential development can be estimated by any one of several different methods. One technique is the case study, whereby knowledgeable local municipal officials are queried to ascertain their best estimate of the immediate public-service expenditures that will be generated by the entry of a new or redeveloped nonresidential facility. These local officials include key operating heads, such as the city managers/business administrators, police/fire chiefs, public-works directors, as well as those charged with less-encompassing responsibilities: building/health inspectors, tax assessors/collectors, and the like. A second method assigns a share of existing local service costs according to a modified, proportional increase in real-property value that a nonresidential facility adds to the value of the community's total real-property base. A third approach projects estimates of local public servicing expenditures by supplying ratios of percent increase in per-capita expenditures that must be applied to the number of employees introduced by the specific commercial or industrial firm.* The three techniques are called the case study (CS), proportional valuation (PV), and employment generation (EG) methods. They are explained in detail in *The Fiscal Impact Handbook*.

All three methods were employed in the projection of primary service expenditures generated by the eleven New Jersey case examples. This was done to provide the fullest range of cost estimates from which to choose a final figure for calculation purposes. The figure selected for primary costs typically is a mid-range value between the high and the low cost estimates. It is not a simple average, however, for in each case the analysis considers the appropriateness of each of the individual costing methods, given the community/project characteristics under study. The cost projections of the more appropriate methods were accorded greater weight in the selection of the final cost figure used in the analysis.

The above discussion focuses primarily on nonresidential cost projection. In several instances, economic-development projects may also include one or more residential components. (This is the case, for instance, in the Marshall and Bale Street UDAG in Paterson.) In such instances, primary service costs can be estimated by the per-capita, service standard, or other method, adjusting procedures for excess or deficient capacity at the site of analysis, as explained in *The Fiscal Impact Handbook*. In Paterson a modified per-capita approach is used, which takes into account the excess service capacity present in the school system as well as the proportion of current residents who previously lived elsewhere in this no-growth community.

In all cases, regardless of the fiscal-impact projection method employed, those undertaking the analysis must take into account the *net new* scale of the economic-development activity.** The counting of costs must limit itself to net additional, development-generated, local cost. If a facility is *expanded* or *reconstructed and expanded* at a new location, only the increment in employment can be counted as requiring local services and thus incurring local costs. This factoring to net employment can usually be accomplished by examining the percentage share of created jobs to total jobs (created plus retained). The new job percentage provides a rough gauge of the share of total facility value to be attributed to the development activity. To illustrate, in the New Jersey case studies, the UDAG Wire-Pro facility in

*Regression coefficients are derived from an analysis of changing community characteristics and municipal costs for New Jersey communities (1978).

**This is a severe test for economic development programs. In the UDAG program a retained job is defined as one which "would not have survived in the absence of assistance." Obviously, this is as good as a new job in the urban redevelopment context; however under the procedures employed above it receives no credit.

Salem helped create 150 *new* jobs, whereas the UDAG grant in Newark to Schnoll Poultry helped *expand* Schnoll's employment from 67 to 137 jobs. Consequently, the redevelopment fiscal-impact analysis considers *all* facility-generated service costs in the Wire-Pro project, but only 51 percent of the public-service costs in the case of Schnoll.

As costs and revenues are treated equally in any fiscal-impact comparison, revenues for an expanded facility are handled in comparable fashion. Total generated revenues are multiplied by the percentage share of new to total jobs in order to identify those revenues generated as a result of the federally stimulated economic expansion.

The calculation procedures for individual revenue sources are explained below.

PROJECTING PRIMARY REVENUES

Local revenues include (1) *local taxes, charges and other revenues*; (2) *state-to-local transfers*; and (3) *federal intergovernmental support*. The revenue calculation considers how the economic-development activity affects all three flows to the host jurisdiction.

In practice, fiscal-impact analyses of nonresidential projects often overstate actual benefits because, although they project local (municipal and school district) costs, they include more than local revenues. A common fallacy of this kind is to count as a local benefit the full property taxes (municipal, school district, county) paid by a facility (assessed valuation multiplied by aggregate local property-tax rate). This treatment is erroneous because the property tax typically is a composite of county, municipal, and school components. The true *local* property-tax benefit consists of the municipal and school-district share of the aggregate property tax and thus excludes the county share of local property taxes. In the New Jersey case studies, counting the full property tax rather than just the municipal and school district share would have fallaciously inflated the true local property-tax benefit by roughly 25 to 33 percent. (In many cases this overcounting appeared in the project's original application for funding.)

LOCAL PROPERTY TAX

The real-property tax is typically the dominant local revenue. It is calculated by multiplying a property's assessed value by the nominal local property tax rate. Alternatively, the property's market value can be multiplied by an equalized or true property-tax rate. Both procedures yield the same property-tax revenue as long as assessment is not discriminatory toward the project.

These calculations are straightforward, but there are a number of practical problems. One is to factor from total project or market value that share which is real as opposed to personal property. This differentiation is important because some jurisdictions do not tax personal property or else tax it at a lower rate than real property. The question and importance of differentiating real versus personal property is pointedly revealed in the interviews with Salem economic-development officials. Somewhat related to Salem's successful Wire-Pro UDAG redevelopment, a local utility has announced that it will construct a $27 million nuclear-operator training facility in the city. In tentative discussion with Salem's assessor, the utility maintains that the training complex is a $3 million structure with $24 million in equipment. The latter would mainly be classified as personal property and hence would be *exempt* from local property taxes. Salem's assessor argues that a larger share of the facility, perhaps as much as one-half, or $13 million, is real property. This negotiation for upwards of a four fold revenue-yield increase from the facility illustrates the importance of definitional differences in local revenue flows.

There are many other practical problems of estimating property-tax revenue, especially in an economic-development context. To illustrate, it is often difficult to estimate either the market or assessed value of a publicly assisted development project. To assume that the true value is equal to total project cost ignores inner-city market realities. An arms-length transaction of a federally sponsored, central-city project—a standard yardstick of market value—will typically yield less than total project cost. The derivation of assessed value is also problematical. Typically, this figure is estimated by multiplying the true value by an equalization ratio—an annual comparison of the assessed and market prices of recent transactions in a local community. This procedure poses two problems, especially in a nonresidential-development situation. First, market value is difficult to estimate, as discussed above. Second, applying the overall community equalization ratio ignores the following confounding factors:

1. Nonresidential property is typically assessed at a higher ratio relative to other classes of property. This disparity is often significant, as revealed by the *Hellerstein* decision in New York.[46] In such cases, applying the overall community equalization ratio will *underestimate* the likely assessment of the nonresidential facility and hence underestimate forthcoming property taxes.
2. A contrasting situation is posed in other cases. To encourage redevelopment activity, communities sometimes de facto assess such projects at a relatively low equalization factor. (This action is not the same as de jure preferred tax assessment sanctioned by law, which is discussed in the next section.) In these instances, applying the overall equalization ratio would *overestimate* assessed value and property taxes generated.

The $1,000,000 Wire-Pro UDAG project in Salem illustrates the second scenario cited above. If we assume that there is a 0.8 ratio between assessed value and project cost, then Wire-Pro should have an $800,000 market value. Subtracting $200,000 to $300,000 in personal property would leave $500,000 to $600,000 in real-property valuation. Multiplying this real-property value basis by Salem's .9729 equalization ratio would mechanically yield an assessment ofapproximately$500,000. In reality, Wire-Pro, Inc. is assessed at $240,000. The 100 percent disparity between the projected and actual Wire-Pro, Inc. assessment illustrates the difficulty of estimating true/assessed value and consequently the actual real-property taxes that will be generated by the specific development.

The Special Case of Preferred Property-Tax Treatment—In some cases, local jurisdictions formally grant preferred property-tax treatment for redevelopment activities. In these situations the property-tax revenue is estimated by referring to the stipulations of the property-tax abatement/deferment statute. New Jersey, for example, allows its most impacted urban cities to offer two types of tax relief.[47] The first, N.J.S.A. 40:55C-40 et seq., is commonly referred to as Fox-Lance. Fox-Lance permits impacted communities to forgive all property taxes for twenty years on urban-renewal projects involving new construction. Instead of property taxes, an annual in-lieu payment is required equal to (1) 15 percent of the project annual gross revenues; or (2) 2 percent of total project cost. The second New Jersey preferred tax treatment is Chapter 12 of the Laws of 1977, commonly referred to as the Persky provision. Persky applies to redevelopment projects involving rehabilitation. It allows a five-year graduated abatement on reassessment resulting from rehabilitation. In year one, there is no reassessment; in year two, 20 percent of the value of improvements is added; in year three, 40 percent, and so on until year six, when 100 percent reassessment is reached. Like Fox-Lance, Persky is allowed only in certain impacted urban communities.

In nine of the eleven New Jersey case studies, state law allowed either Fox-Lance or Persky tax treatment. In six of these nine, tax relief has been or likely will be accorded (see Exhibit 21). Tax relief is not used in conjunction with the New Jersey FmHA programs—the agricultural communities where FmHA typically operates are not allowed to offer Fox-Lance or Persky. (The one exception is Salem.) The New Jersy EDA and HUD projects, in contrast, often integrate some measure of preferred tax treatment—this was found in three out of four EDA- and HUD-sponsored projects.

The presence or absence of special tax treatment can mean a significant difference in property-tax revenue. To illustrate, the Raritan River Steel Company, a $140 million steel fabricating plant pays $250,000 in-lieu taxes

EXHIBIT 21

PREFERRED PROPERTY-TAX TREATMENT IN NEW JERSEY ECONOMIC-DEVELOPMENT PROJECTS

Federal Agency Assisting Economic Development	Economic Development Projects	Treatment for City Location	City Allowed to Grant Preferred Property-Tax Treatment for Economic Development	Preferred Tax Treatment
HUD	Wire-Pro	Salem	Yes	Not Granted
HUD	Schnoll Poultry	Newark	Yes	Fox-Lance
HUD	Balco-RAR	Newark	Yes	Persky
HUD	Marshall St. and Bale Ave.	Paterson	Yes	Persky
EDA	ATP	Paterson	Yes	Not Granted
EDA	Lakewood Industrial Campus	Lakewood	Yes	Persky
EDA	Great Falls Historic District	Paterson	Yes	Persky
EDA	Raritan River Steel	Paterson	Yes	Fox-Lance
FmHA	Breen Color Concentrate	West Amwell	No	Not Allowed
FmHA	Foster Glass	Salem	Yes	Not Granted
FmHA	Tencor	Hopewell	No	Not Allowed

Source: New Jersey case examples

each year for twenty years, under the Fox-Lance tax schedule. Without Fox-Lance, Raritan Steel would remit at least double or triple this amount in annual property taxes.

OTHER LOCAL REVENUES

Whereas the property tax remains the largest individual local revenue resource, there are several other local taxes (income, sales, franchise), as well as miscellaneous revenues (interest earnings and fees, fines and permit revenue) and user charges, which also are affected by local development. These revenue sources, in the aggregate, constitute approximately 30 percent of local revenues.

The first step is to determine which nonproperty taxes are affected* by the incoming economic-development project. This clarification involves not only checking what taxes/charges are imposed (for example, Newark is the only city in New Jersey with a payroll tax; no city in the state imposes a local sales tax), but also determining whether the entry of a particular facility will actually increase/decrease a particular type or form of revenue.

The New Jersey case studies revealed that several important local revenues, such as business personal-property and public-utility gross-receipts/franchise taxes would *not* increase due to nonresidential redevelopment. To illustrate, public-utility franchise revenue is collected by the state and consists of a 2 to 5 percent tax on public-utility gross receipts. This statewide revenue pool is then redistributed to local communities based on their proportional share of the utility's lines/mains throughout the state. The value of service connections is *not* counted, however. This is an important exclusion because redevelopment in central cities, as opposed to new construction in the suburbs, typically does not entail the provision of new utility central-feeder mains or lines. Although new utility service connections will be made, these are not counted for the purpose of local utility-tax redistribution. Consequently, redevelopment will usually not increase public-utility franchise revenue to the host community, whereas a new development frequently will.

A similar situation characterizes road-repair or street-lighting aid when the basis for local allocation or redistribution is the value or length of local capital infrastructure in the form of roads and streets. It is ironic that one of the characteristic benefits of urban redevelopment—that the urban capital infrastructure is in place as opposed to the voracious new capital demands of suburban or exurban development—has the practical effect of denying a city income from revenue sources that increase only if this segment of local capital infrastructure is expanded.

Once a determination is made as to what revenues are present and will be affected by new construction or redevelopment, it is a simple matter to calculate the additional increases or decreases in other local revenues.

INTERGOVERNMENTAL TRANSFERS: STATE

There are numerous state intergovernmental revenue sources. Several flow to municipal governments. Prominent examples include sales, income, motor-fuels and cigarette/alcohol taxes. These revenues are collected by the state and redistributed to localities based on such proportional local factors as the share of local sales of the product to total state product sales, the

*All local revenues are not affected by nonresidential redevelopment. In New Jersey only approximately one-third of "other local revenues" are impacted by redevelopment activities.

share of local population to total state population, and so on. The specific projection procedures for each of these types of revenues is detailed in *The Fiscal Impact Handbook*.

New Jersey does not redistribute sales or income taxes to municipalities. Although there are other significant intergovernmental transfers to municipal government, such as business-personal income, utility franchise, and utility gross-receipts taxes, these are not typically triggered by new or revitalized nonresidential development.

In addition to transfers to municipal government, all states grant considerable aid to local school districts. To give some order of magnitude, as of 1979 total elementary and secondary educational expenditures in the United States totaled about $80 billion and of this figure about half was paid for by state governments.[48] Given the importance of state school aid, it is important to examine how it is allocated and whether it is affected by nonresidential development.

Whereas states typically offer dozens of educational subsidies, such as categorical aid for the handicapped or for transportation purposes, the most significant aid, commonly called basic support, is for general operating expenditures. Since the *Serrano* and *Robinson* court decisions of the 1970s, basic support is increasingly granted *inversely* to local wealth—that is, poorer districts get more; wealthier districts, less.[49]

There are many variations in the actual procedures through which state aid is allocated in a wealth-sensitive manner. In some cases there are funding maxima whereby the state will fund varying amounts of a state-established maximum stipend, called a foundation amount, depending on relative local wealth. More popular are percentage-equalization programs where, instead of a given stipend, the state pays for varying percentages of locally determined total educational expenditures. The state percentage, in turn, varies inversely to local wealth.

The New Jersey state school-aid program illustrates a wealth-sensitive, percentage-equalization subsidy. The state school-aid percentage equals 100 percent minus a quotient derived from dividing local property valuation per pupil* by a state-determined, per-pupil amount called the state guaranteed property valuation per pupil. The same denominator, the state guaranteed valuation, is used in all school-district calculations. Consequently, the quotient of local wealth divided by the common denominator is *higher* in *wealthier* districts and *lower* in *poorer* districts. Because this quotient is subtracted from 100 percent, the state funding percentage is lower in wealthier districts and higher in poorer districts.

---

*This figure is determined by dividing total local property valuation by the total number of local pupils.

To illustrate the operation of this particular formula, as of 1978, Paterson had $32,029 equalized valuation per pupil. The state guaranteed valuation was $106,000 per pupil. Consequently, the state funding percentage was 70 percent, or about $1,100 of the $1,500 school cost per pupil. This is a very high percentage of state support. Because Paterson had a 1978 enrollment of 27,000, total school aid amounted to $30 million. In contrast, Hopewell Township, a comparatively wealthy district, had only 10 percent of its educational expenditures paid for by the state.

With the exception of Hopewell and West Amwell townships (sites of two FmHA projects), all of the New Jersey case example communities receive considerable state support. This support is not surprising since, in most instances, these communities are eligible for federal economic-development assistance precisely because they are economically distressed.

In short, a major portion of state school aid is granted inversely to local wealth. Because federal economic-development assistance is designed to strengthen the local tax base, it has the potential of decreasing state school aid. As state school aid is a significant local intergovernmental revenue, the effect of an economic development stimulus could be to deny more local revenues than it is bringing into the community itself.

The New Jersey case examples illustrate how economic-development projects can affect state school support. In all but five cases, at the *primary impact* level, the projects resulted in significantly *decreased* school aid to host jurisdictions (see Exhibit 22). There were large losses because the nonresidential projects increased the local real-property valuation per pupil. The increase in this local wealth measure had a critical effect because most case-example communities were poor and had large school enrollments. They therefore received larger aggregate amounts of state school aid, which were vulnerable to cuts brought about by the increasing wealth of the district after economic development.

As indicated above, in five cases state school aid did *not* decrease at the primary impact level. This occurred for the following reasons:

1. Two projects were accorded Fox-Lance preferred tax treatment (Schnoll Poultry and Raritan Steel). When Fox-Lance is applied, the real-property assessed value of the economic-development project is not added to the community's total property-tax base.* Consequently, the redevelopment does not affect local valuation per pupil.**
2. Two projects (Breen Color Concentrate and Tencor, Inc.) were located in

*Actually, the value of the land is added, not the value of improvements, to the real-property sector where the redevelopment funds are spent.

**This stands in contrast to Persky preferred tax treatment where, within a short period (two–three years), most of the assessment from the redevelopment improvements are counted in computing the new local valuation per pupil.

EXHIBIT 22

IMPACT OF ECONOMIC DEVELOPMENT ON STATE SCHOOL AID

Federal Agency Assisting Economic Development	Economic Development Projects	City Location	Change in State School Aid
HUD	Wire-Pro	Salem	−$ 4,500
HUD	Schnoll Poultry	Newark	[1]
HUD	Balco-RAR	Newark	−$ 42,880
HUD	Marshall St. and Bale Ave.	Paterson	−$ 45,563
EDA	ATP	Paterson	−$ 27,000
EDA	Lakewood Industrial Campus	Lakewood	−$457,920
EDA	Great Falls Historic District	Paterson	−$ 60,750
EDA	Raritan River Steel	Perth Amboy	[1]
FmHA	Breen Color Concentrate	W. Amwell	[2]
FmHA	Foster Glass	Salem	− 19,500
FmHA	Tencor	Hopewell	[2]

[1]State school aid is *not* affected because project has been accorded Fox-Lance preferred tax treatment. In these situations, the real-property assessment of the improved facility is not add ed to the total community property-tax base. Consequently, there is no change to the equalized valuation per pupil and therefore no change in state school aid.

[2]Community receives minimum state aid, and therefore the addition to the community real-property tax base and the consequent increase in the valuation per pupil does not affect state school support.

communities receiving minimum state school aid. They therefore could not be penalized further by the introduction of new tax ratables that would increase the wealth of these communities.

3. One project, the Marshall Street and Bale Avenue UDAG Development, includes both nonresidential and residential components.

The inclusion of residential development housing large or elderly moderate-income families has the effect of *decreasing* Paterson's valuation per pupil and therefore increasing state school aid.

Similar changes in state school aid as a consequence of development will occur in other states besides New Jersey because most states incorporate wealth-sensitive channeling devices to direct school aid to local jurisdictions. It is important, however, to check the specific state school-aid regulations because certain administrative/statutory provisions may inhibit the development-induced changes described above. Examples include a hold-harmless provision, whereby state aid to local districts cannot be reduced, or a phased hold-harmless provision, where this reduction will be implemented over a number of years in order to lessen the immediate hardship. These types of provisions are currently not in effect in New Jersey.

INTERGOVERNMENTAL TRANSFERS: FEDERAL

Municipalities receive various types of federal intergovernmental revenues. In several cases these are categorical grants, for example, job-training funds for the physically handicapped or for mass transit, and are not likely to be affected by new development.

Other federal support for municipalities is much more general and can be definitely affected by economic-development activities. Revenue Sharing is a good example. This source of federal funds typically acts as a broad-based general revenue to be spent as deemed necessary by local officials. Revenue Sharing is allocated to local communities on the basis of three local criteria: (1) relative population; (2) relative general tax effort; and (3) relative resident income. Economic development affects most directly the tax effort variable—the new facility generates service demands and introduces added revenues—both factors resulting in added local taxation. Although the redevelopment project may influence the other Revenue Sharing variables of local population and resident income, these effects are indirect and of much less magnitude.

The impact of redevelopment on Revenue Sharing can be estimated by multiplying the current Revenue Sharing allotment by the ratio of the economic-development facility's real-property value to total local real-property value. Changes in the local property-tax base are the single best indicators of forthcoming community tax revenues. The proportional increase in the local property-tax base is therefore a good advance indicator of the extent of the increase in total local taxation—the change which will then increase the Revenue Sharing allotment to the municipality (assuming relative tax-base changes continue to take place as they have in the past).

It is important to check that the local projected increase will not violate Revenue Sharing's "145 percent rule," which restricts the local per-capita Revenue Sharing amount to 145 percent of the statewide average. To illustrate, for the New Jersey case-example cities, Newark was already at the 145 percent maximum and, so "constrained," could not receive additional

Revenue Sharing funds as a result of either the Balco-RAR or Schnoll Poultry economic-development efforts.

Extremely large economic-development projects with significant labor forces that choose to reside locally may affect other types of intergovernmental support. To illustrate, a massive residential renewal complex could influence the population, growth lag, and crowding variables of the CDBG formula. In most cases, however, only changes in Revenue Sharing funds have to be traced in examining the fiscal impact of most nonresidential economic-development efforts.

PROJECTING SECONDARY COSTS AND REVENUES

SIMILARITIES IN PROJECTING PRIMARY COSTS AND REVENUES

The analysis at this stage considers the second round of consequences brought about by the primary economic-development activities. To illustrate, a nonresidential facility locating in a city can be expected to induce secondary local residential growth from a share of its employees moving into the community and from the increased wealth of employees already residing there. The nonresidential facility also acts to support local commercial and industrial service establishments, both directly from services/goods the facility purchases locally, as well as indirectly, from the local purchases of its employees (see Exhibit 20).

The costs and revenues of these secondary effects are traced by similar procedures as those used at the primary level. Secondary residential costs are determined by either per-capita, service-standard or other methods, depending on the community/facility being examined. Secondary nonresidential costs are calculated by either case-study, proportional-valuation, or employment-generation techniques, with the choice of method also keyed to the context of the analysis. Similarly, the revenue impacts of secondary residential or nonresidential growth are estimated following the procedures utilized at the primary level: local property-tax and other revenues are calculated; changes in state intergovernmental assistance are projected; and reductions/additions to federal intergovernmental support are also factored.

In addition to the similarity in fiscal-impact procedures used at the primary and secondary levels, the secondary cost/revenue calculations often utilize data already gathered or derived for the primary cost/revenue projections. Common data sources include the community's real-property tax base, the local property-tax rate, the sum of other local revenues, state school-aid figures, and the Revenue Sharing allotment per capita. In short, from both procedural and informational perspectives, the secondary fiscal-impact projections build on the base of calculations already undertaken in the primary fiscal analyses. It should be noted however, that as one moves from primary to other rounds of impact the ability to project with accuracy decreases significantly.

PROJECTING SECONDARY COSTS

Secondary residential costs are generated by new residents attracted to a community. These are least important for small facilities in delcining communities; most important for large facilities in growing communities. These costs are derived using one or more of the residential fiscal-impact techniques discussed in the *Fiscal Impact Handbook*. Although the procedures are straightforward, it is important to be sensitive to existing levels of local excess service capacity—a characteristic common to large communities that are losing population.* The presence and degree of excess service capacity is estimated by interviewing municipal officials as well as from secondary data sources, that is, school populations or municipal labor-force tallies over time, specific school-district or municipal studies indicating enrollment/population shifts, and the like. Once excess capacity is identified, future secondary residential costs, estimated initially on a per-capita or other basis, can be adjusted as necessary to reflect the true capacity of the local service system to absorb additional service demand.

Secondary commercial costs are the expenditures generated by those commercial establishments, receiving business from incoming secondary-round residents as well as from the primary nonresidential facilities. As in the case of extant local public services, where applicable (i.e., larger declining cities), a certain absorption capacity of existing commercial facilities must be assumed. The secondary commercial costs are calculated via a multistep process. First, the total income of the incoming population is estimated along with a projection of what share of that income will be spent on local commercial purchases. Identifying the magnitude of the local commercial sales volume permits projection of how much local commercial space is supported at the secondary impact level. This initial space estimate is tempered by the absorption capacity of the local commercial sector. The revised amount of space is then converted to a real-property value. The latter figure allows the estimation of induced local expenditures via a proportion of real-property-value, cost-assignment technique.

*Excess service capacity exists in a declining community in three forms: (1) system-wide personnel excesses, which may decrease over time; (2) system-wide infrastructure excesses, which may or may not decrease over time; and (3) geographic-specific excess capacity, which will only decrease due to renewed site-specific demand or to local phaseout of the excess capacity.

To illustrate, assume that 500 employees moving to a city as a result of a federal economic-development project have an income of $5,000,000. Consumer surveys report that, on average, residents spend 20 percent of their income on convenience goods and 10 percent of their income on shopping goods—two major commercial purchase components. The 100 residents therefore purchase $1,000,000 in convenience goods and $500,000 in shopping goods. Consumer surveys also indicate that residents commit approximately 75 percent of their total expenditures for convenience foods to local vendors; the figure is assumed to be approximately 25 percent for local shopping goods. In our example, the new residents would therefore spend $750,000 on local convenience goods and $125,000 on local shopping purchases—a total of $875,000. If local surveys indicate that commercial establishments have $150 in sales per square foot, then the $875,000 of induced sales translates into 5,833 square feet of supported commercial space. The local commercial sector can absorb about one-half of this new growth without expansion. If construction costs are $40 per square foot, then one-half of the initially estimated commercial footage has a value of $116,510. This last figure would then be used to estimate local costs via a proportional cost-assignment technique. A similar overall procedure would be used to estimate the secondary industrial/service facilities supported by the expenditures of the primary nonresidential facility.

PROJECTING SECONDARY REVENUE: SUMMARY OF PROCEDURES

The projection of secondary revenues considers the same sectors—residential, commercial and industrial/service—analyzed in the estimation of secondary costs.

There are numerous secondary residential revenues. Incoming households rent apartments or purchase homes and thus contribute to local property taxes. The amount of property taxes paid can be estimated by a six-step procedure consisting of (1) estimating the proportion of the labor force that resides locally; (2) the number of those who are net new additions to the community; (3) of these, the number that are worker household heads; (4) projecting the income of the new, worker household heads; (5) multiplying this household income by a housing, expense-to-income ratio to derive the incurred housing expenditures; and finally, (6) multiplying the projected housing outlay by that portion typically allocated to property-tax payments.

New residents also generate other local revenues, such as added fees, fines, alcoholic-beverage and cigarette taxes, and so forth. The increment of these revenues is projected by multiplying the current per-capita amount of these revenues by the projected number of resident-worker heads of households.

New permanent households will introduce additional school children and thus state school aid must also be calculated. In most cases, the additional families will have the effect of increasing state school assistance. This is brought about because new residential development almost invariably reduces the local property valuation per pupil. A reduction is especially likely when the housing in question is modest or is likely to be occupied by large families—two common characteristics of the housing of residents moving into a community as a result of federal economic development. Because state school aid is granted inversely to local wealth, an induced reduction in the local valuation per pupil will increase state school aid.

The projection of secondary commercial and industrial/service revenues is much simpler than the estimation of secondary residential revenues. The secondary commercial benefit consists of the property tax and other revenues paid by commercial expansions (after absorption is considered), supported by the incoming primary residential or nonresidential growth. The calculation is a multiple-step procedure consisting of estimating the total commercial purchases of, for example, the incoming households; factoring from this figure the share of local purchases; using this sales base to project the amount of supported commercial space; refining this figure by the local potential for commercial absorption, and using the refined space figure to estimate net new value and net new property and other tax dollars. Similar calculations have already been made in considering secondary residential costs and thus need not be repeated here.

Secondary industrial/service revenues are counted following a comparable strategy of first determining what is spent, then translating sales to supported local industrial/service space, refining this figure by local capacity for absorption and, finally, estimating what this industrial/service space at an estimated value will contribute to local revenues.

SUMMARIZING THE LOCAL IMPACTS OF FEDERAL ECONOMIC DEVELOPMENT

The cost/revenue calculations at the primary and secondary levels are the basis for summarizing the local fiscal impacts of federal economic development. The difference between total primary costs and revenues is the total primary fiscal impact. Comparing secondary costs/revenues yields the secondary fiscal impact.

The local return to federal outlay analysis follows the fiscal-impact analysis. It calculates the net local return—the sum of the total fiscal impact as well as any additional local costs or revenues (street/road improvements or loan repayments and the like). The net local return is then compared to the federal outlays that contributed to the local effect. This comparison is expressed as a net local return to federal outlays ratio. This ratio provides a preliminary handhold on the multiplier effect of federal economic-development efforts.

IV. THE FISCAL AND ECONOMIC IMPACTS OF ECONOMIC-DEVELOPMENT ACTIVITIES—RESULTS OF THE ANALYSES/IMPLICATIONS FOR POLICY

INTRODUCTION—RESULTS/POLICY

The purpose of this section is to analyze the results of the fiscal-impact analyses conducted on the specifically chosen case examples. From this analysis statements may be made on the overall fiscal implications of economic development, the types of projects that appear to have the greatest or least fiscal benefits, the differences in scale of benefit/loss between primary and secondary fiscal impacts, and, finally, the relationship at the local level between local revenue generation and federal economic commitment. Exhibit 23 presents an overview of the local impacts of the eleven case studies. It includes primary and secondary local fiscal impacts as well as a comparison of local dollar outputs to federal dollar impacts. It is grouped by agency (vertical axis) and by form of resource allocation (horizontal axis). Details of the calculations for the individual projects, as well as the methodologies employed, are available from the Center for Urban Policy Research.

RESULTS OF THE ANALYSES

OVERALL (see Exhibit 23)

Of the eleven case examples, ten exhibited a positive, primary fiscal impact. Thus, when the local public-servicing costs (police, fire, public works, and so on) of economic-development projects were pitted against the local revenues generated by the projects (property tax, other taxes, user charges, miscellaneous revenues, federal/state intergovernmental revenues, and the like), in 90 percent of the cases they provided more revenues than they occasioned in costs.

	Positive	Negative
Primary Fiscal	10	1
Secondary Fiscal	8	3

The primary revenue/local cost ratio ranged from slightly over 1 to 1 to a projected ratio for a yet-to-be-completed industrial-park project of close to

EXHIBIT 23

SUMMARY: FISCAL IMPACTS AND RETURN TO OUTLAY RATIOS OF SELECTED, FEDERALLY-SPONSORED ECONOMIC DEVELOPMENT PROGRAMS

	U.S. DEPARTMENT OF HOUSING AND URBAN DEVELOPMENT (HUD)		ECONOMIC DEVELOPMENT ADMINISTRATION (EDA)		FARMERS HOME ADMINISTRATION (FmHA)	
PRIMARY FISCAL IMPACT	−$2,182	*Grant* Wire-Pro, Inc. Salem, N.J.	+$7,627	*Loan* ATP Processors, Inc. Paterson, N.J.	+$4,246	*Guarantee* Breen Color Concentrate, Inc., West Amwell, N.J.
	+$8,233	*Grant* Schnoll Poultry Newark, N.J.	+$2,660,866	*Grant* Lakewood Industrial Campus, Lakewood, N.J.	+$27,281	*Guarantee* Tencor, Inc. Hopewell, N.J.
	+$60,048	*Grant* Balco-RAR Newark, N.J.	+$52,262	*Grant* Great Falls Historic District, Paterson, N.J.	+$8,580	*Guarantee* Fosterglass Salem, N.J.
	+$26,418	*Grant* Marshall St. and Bale Ave. Paterson, N.J.	+$735,750	*Guarantee* Raritan River Steel Co. Perth Amboy, N.J.		
PRIMARY RETURN TO FEDERAL OUTLAYS (RATIO)	−0.1	*Grant* Wire-Pro, Inc. Salem, N.J.	0.7	*Loan* ATP Processors, Inc. Paterson, N.J.	3.5	*Guarantee* Breen Color Concentrate, Inc., West Amwell, N.J.
	0.3	*Grant* Schnoll Poultry Newark, N.J.	12.2	*Grant* Lakewood Industrial Campus, Lakewood, N.J.	16.2	*Guarantee* Tencor, Inc. Hopewell, N.J.
	0.6	*Grant* Balco-RAR Newark, N.J.	0.0	*Grant* Great Falls Historic District, Paterson, N.J.	1.0	*Guarantee* Fosterglass Salem, N.J.
	0.1	*Grant* Marshall St. and Bale Ave. Paterson, N.J.	10.2	*Guarantee* Raritan River Steel Co. Perth Amboy, N.J.		

EXHIBIT 23 (*Continued*)

SUMMARY: FISCAL IMPACTS AND RETURN TO OUTLAY RATIOS OF SELECTED, FEDERALLY-SPONSORED ECONOMIC DEVELOPMENT PROGRAMS

SECONDARY FISCAL IMPACT	+$18,083	*Grant* Wire-Pro, Inc. Salem, N.J.	+$19,074	*Loan* ATP Processors, Inc. Paterson, N.J.	−$1,193	*Guarantee* Breen Color Concentrate, Inc., West Amwell, N.J.
	+$10,835	*Grant* Schnoll Poultry Newark, N.J.	−$1,250,603	*Grant* Lakewood Industrial Campus, Lakewood, N.J.	−$751	*Guarantee* Tencor, Inc. Hopewell, N.J.
	+$62,837	*Grant* Balco-RAR Newark, N.J.	+$81,336	*Grant* Great Falls Historic District, Paterson, N.J.	+$14,592	*Guarantee* Fosterglass Salem, N.J.
	+$18,493	*Grant* Marshall St. and Bale Ave. Paterson, N.J.	+$35,163	Guarantee Raritan River Steel Co. Perth Amboy, N.J.		
SECONDARY RETURN TO FEDERAL OUTLAYS	1.1	*Grant* Wire-Pro, Inc. Salem, N.J.	1.7	*Loan* ATP Processors, Inc. Paterson, N.J.	−1.0	*Guarantee* Breen Color Concentrate, Inc., West Amwell, N.J.
	0.4	*Grant* Schnoll Poultry Newark, N.J.	−5.7	*Grant* Lakewood Industrial Campus, Lakewood, N.J.	−0.4	*Guarantee* Tencor, Inc. Hopewell, N.J.
	0.6	*Grant* Balco-RAR Newark, N.J.	0.1	*Grant* Great Falls Historic District, Paterson, N.J.	1.7	*Guarantee* Fosterglass Salem, N.J.
	0.0	*Grant* Marshall St. and Bale Ave. Paterson, N.J.	0.5	*Guarantee* Raritan River Steel Co. Perth Amboy, N.J.		

Source: Rutgers University, Center for Urban Policy Research, Winter 1980.

60 to 1.* Except for cases where local tax abatement was granted to the economic-development facility, the revenue/local cost ratio increased in direct proportion to the scale or value of the project. The large majority of cases fell between revenue/local cost ratios of 4 to 1 and 1 to 1. Only in the case of a modest economic-development grant to rehabilitate and reoccupy an abandoned factory in Salem, N.J., a small nonmetropolitan city, was the primary local fiscal impact a negative one. This was due largely to a significant underassessment of the rehabilitated facility and resulting low property-tax yields.

Secondary fiscal impact, the local costs versus revenues to publicly service activities (residences, businesses, secondary industry, etc.) that may be spawned by primary development was positive in eight of eleven instances (70 percent). In six of the eight cases of positive cost revenue, the revenue/local cost ratios were slightly above 1 to 1; in the two other cases, the ratios were just less than 2 to 1. It was not uncommon for both secondary costs and revenues to individually exceed those of primary costs and revenues by a sizeable margin. The three negative secondary fiscal impacts occurred in the cases of (1) a large grant for an industrial park in a growing community (large, new labor force attracted to "service spent" community); (2) an average-size loan guarantee for a commercial dye corporation in a small rural township (negative impact on small local public-service system); and (3) a medium-size loan guarantee for a recreational facility in an exurban, developing setting. In the last case, a small, lowly paid labor force lived locally in a middle-class community and tipped the fiscal balance slightly negatively as a result of their impact on a school system that was at capacity and in a district not receiving a great deal of school aid.

However, it should be emphasized that preferential tax treatment was provided by local governments in six out of the eight projects assisted by EDA and HUD. These tax preferences reduced the fiscal impacts of the projects on the communities and distorted patterns of fiscal impacts, both among programs and among communities. Preferential tax treatment had especially great effects on the fiscal impacts of the four projects located in Newark and Paterson, two highly distressed cities with heavy property-tax burdens. Even with favorable tax treatment, these projects yielded positive primary fiscal benefits for the cities. Projected secondary impacts were also positive in their fiscal effects. The projects that generated the greatest primary fiscal benefits per dollar of federal outlay were projects in

*These details are found in the full study conducted by the authors for the U.S. Department of Housing and Urban Development.

**The large majority of cases of primary fiscal impact were found to exhibit revenue-cost ratios of 1.5–3.0 to 1.

economically less distressed or healthy communities, such as Hopewell or Lakewood Township. Tax preferences were not significant for either of the projects in these cities.

PRIMARY FISCAL IMPACTS

The direct public costs to service a new or revitalized nonresidential facility are borne primarily by the municipal service system of the host municipality. Essentially, they consist of additional police equipment for patrol or traffic control; standby fire-protection personnel/equipment; support for public-works activities, such as sanitation services and road maintenance/repair; funding for a small portion of administrative staff time (tax assessor/collector, clerk, inspectors) for record maintenance and processing; and extra utilities of the nonresidential facility's product production/dissemination (electricity, water). These costs usually are not severe local outlays and, except for fire and police, are absorbed by service excesses in one or more components of the existing service system. The latter utility costs (and occasionally those for sanitation services), are assigned via user charges, and unless the system needs significant upgrading to handle additional loads, the transaction is frequently a wash locally—occasioning neither direct costs nor revenues to the local jurisdiction. The cost of primary service extensions to the nonresidential facilities in the eleven case examples ranged from $1,500 to $50,000 annually, and although these costs varied with the scale (or value) of the facility, this variation was far from linear. A factory with an assessed value of $100,000 imposed $7,500 in local costs; a steel mill whose assessed value was $80,000,000 occasioned $50,000 in local costs.

As a result, absent any preferred tax treatment, the excess of primary revenues over costs varies almost logarithmically with the scale of the nonresidential facility. Large nonresidential developments also tend to privatize "public" services as scale increases, further enhancing the revenue cost superiority of large projects. Private security forces, garbage-collection arrangements, and advanced fire protection, water treatment, and sewage systems usually lessen the on-site time requirements of members of the host municipal labor force.

The two mechanical methods used to project primary costs, proportional-valuation and employment-generation techniques, tended to diverge from the case-study approach (proportional valuation, higher; employment generation, lower) as project scale (value) increased. The most reasonable results seemed to emerge from case-study analysis.

School-aid changes due to primary impact were negative with the exception of projects that received Fox-Lance tax treatment (property value subject to Fox-Lance not added to local tax roles). Revenue Sharing allocations evidenced positive gains due to primary impact in all communities except for Newark, which was constrained at maximum limits set by a ratio to the statewide average.

SECONDARY FISCAL IMPACTS

The indirect public costs to service additional nonresidential growth consist of municipal and school-district services to the resident labor force and municipal services to support commercial and secondary industrial growth spawned by the expenditures of the resident and nonresident labor force and also by the goods/product purchases of the primary nonresidential facility.

Secondary residential costs accrue from police/rescue, fire, public-works, administrative, recreational, and public-educational services to those primary wage earners whose families would not otherwise live locally in the absence of the projects. These costs are most pronounced in growing communities receiving an economic-development facility with a large labor force. Because the family size of these workers is normally higher than average and public-school participation rates of their children is also high, residential servicing costs, when they occur, are relatively steep.

With wages modest and a high proportion of renters, derived local property tax/other revenues are usually low. Fortunately, state intergovernmental transfers for education may be significant because of (1) increases in per-pupil funding due to low relative property value of workers' housing, and (2) additional pupils due to the public educational needs of the families of resident workers. In most instances, secondary residential costs were on a par with derived secondary revenues, that is, the value of the housing of resident workers contributed at least as much in revenues as was required to finance local service extensions. The one instance where there was an observable imbalance of costs over revenues was in the previously mentioned, growing community that received grant funds to support a large industrial park. Here, small service systems (both educational and municipal) were at capacity and would have to undergo major expansion to satisfy additional demand.

The costs versus revenues of the additional commercial and industrial/service facilities supported by the resident/nonresident labor force and the nonresidential facility itself bulked high in favor of revenues. The costs, estimated by the proportional-valuation technique, were modest in all cases, and derived revenues, relatively high. Revenues exceeded costs, typically by factors of 10 to 1. Thus, secondary impacts due to the costs to service residences occupied by workers are significant but essentially break even. Those due to additional commercial and industrial/service growth are more modest in scale but, very frequently, derived local revenues far outdistance assigned public-service costs.

LOCAL REVENUE RETURNS TO FEDERAL OUTLAYS

The local return to federal outlay analyses attempt to estimate the multiplier effect of indirect federal grant, loan, and guarantee expenditures. Federal outlays are defined differently for each category of resource allocation. The federal outlay for a guarantee is the dollar loss due to an imputed program default rate. The default rate for FmHA guarantee programs is estimated at 4.5 percent; for EDA guarantees (reflecting "credit not-available-elsewhere" type of lending situations) the figure is 12.0 percent. For a loan, federal outlays are defined as the difference in cost between federal borrowing and lending rates (when the federal government lends at below-market interest rates) plus the dollar loss due to an imputed program default rate. The default rate for EDA loan programs (the only ones analyzed) is estimated at 12.0 percent. The federal outlay for grants is the current federal cost of borrowing on the face amount of the grant. This is assumed to be 10 percent. Where grants are transferable to a third party and repayment benefits flow to the host community (second party), a default rate of 10.5 percent is assumed. Thus, for EDA and HUD communities that employ a revolving loan with a portion of their grant funds, the amount of the loan repayment is lessened by the assumed default rate. All costs are expressed in current annual amounts. Current, annualized amounts are identical, assuming an inflation rate and applying discounted present value. Local returns are defined as the net local fiscal-impact revenue surplus plus any additional locally accruing revenues (direct grant to city; loaned by city to third party; repaid with interest to city).

In accordance with the above definitions, local returns to federal outlays were positive in nine of eleven cases. Due in large part to tax preferences granted by local government, a large, HUD UDAG grant in Paterson and a large EDA Title IX grant in the same city provided only one-half to one-fifth of the local revenues that it "cost" the federal government to spur these particular projects. Overall, local return to federal outlays are quite favorable, however, especially given the magnitude of some of the UDAG and EDA direct grants.

What is apparent here, albeit from limited case-study analyses, is the potentially greater multiplier effect from economic-development programs than from direct revenue transfers, such as Revenue Sharing. In most instances economic-development returns to outlays are greater than one, pointing to increased "output" dollars via this type of subsidy. Obviously, more research needs to be undertaken to extend this finding to other fiscal contexts.

POLICY IMPLICATIONS

The remaining portion of this section discusses when fiscal-impact analyses of economic-development projects should be conducted; which methods are most applicable when a decision is made to compare local costs and revenues; and how both state and the federal government can affect more positively the local fiscal impact of economic-development activity.

WHEN SHOULD A FISCAL IMPACT ANALYSIS BE CONDUCTED

In all cases, the property taxes generated by economic development should be considered, with attention paid to specifying what share of those property taxes flow to the local jurisdiction. This calculation is simple, requiring data that are readily available. The property-tax rate can be obtained with a single telephone call to the municipal clerk, and although it is sometimes difficult to estimate the *exact* market or assessed value of an economic-development project, a rough figure suffices for projecting the order of magnitude of forthcoming property taxes. Whereas the property-tax calculation is simple, it is essential because it typically is the most important local revenue.

The ability and likelihood of local jurisdictions to grant preferred property-tax treatment should also always be noted, for such abatement on required payments clearly affects the actual property-tax yield. In addition, this side-by-side comparison then gives a direct basis for considering what the local community is giving up by granting preferred property-tax treatment—a figure that can be compared to the project's local benefits.

The calculations discussed above are the minimum required and clearly do not constitute a comprehensive fiscal analysis. The latter, however, is expensive and time consuming and, therefore, it is important to consider under what conditions a full fiscal-impact projection should be conducted. It is recommended that such an analysis always be conducted when there is likelihood of a local fiscal deficit. This recommendation is based on the belief that it is more important to flag a local loss than to document a local benefit.

The findings of this study indicate that economic development typically will result in a local surplus. The exception is the case of growing, affluent communities with economic-development projects characterized by a highly paid labor force that is likely to reside locally. Under these conditions, it may well be that an economic-development project will occasion a local fiscal deficit and, consequently, a full fiscal project analysis should then be conducted. It might well be that these types of communities should be excluded from most economic-development grant subsidies on pure policy grounds.

STATE ROLE IN INFLUENCING THE LOCAL FISCAL IMPACT OF ECONOMIC DEVELOPMENT

Consideration of the local fiscal impact of economic development has understandably focused on the dynamic of actions, interactions, and cost-revenue characteristics at the local level. These factors included the level of the local property-tax rate, the value that the local assessor assigns to incoming properties, the degree to which excess capacity will be found to exist in the local public-service delivery system, and so on.

By comparison, the state role in influencing the local fiscal impact of economic development has often been overlooked. State statutes and programs do, however, occasion local fiscal effects in several ways. State revenue-redistribution formulas, for example, affect whether communities experiencing economic development will receive such revenues as personal-property, sales, income, or utility-franchise/income taxes. States also have the power to decide whether and which classes of communities can grant preferred property-tax treatment to economic-development projects—a factor with significant bearing on the local fiscal bottom line.

The most important state influence on the local fiscal impact of economic development concerns the distribution of state school aid. This significant state-to-local transfer is typically distributed inversely to local wealth as measured by the average property value per pupil. Poorer school districts, with relatively low property valuation per pupil, get more aid; wealthier districts, with relatively high property value per pupil, receive less assistance. This allocation strategy provides an important prop to central cities and other communities experiencing economic distress, especially losses in their property-tax base. At the same time, however, the state school-aid programs act to penalize distressed communities when they experience increases in their revenue-raising bases as a result of economic development. In short, one of the principal objectives of the federal economic-development programs—to improve the fiscal health of impacted communities— can be circumvented by states' withdrawing school support from these same communities.

Various strategies should be considered for addressing a situation that has state and federal governments working at cross purposes. One approach is for the federal government to require, as a quid pro quo of continued economic-development assistance to communities within a state, that changes be made by the state in its distribution of school aid. The change could take the form of the state providing a hold-harmless provision protecting communities from school-aid reductions as a result of federally assisted economic development. The hold-harmless provision does not have to be blanket—covering all communities—but at minimum it should be extended to those most economically distressed, that is, communities eligible for federal UDAG assistance or state urban aid. The hold-harmless provision also does not have to extend protection without regard to the improving economic status of a community. Thus, hold-harmless could be maintained only during the period that a community kept its eligibility for the relief programs cited above. Alternatively, continuation of hold-harmless could be tied directly to the state school-aid formula. To illustrate, the hold-harmless provision could terminate when the local valuation per pupil equaled the average state valuation per pupil.

In addition or as an alternative to the hold-harmless guarantee, states could avoid penalizing impacted communities involved in economic development by incorporating an explicit municipal overburden provision in their school-aid allocation. This provision incorporates sensitivity to a wide range of community distress factors in the distribution of state school aid. It does this by expanding the measure of local economic status from simply valuation per pupil to include other local factors, such as unemployment, welfare dependency, tax burden per capita. It also incorporates special measures of local need, such as the high cost of educating children from disadvantaged families and the presence of inadequate school capital facilities, etc. With a municipal overburden mechanism in place, distressed communities engaged in economic development would experience little or no reduction in state school support. Whereas their local valuation per pupil would increase, other measures, such as the need variables cited above, would not change, and therefore the community would not be penalized.

FEDERAL ROLE IN INFLUENCING THE LOCAL FISCAL IMPACT OF ECONOMIC DEVELOPMENT

Federal intergovernmental flows to local communities are also affected by local economic development projects. The most prominent example is Revenue Sharing. Communities with economic-development activity usually gain Revenue Sharing funds because they experience an increase in their tax effort—one of the local characteristics considered by the Revenue Sharing allocation formula.

The *increase* in federal intergovernmental flows, as a consequence of economic development, stands in contrast to the *decrease* of state school aid. Thus, in contrast to state governments, the federal government can *not* be accused of penalizing communities engaged in economic revitalization. The federal response, however, raises another issue. Is it not an unfair windfall that communities receiving one measure of federal largesse—economic-development assistance—are given a further transfer of federal aid—added Revenue Sharing? The question is even more pertinent in view of the fact that the additional Revenue Sharing comes at the expense of other communities in the local Revenue Sharing pool that will experience a *reduction* in their allotment.* In short, local jurisdictions engaged in economic development may receive a compounding of added federal support. In contrast, sister communities, not receiving federal economic-development assistance, may be the object of a compounding chain of reduced federal aid.

The results discussed above are not necessarily inequitable if the multiple increases work to the benefit of distressed communities while reductions are experienced only by more affluent jurisdictions. The important point is that it is not known exactly who is benefiting and who is losing from the interaction of federal economic-development assistance with other federal intergovernmental programs. This interface clearly needs additional crosscut research, considering the extent to which the multiple federal programs interact in practice to affect different classes of communities.

WHICH METHOD IS MOST EFFECTIVE FOR CONSIDERING THE FISCAL IMPACT OF ECONOMIC DEVELOPMENT?

There are three methods for projecting the local costs generated by nonresidential economic development—case study, proportional valuation, and employment anticipation. Of the three, the case study is the most appropriate. The major reason for this is the presence of excess service capacity common to many communities where economic development is taking place. These communities often have experienced a sharp population loss and thus can accommodate growth without having to significantly expand their existing service system. The case study is sensitive to the presence of excess service capacity because it relies on municipal department head interviews.** In these interviews local officials are asked specifically whether an incoming project will force them to hire staff, purchase equipment, or build new capital facilities. Other methods, not sensitive to slack capacity, would overestimate the expenditures generated by eonomic development.

Although the case study is preferable, it sometimes is impractical where time and resources do not permit on-site interviews. In such instances an employment-generation approach should be considered. This method assigns costs according to the magnitude of the employment generated by a nonresidential facility. It is based on regression analysis of the actual service

*Except for very large economic-development facilities, which receive no form of preferred tax treatment, the impact on future Revenue Sharing allocations will usually be relatively small.

**Excess service capacity exists in declining communities because (1) unions and other employee organizations retard personnel cutbacks; (2) it cannot be reduced because of system-wide dependence; or (3) it cannot be drawn on because of geographic location.

expenditures incurred by different communities as a result of measured additions to their employment base. Separate results are derived for different types of communities (depending on their size and direction/magnitude of growth) and for different categories of employment (commercial versus industrial).

The employment-generation approach is not directly sensitive to excess service capacity, but by differentiating the impact of employment by community size and direction of growth it is indirectly incorporating the service reserve of large cities with a declining population. The employment-generation approach also offers a number of practical advantages. It can be implemented in much less time and at a much lower cost than the case study. In addition, one important required data element—generated employment—is a figure given prominent attention in economic-development project applications and thus is usually readily available to the analyst.

If an employment-generation technique is used on more than an infrequent basis, then expenditure multipliers per employee should be derived for the location where the method is used. In addition, refinements in the classification of communities and the categories of employment should be considered. The methodological and procedural bases for these analyses are contained in the *Fiscal Impact Handbook*.

NOTES

1. U.S. Department of Housing and Urban Development, Office of Community Planning and Development, *Economic Development Crosscut: Overview of Federally-assisted Economic Development: Purposes, Issues and Performance* (Washington, D.C.: The Office, 1980), p. 1.
2. Ibid., p. 2.
3. Ibid., p. 3.
4. Urban Land Institute, *UDAG Marketplace: Nine Case Studies* (Washington, D.C.: ULI, 1979), p. I.
5. U.S. Department of Housing and Urban Development, Office of Community Planning and Development, *Urban Development Action Grant Program: Second Annual Report* (Washington, D.C.: Government Printing Office, 1980), p. 1.
6. Ibid., p. i.
7. Ibid., p. ii.
8. ULI, *UDAG Marketplace*, p. III.
9. Ibid., p. IV.
10. U.S. Department of Housing and Urban Development, Office of Community Planning and Development, *Economic Development Crosscut: Remarks Summarizing Program Profile Questionnaire for 1981 Economic Development Crosscut* (Washington, D.C.: The Office, 1980), p. 5.

11. U.S. Department of Commerce, Economic Development Administration, *Economic Development Administration: 1979 Annual Report* (Washington, D.C.: The Administration, 1980), p. 2.
12. Ibid., p. 3.
13. Ibid., p. 7.
14. U.S. Department of Housing and Urban Development, Office of Community Planning and Development, *Economic Development Crosscut: Program Profile Questionnaire: Summary Outline* (Washington, D.C.: The Office, 1979), p. 3.
15. EDA, *1979 Annual Report,* p. 47.
16. Ibid., p. 48.
17. Ibid., p. 4.
18. Ibid., p. 5.
19. Ibid., p. 46.
20. HUD, *Economic Development Crosscut: Program Profile Questionnaire: Summary Outline,* p. 2.
21. Ibid., p. 3.
22. EDA, *1979 Annual Report*, p. 50.
23. Ibid., p. 5l.
24. HUD, *Economic Development Crosscut, Program Profile Questionnaire: Summary Outline,* p. 6.
25. Ibid., p. 7.
26. U.S. Farmers Home Administration, *An FmHA Report on the Business and Industrial Loan Program* (Washington, D.C., FmHA, 1980 [unpublished]), p. 2.
27. Ibid., p. 3.
28. Ibid.,
29. Ibid., p. 5.
30. Ibid., p. 13.
31. HUD, *Economic Development Crosscut: Program Profile Questionnaire: Summary Outline*, p. 4.
32. Ibid., p. 3.
33. FmHA, *An FmHA Report,* p. 11.
34. Ibid., p. 3.
35. HUD, *Summary Outline,* p. 6.
36. FmHA, *An FmHA Report,* p. 3.
37. Ibid., p. 2.
38. Ibid., p. 6.
39. EDA, *1979 Annual Report* p. 2.
40. FmHA, *An FmHA Report*, p. 8.
41. New Jersey Department of Community Affairs, Division of Local Government Services, *Budget Manual for New Jersey Municipalities Promulgated by the Local Finance Board for the Year 1978* (Trenton, N.J.: The Division, 1979), p. ii.
42. New Jersey, Division of Taxation, *Annual Report of the Division of Taxation in the Department of the Treasury for the Fiscal Year 1979* (Trenton, N.J.: The Division [1980]), p. 600.
43. Robert W. Burchell and David Listokin, *The Fiscal Impact Handbook* (New Brunswick, N.J.: Rutgers University Center for Urban Policy Research, 1978).
44. Interview with the Newark Associate Tax Assessor, October, 1980.
45. See note 43.
46. *Hellerstein v. Assessor of Town of Islip*, 37 N.Y. 2d—1—(1975).

47. Interview with Ami Golubtchik, counsel to the Paterson (N.J.) Restoration Corporation, Oct. 1980.
48. New Jersey Education Association, *Where New Jersey Ranks—Basic Statistical Data* (Trenton, N.J.: NJEA, 1979).
49. See, for example, *Robinson v. Cahill* 62 N.J. 473, 303 A. 2d 273.

BIBLIOGRAPHY

Alexander, James, Jr., et al. *The Municipal Budget Process.* New Brunswick, N.J.: Rutgers University, Bureau of Government Research, 1980.

Bahl, Roy, and Montrone, William. *Forecasting Municipal Revenues and Expenditures: A Primer and Handbook.* Boston: Coalition of Northeast Municipalities, 1980.

———, and Schroeder, Larry. "Local Government Revenue and Expenditure Forecasting." *Urban Interest* 2(2) (Fall 1980): 59-65.

Brookings Institution. *Case Studies of the Impact of Federal Grants in Large Cities, 1978: Transcripts of Working Conference Proceedings, Washington, D.C., February 2, 1978.* Springfield,Va. NTIS, 1978.

———. *Report on Allocation of Community Development Funds to Small Cities.* Washington, D.C.: U.S. Department of Housing and Urban Development, 1979.

Black, Thomas J., et al. *UDAG Marketplace: Nine Case Studies.* Washington, D.C.: Urban Land Institute, 1979.

Burchell, Robert W., and Listokin, David. *The Fiscal Impact Handbook: Estimating Local Costs and Revenues of Land Development.* New Brunswick, N.J.: Rutgers University Center for Urban Policy Research, 1978.

———. "Methods for Analyzing Fiscal Impacts: State of the Art and State of The Practice." *Urban Interest* 2(2) (Fall 1980): 49–58.

Butler, Robert. Statement of Robert Butler, Farmers Home Administration, U.S. Department of Agriculture before the Subcommittee on Antitrust, Consumers and Employment, Committee on Small Business, U.S. House of Representatives, Sept. 26, 1978. (n.p.)(n.d.)

Coopers & Lybrand. *Developmental Aspects of the Business and Industry Loan Guarantee Program to the Farmer's Home Administration.* Washington, D.C.: The Farmer's Home Administration, 1979.

DeLeon, Richard, et al. "Economic Development Projects and CDBG Program Benefit Analysis." *Clearinghouse Review*, Nov. 1979, pp. 499–505.

Dulton, William H., et al. "Fiscal Impact Models and the Policy Making Process." *Urban Interest* 2(2) (Fall 1980): 66–74.

E. A. Jaenke and Associates, Inc. *A Feasibility Study to Determine Whether or Not FmHA Should Extend Its Business and Industry Guaranteed Loan Program to Include All Facets of Livestock, Poultry and Turkey Production.* Washington, D.C.: Farmers Home Administration, 1979.

Galambos, Eva C., and Schrieber, Arthur F. *Making Sense Out of Dollars: Economic Analysis for Local Government.* Washington, D.C.: National League of Cities, 1978.

Hughes, James W. *Methods of Housing Analysis: Techniques and Case Studies*. New Brunswick, N.J.: Rutgers University Center for Urban Policy Research, 1979.

Jackson, Stephen T. *Evaluation of the Administration of the Title X Program (Public Works and Economic Development Act of 1965)*. Washington, D.C.: U.S. Economic Development Administration, 1977.

Kirlin, John J., and Chapman, Jeffrey I. "Active Approaches to Local Government Revenue Generation." *Urban Interest* 2(2) (Fall 1980) 83–91.

Lund, Leonard, and Winter, Linda. *The Public-Private Partnership in Action: Some Views by Participants and Observers of the Community Economic Development Program*. New York: The Conference Board, 1979.

Mechling, William. *Can Community Economic Development Meet the Fiscal Needs of Municipalities? Economic Growth and Fiscal Stress in Three Northeast Cities*. Boston: Coalition of Northeast Municipalities, 1980.

Mercure, Alex P. Statement by Alex P. Mercure, Assistant Secretary for Rural Development, before the Senate Committee on Agriculture, Nutrition, and Forestry, Subcommittee on Agricultural Credit and Rural Electrification, U.S. Senate, Nov. 8, 1979. (n.p.) (n.d.)

Montrone, William. *Can the Local Property Base Continue to Support Municipal Government?: An Analysis of the Relationship between Growth in Expenditures and Property Values for Northeast Municipal Governments*. Boston: Coalition of Northeast Municipalities, 1980.

Nathan, Richard P. "Research Issues in the Evaluation of Broad-Gauged and Multi-Purpose Federal Grants-in-Aid." (Paper prepared for the Committee on Taxation, Resources, and Economic Development, Sept. 26, 1980, Cambridge, Mass.)

National Council for Urban Economics. *Development Coordinated Urban Economic Development: A Case Study Analysis*. Washington, D.C.: The Council, 1978.

New Jersey Department of Community Affairs, Division of Local Government Services. *Budget Manual for New Jersey Municipalities Promulgated by the Local Finance Board for the Year 1978*. Trenton, N.J.: The Division, 1979.

New Jersey, Division of Taxation. *Annual Report of the Division of Taxation in the Department of the Treasury for the Fiscal Year 1979*. Trenton, N.J.: The Division, 1980.

New Jersey Education Association. *Basic Statistical Data of New Jersey School Districts, 1979 Edition: Part 1: 1977–78 Per Pupil, Wealth, Expenditures, Staffing, Enrollments*. Trenton, N.J.: The Association, 1979.

———. *Basic Statistics of New Jersey School Districts, 1978 Edition: Part 2: Tax Rates; State Aid 1977–78; Net Valuation Taxable 1978; Enrollments—Sept. 30, 1977*. Trenton, N.J.: The Association, 1978.

Phillip B. Hert & Associates. *Negotiating Fiscal Impacts: A Handbook for Evaluating City Development*. Boston: Coalition of Northeast Municipalities, 1980.

Racial America, Inc. *Limited Access: A Report on the Community Development Block Grant Program in Non-Metropolitan Areas*. Washington, D.C.: U.S. Community Services Administration, 1978.

Salterthwaite, Ann. "UDAG: Is It the New Urban Renewal?" *Preservation News*, Dec. 1979, pp. 1-2.

Sternberg, Carl, et al. *Block Grants: A Comparative Analysis*. Washington, D.C.: U.S. Advisory Commission on Intergovernmental Relations, 1977.

U.S. Conference of Mayors. *Economic Development: New Roles for City Government: A Guidebook for Local Government*. Washington, D.C.: U.S. Department of Housing and Urban Development, 1979.

U.S. Congress. House. Committee on Banking, Finance and Urban Affairs, Subcommittee on Economic Policy. *Effectiveness of Economic Stimulus Programs: Hearings* . . . 95th Cong., 2d sess., Feb. 18 and 20, 1978. Washington, D.C.: Government Printing Office, 1978.

———, Subcommittee on the City. *Impact of the Federal Budget on Cities*. Washington, D.C.: Government Printing Office, 1977.

U.S. Congress, Joint Economic Committee. *State and Local Budget Surpluses and the Effect of Federal Macroeconomic Policies*. Washington, D.C.: Government Printing Office, 1979.

———, Subcommittee on Fiscal and Intergovernmental Policy. *Keeping Business in the City: Hearings* . . . 95th Cong., 2d sess. Washington, D.C.: Government Printing Office, 1978.

U.S. Department of Commerce, Economic Development Administration. *Annual Report*, Washington, D.C.: The Administration, 1978.

———. *Economic Development Administration: 1979 Annual Report*. Washington, D.C.: The Administration, 1980.

———. *EDA Directory of Approved Projects: April 1–September 30, 1978*. Washington, D.C.: The Administration, [1978].

———. *EDA Directory of Approved Projects as of March 31, 1978*. Washington, D.C.: The Administration, 1978.

———. "Local Public Works Program: Status Report." 1978.

U.S. Department of Housing and Urban Development. *Fifth Annual Community Development Block Grant Report*. Washington, D.C.: The Department, 1980.

———, Office of Community Planning. *Action Grant Information Systems: Data Element Definitions*. Washington, D.C.: The Office, 1980.

———, Office of Community Planning and Development. *Community Development Block Grant Program—Urban Counties: The First Year Experience*. Washington, D.C.: Government Printing Office, 1977.

———. *Economic Development Crosscut: Program Profile Questionnaire: Summary Outline*. Washington, D.C.: The Office, 1979.

———. *Economic Development Crosscut: Remarks Summarizing Program Profile Questionnaire for 1981 Economic Development Crosscut*. Washington, D.C.: The Office, 1980.

———. *Urban Development Action Grant Program: First Annual Report*. Washington, D.C.: Government Printing Office, 1979.

———. *Urban Development Action Grant Program: Second Annual Report*. Washington, D.C.: Government Printing Office, 1980.

———. *Pockets of Poverty: An Examination of Needs and Options*. Washington, D.C.: The Department, 1979.

———. *UDAG National Project Summaries: Dollars and Jobs 1978–1980*. Washington, D.C.: The Office, 1980.

———, Office of Management, Division of Data Systems and Statistics. *UDAG Project Data: Coding Sheet*. Washington, D.C.: The Division, 1980.

———. *Urban Development Action Grant Program, Quarterly Progress Report: Report Preparation Instructions*. Washington, D.C.: The Division, 1980.

———, Office of Policy Development and Research. *Methods of Urban Impact Analysis: The President's Tax Program*. Washington, D.C.: Government Printing Office, 1979.

U.S. Farmer's Home Administration. *Instructions for Preparation of "Rural Community Facility Activity Card."* Washington, D.C.: U.S. Department of Agriculture, [n.d.].

U.S. General Accounting Office. *Criteria for Participation in the Urban Development Action Grant Program Should be Refined*. Washington, D.C.: The Office, 1980.

U.S. General Accounting Office. *Improvements Needed in Selecting and Processing Urban Development Action Grants*. Washington, D.C.: The Office, 1979.

U.S. Office of Management and the Budget. *Economic Development Performance Indicators: Data Element Questionnaire*. Washington, D.C.: The Office, 1980.

Wolman, Harold, and Peterson, George. "Policy Consequences of Local Government Constraints." *Urban Interest* 2(2) (Fall 1980): 75–82.

Vernez, George, et al. *Federal Activities in Urban Economic Development*. Prepared for Economic Development Administration. Santa Monica, Calif.: Rand Corp., 1979.

Index